Fluency Instruction

Research-Based Best Practices

Edited by
TIMOTHY RASINSKI
CAMILLE BLACHOWICZ
KRISTIN LEMS

THE GUILFORD PRESS
New York   London

© 2006 The Guilford Press
A Division of Guilford Publications, Inc.
72 Spring Street, New York, NY 10012
www.guilford.com

Printed in the United States of America

This book is printed on acid-free paper.

Last digit is print number: 9   8   7   6   5   4   3   2

Library of Congress Cataloging-in-Publication Data is available from
the Publisher.

ISBN 1-59385-253-3 (pbk.); 1-59385-254-1 (hardcover)

About the Editors

Timothy Rasinski, PhD, is Professor of Literacy Education at Kent State University. He also helps direct Kent State's Reading Clinic, which recently won the Ohio's Best Award for its effectiveness and innovations in working with students who struggle with reading. Dr. Rasinski has written over 150 articles and has authored, coauthored, or edited 15 books on reading education. His scholarly interests include reading fluency and word study and reading in the elementary and middle grades. Dr. Rasinski's research on reading has been cited by the National Reading Panel and has been published in journals such as *Reading Research Quarterly, The Reading Teacher, Reading Psychology,* and the *Journal of Educational Research.* He recently served a 3-year term on the Board of Directors of the International Reading Association and currently serves as coeditor of the *Journal of Literacy Research.*

Camille Blachowicz, PhD, is Professor of Education at National-Louis University, where she also directs the Reading Specialist Program and the Reading Center. She is the author of several books and numerous chapters, monographs, and articles on vocabulary and comprehension instruction and on working with at-risk readers. Dr. Blachowicz was a Fulbright Fellow in Italy and is active in professional organizations and staff development nationally and internationally.

Kristin Lems, EdD, is Program Coordinator and Associate Professor in the English as a Second Language/Bilingual Education Program in the Department of Curriculum and Instruction at National-Louis University. Previously, she taught in an intensive postsecondary English as a Second Language program. Dr. Lems was a Fulbright Scholar in Algeria for 2 years, and has authored a book on Teaching English as a Foreign Language methodology for the Peace Corps.

Contributors

Richard L. Allington, PhD, Department of Theory and Practice in Teacher Education, College of Education, University of Tennessee, Knoxville, Tennessee

Gwynne Ellen Ash, PhD, Department of Curriculum and Instruction, College of Education, Texas State University, San Marcos, Texas

Jessica Bevans, PhD, Department of Teacher Education, Brigham Young University, Provo, Utah

Camille Blachowicz, PhD, Department of Reading and Language, National College of Education, National-Louis University, Evanston, Illinois

Lila Ubert Carrick, EdD, Department of Early Childhood Education, New Jersey City University, Jersey City, New Jersey

David J. Chard, PhD, Department of Special Education, College of Education, University of Oregon, Eugene, Oregon

Randal Donelson, PhD, Department of Early Childhood Education, College of Education, Ashland University, Ashland, Ohio

Charles W. Fisher, PhD, School of Education, University of Michigan, Ann Arbor, Michigan

Peter Fisher, PhD, Department of Reading and Language, National College of Education, National-Louis University, Evanston, Illinois

Ellen Fogelberg, MS, Evanston–Skokie School District 65, Evanston, Illinois

Elfrieda H. Hiebert, PhD, School of Education, University of California, Berkeley, California

Susan Johnston, MS, Educational Service Unit 3, Omaha, Nebraska

Melanie R. Kuhn, PhD, Graduate School of Education, Rutgers—The State University of New Jersey, New Brunswick, New Jersey

Kristin Lems, EdD, English as a Second Language/Bilingual Education, Department of Curriculum and Instruction, National-Louis University, Chicago, Illinois

Jennifer R. Massarelli, MEd, National College of Education, National-Louis University, Evanston, Illinois

Danielle V. Mathson, MEd, Department of Theory and Practice in Teacher Education, College of Education, University of Tennessee, Knoxville, Tennessee

Sarah H. McDonagh, PhD, School of Teacher Education, Charles Sturt University, Bathurst, Australia

Kouider Mokhtari, PhD, Department of Teacher Education, Miami University, Oxford, Ohio

Mary Kay Moskal, EdD, School of Education, St. Mary's College of California, Moraga, California

Connie M. Obrochta, MEd, Evanston–Skokie School District 65, Evanston, Illinois

Nancy Padak, EdD, Ohio Literacy Resource Center, Kent State University, Kent, Ohio

John J. Pikulski, PhD, School of Education, University of Delaware, Newark, Delaware

Meryl-Lynn Pluck, MPhil, Rainbow Reading Program, Nelson, New Zealand

Timothy Rasinski, PhD, Department of Teaching, Leadership, and Curriculum Studies, Kent State University, Kent, Ohio

D. Ray Reutzel, PhD, Emma Eccles Jones Center for Early Childhood Education, Utah State University, Logan, Utah

S. Jay Samuels, EdD, Department of Educational Psychology, University of Minnesota, Minneapolis, Minnesota

Stephan Sargent, EdD, Department of Curriculum and Instruction, Northeastern State University, Broken Arrow, Oklahoma

Timothy Shanahan, PhD, College of Education, University of Illinois at Chicago, Chicago, Illinois

Kathryn L. Solic, MEd, Department of Theory and Practice in Teacher Education, College of Education, University of Tennessee, Knoxville, Tennessee

Bruce Stevenson, PhD, Worthington Schools, Worthington, Ohio; Education Department, Capital University, Columbus, Ohio

Patsy Todt, MEd, Department of Teacher Education, Shawnee State University, Portsmouth, Ohio

Keith J. Topping, PhD, Faculty of Education and Social Work, University of Dundee, Dundee, Scotland

Barbara J. Walker, EdD, Department of Curriculum and Instruction, Oklahoma State University, Tulsa, Oklahoma

Jerry Zutell, PhD, Department of Teaching and Learning, College of Education, Ohio State University, Columbus, Ohio

Preface

Until recently, reading fluency had not been a priority in American reading instruction. Despite periodic calls for a reexamination of reading fluency (e.g., Allington, 1979; Zutell & Rasinski, 1991), fluency was not able to capture the attention or imagination of most reading educators. This may have been due to the way that fluency was defined. For many educators, fluency was nothing more than reading fast or with good oral expression. Neither of these seemed even remotely connected to the well-accepted goal of reading: comprehension.

Things began to change when reading researchers began to show that reading fluency was a necessary precondition for good comprehension (e.g., LaBerge & Samuels, 1974; Stanovich, 1980). More recently, the meta-analysis conducted by the National Reading Panel (2000) concluded that existing research demonstrated that reading fluency was indeed an important component of the reading process and that it was essential that it be taught to developing readers. Thus, since the beginning of the 21st century, reading fluency has taken its place with phonemic awareness, word decoding, vocabulary, and comprehension as critical components of effective reading instruction.

Despite the prominence given to reading fluency by the National Reading Panel, the fact of the matter is that most teachers in the United States do not have an accurate idea of what fluency is or how it can best be taught. And it is not their fault that they do not have a solid conception of reading fluency. For the most part, fluency has not been a visible part of teacher preparation programs or the textbooks that support such programs. Until recently, teachers simply had not been exposed to fluency instruction in their undergraduate and graduate reading education programs.

That is where this book comes in. We have assembled some of the best-known scholars in reading fluency and asked them to share with readers their thoughts on fluency and fluency instruction. We have also asked practitioner colleagues, who are doing innovative, research-based work with fluency programs in real classrooms, to share their perspectives on fluency instruction and assessment. Finally, we have invited diverse educators to look at some specific populations in greater detail. The chapter authors—with backgrounds in universities, school districts, and classrooms at all age levels—are drawn from all across the United States, Australia, New Zealand, and Scotland.

The book is divided into three parts. Part I—Fluency Theory, Fluency Research—is focused on some of the ways in which fluency has come to be understood, and the educational areas in which it has become situated. The second part—Best Programs, Best Practices—highlights some instructional programs and classroom practices that are widely varied in their approach but are all built on a deep understanding of how fluency works. Finally, Part III—Special Populations, Special Issues—explores the applications of fluency research and practice to some populations not typically associated with fluency instruction. The book fittingly opens with a historical overview of fluency by S. Jay Samuels, who first brought the issue into literacy education and continues to be one of its most articulate voices.

We believe that this book makes a significant contribution to the important work of raising readers by providing a conceptual and research base for fluency instruction and effective and engaging instruction in fluency. Readers of this book will come away with a better understanding of reading fluency and some of the problematic issues in both its conceptualization and application in the classroom. The chapters also touch on some of the pitfalls and concerns associated with reading fluency, how to assess fluency and monitor student progress in fluency, and, most importantly, how to teach fluency effectively to different populations of students.

Developing this book has been a labor of love and a marvel of modern technology, as we have collaborated, long distance, with some of the finest minds in reading fluency in the English-speaking world. We hope you will enjoy this journey into the complex realm of fluency as much as we have enjoyed preparing the paths to guide you on your way.

TIMOTHY RASINSKI
CAMILLE BLACHOWICZ
KRISTIN LEMS

REFERENCES

Allington, R. L. (1983). Fluency: The neglected reading goal. *The Reading Teacher, 36*, 556–561.

LaBerge, D., & Samuels, S. A. (1974). Toward a theory of automatic information processing in reading. *Cognitive Psychology, 6*, 293–323.

National Reading Panel. (2000). *Report of the National Reading Panel: Teaching children to read. Report of the subgroups.* Washington, DC: U.S. Department of Health and Human Services, National Institutes of Health.

Stanovich, K. E. (1980). Toward an interactive–compensatory model of individual differences in the development of reading fluency. *Reading Research Quarterly, 16*, 32–71.

Zutell, J., & Rasinski, T. V. (1991). Training teachers to attend to their students' oral reading fluency. *Theory to Practice, 30*, 211–217.

Contents

Introduction

TIMOTHY RASINSKI
CAMILLE L. Z. BLACHOWICZ
KRISTIN LEMS

Until recently, reading fluency had not been a priority in reading instruction in the United States. Despite periodic calls for a reexamination of reading fluency (e.g., Allington, 1983; Zutell & Rasinski, 1991), fluency was not able to capture the attention or imagination of most reading educators. This may have been due to the way that fluency was defined. For many educators, fluency was nothing more than reading fast or with good oral expression. Neither of these seemed even remotely connected to the well-accepted goal of reading—comprehension.

Things began to change when reading researchers began to show that reading fluency was a necessary precondition for good comprehension (e.g., Laberge & Samuels, 1974; Stanovich, 1980). Most recently, the meta-analysis conducted by the National Reading Panel (2000) concluded that existing research demonstrates that reading fluency is indeed an important component of the reading process and that it is essential that it be taught to developing readers. Thus, since the beginning of the 21st century, reading fluency has taken its place with phonemic awareness, word decoding, vocabulary, and comprehension as critical components of effective reading instruction.

Despite the prominence given to reading fluency by the National Reading Panel, the fact of the matter is that most teachers in this country do not have an accurate idea of what fluency is or how it can best be taught. And it is not their fault that they do not have a solid conception of reading fluency. For the most part, fluency has not been a visible part of teacher preparation programs or the textbooks that support such programs. Until recently, teachers had simply not been exposed to fluency instruction in their undergraduate and graduate reading education programs.

That is where this book comes in. We have assembled some of the best-known scholars in reading fluency and have asked them to share with readers their thoughts on fluency and fluency instruction. We have also asked practitioner colleagues who are doing innovative, research-based work with fluency programs in real classrooms to share their perspectives on fluency instruction and assessment. Finally, we have invited diverse educators to look at some specific populations in greater detail. The authors, with backgrounds in universities, school districts, and classrooms at all age levels, are drawn from all across the United States, Australia, New Zealand, and Scotland.

The book is divided into three sections. The first focuses on some of the ways in which fluency has come to be understood, and the educational areas in which it has become situated. The second section highlights some instructional programs and classroom practices that are widely varied in their approach, but all built on a deep understanding of how fluency works. Finally, the third section explores the applications of fluency research and practice to some populations not typically associated with fluency instruction. The book fittingly opens with a historical overview of fluency by Jay Samuels, who first brought the issue into literacy education and continues to be one of its most articulate voices.

We believe that this book makes a significant contribution to the important work of raising readers' awareness by providing a conceptual and research base for fluency instruction, and effective and engaging instruction in fluency. Readers will come away with a better understanding of reading fluency and some of the problematic issues in both its conceptualization and application in the classroom. The chapters also touch on some of the pitfalls and concerns associated with reading fluency, how to assess fluency and to monitor student progress in fluency, and, most importantly, how to teach fluency to different populations of students effectively. Developing this book has been a labor of love and a marvel of modern technology as we have collaborated, long-distance, with some of the finest minds in reading fluency in the English-speaking world. We hope our readers will enjoy this journey into the complex realm of fluency as much as we have enjoyed preparing the paths to guide you on your way.

REFERENCES

Allington, R. L. (1983). Fluency: The neglected reading goal. *Reading Teacher, 36,* 556–561.

LaBerge, D., & Samuels, S. A. (1974). Toward a theory of automatic information processing in reading. *Cognitive Psychology, 6,* 293–323.

National Reading Panel. (2000). *Report of the National Reading Panel: Teaching children to read. Report of the subgroups.* Washington, DC: U.S. Department of Health and Human Services, National Institutes of Health.

Stanovich, K. E. (1980). Toward an interactive-compensatory model of individual differences in the development of reading fluency. *Reading Research Quarterly, 16,* 32–71.

Zutell, J., & Rasinski, T. V. (1991). Training teachers to attend to their students' oral reading fluency in. *Theory Into Practice, 30,* 211–217.

PART I

Fluency Theory,
Fluency Research

CHAPTER 1

Reading Fluency
Its Past, Present, and Future

S. Jay Samuels

In the last few years, reading fluency has become a topic of great interest to teachers. An article by Cassidy and Cassidy (2003/2004) that appeared in the International Reading Association publication *Reading Today* was entitled "What's Hot, What's Not for 2004." For this article, numerous reading experts were asked their views about what is in and what is out in reading instruction. For the first time, reading fluency was added to the list of terms that were evaluated by these experts. This field of experts was of the opinion that not only was fluency a hot topic, but that it also deserved to be a hot topic.

With its new popularity, however, fluency is going through a period of what may be thought of as "growing pains." One problem has to do with the definition of fluency and another has to do with how it is measured, and both problems are interrelated. Since both problems are part of the history of fluency, I begin this chapter by defining it. Then I describe what was happening a century ago in the area of fluency, from the 1900s to about the 1970s. Using the year 1970 as a benchmark leading to the present, I explain what has been happening with regard to developing and measuring fluency. Finally, I gaze into my crystal ball and attempt to predict some future developments in reading fluency.

DEFINITION OF FLUENCY

Automaticity theory attempts to explain how people become highly skilled at difficult tasks such as driving a car, typing on a computer keyboard, or reading a book. If we examine the developmental stages in learning a complex skill, we usually find that good instructors break the complex skill into subskills, and the student is given instruction in how to perform each of the subskills. During the beginning phase, while learning to perform to the level of accuracy, the student has to put so much effort and attention into the task that only one task can be performed at a time. For example, beginning drivers find that when driving in traffic, they usually dislike taking on another task such as talking to another person, or listening to a talk radio show. This focus on one task at a time is somewhat reminiscent of President Theodore Roosevelt's comments about running the country or taking care of his daughter, who was giving her family some problems. The President said, "I can either run the country, or I can take care of Alice, but I cannot do both."

While it is true that in beginning stages of learning a complex task the student can perform only one task at a time, with practice, that situation changes. With practice, the mechanics of driving a car becomes easier, and tasks such as use of lane-change signals, watching for traffic lights, steering to avoid accidents, and choosing routes to one's destination can be done with speed, accuracy, and little attention. As the student becomes automatic at the mechanics of driving, he or she finds it is possible to do two things simultaneously. For example, the person can drive the car through traffic and at the same time engage in conversation with another person or listen to talk shows on the radio. In other words, skilled drivers can do two or more things at the same time, whereas novice drivers cannot.

In order to explain the transition from beginner to expert, automaticity theory makes certain assumptions. For example, it assumes that the human mind has only a limited capacity to perform difficult tasks. Second, it assumes that in order to perform difficult tasks such as recognizing words in a text or understanding their meaning, mental effort must be expended, and this effort consumes some of the limited capacity of the mind. Third, with continued practice over time, the amount of effort required to perform these tasks becomes less and less. And finally, when the amount of effort used in performing a task drops sufficiently, that person can then take on a new task *at the same time*. These few simple rules allow us to describe fluent reading.

The reading process requires that two tasks get done. The first task the student must perform is to recognize the printed words (i.e., decode). The second task is that the student must be able to construct meaning for the words that were decoded (i.e., comprehend). For a beginning reader, the decoding task is so hard that all of the student's mental capacity is used up in the word recognition process. When the entire capacity of the mind is used for decoding, the student cannot construct meaning. However, having decoded the words, the student can then switch attention to getting meaning. So, for beginners, the reading process is one of switching attention back and forth from decoding to meaning. This process is slow, effortful, and hard on memory.

When the student has had lots of practice at reading high-frequency common words found in easy reading material, the decoding process becomes easier and easier, to the point where we can say that decoding is automatic. By "automatic" we simply mean that the words in the text can be decoded with ease, speed, and accuracy. Since the decoding task has become so easy and has not consumed all of the processing capacity of the mind, the student can then direct the unused portion of the mind toward constructing meaning. In other words, the most important characteristic of the fluent reader is the ability to decode and to comprehend the text at the same time. Of course, there are other characteristics of fluency such as accuracy of word recognition, speed of reading, and the ability to read orally with expression, but these are simply indicators of fluency. These indicators of fluency are like the temperature readings in a thermometer when administered to a sick person. The high temperature on the thermometer is not the disease itself, but only an indicator that a person is sick. Reading speed and proper expression in oral reading are indicators of fluency. The essence of fluency is not reading speed or oral reading expression, but the ability to decode and comprehend text at the same time.

READING FLUENCY: 1900–1970

About a century ago, a truly remarkable book about reading was written by Edmund Burke Huey (1908/1968), entitled *The Psychology and Pedagogy of Reading*. The book was so remarkable that the Massachusetts Institute of Technology, one of the leading universities in the world, reissued the book in 1968 with a foreword by John B. Carroll and an introduction by Paul A. Kolers, both of whom were early pioneers in the field of cognitive psychology. One of the remarkable aspects of Huey's book was his keen insight into what would later become automaticity theory. For example, on page 104 of the MIT publication, we find Huey's description of how students become fluent readers:

> Perceiving being an act, it is, like all other things that we do, performed more easily with each repetition of the act. To perceive an entirely new word or other combination of strokes requires considerable time, close attention, and is likely to be imperfectly done, just as when we attempt some new combination of movements, some new trick in the gymnasium or new serve in tennis. In either case, repetition progressively frees the mind from attention to details, makes facile the total act, shortens the time, and reduces the extent to which consciousness must concern itself with the process.

Without invoking what would later become automaticity theory, Huey described the student's progress from beginner, where close attention to the details of words was required for recognition, to the fluency stage, where words could be recognized automatically, with speed and accuracy.

Huey even described how the fluent reader had available a number of options with regard to what unit of word recognition to use in recognizing a word (p. 81). For example, a person can recognize a word letter by letter, in which case the unit of word recognition is the letter. Or a person can recognize a word as a holistic unit, in which case the unit is the entire word. There is evidence that for beginning readers, the letter is the unit used in word recognition, whereas the unit of word recognition for fluent readers is the word itself (Samuels, LaBerge, & Bremer, 1978). With prescience, Huey wrote (p. 81) that

> the more unfamiliar the sequence of letters may be, the more the perception of it proceeds by letters. With increase of familiarity, fewer and fewer clues suffice to touch off the recognition of the word or phrase, the tendency being toward reading in word-wholes. So reading is now by letters, now by groups of letters or by syllables, now by word-wholes, all in the same sentence some times, or even in the same word, as the reader may most quickly attain his purpose.

What Huey was actually describing was how fluent readers read a text. Fluent readers have the option of using a variety of units as the need arises, ranging from the whole word to the single letter. Beginning readers, on the other hand, do not have these options and are limited to the single letter, at least in the beginning stage of reading development.

Until recently, many texts on reading instruction failed to have an entry in their index for "fluency" or "reading fluency." As Allington

(1983) stated some years ago, reading fluency was one of the most neglected areas of the reading curriculum. However, in Huey's 1908 book, there is an entry for "fluent reading" (p. 292). Turning to page 292 in Huey's book, one finds a description of a technique that is reminiscent of a famous experiment designed to find out how chess masters were different from the run-of-the-mill chess player. In this experiment, DeGroot (1965) had chess experts and nonexperts look at a chessboard in which the chess pieces were positioned in well-established positions commonly used by experienced players. After allowing the people in the experiment to view the board for a few moments with the pieces in patterns commonly used in chess, the pieces were knocked off the board, and the task was to recreate the positions as they were originally.

The chess expert was able to recreate the original position, but the nonexpert could not. At first it was thought that the expert had superior memory. But then the second part of the study was done. The same number of pieces was put on the chessboard, only now they were in a random order. Again, the two groups were asked to recreate the chess positions. However, now the expert and the nonexpert did equally poorly. The interpretation for these findings was that chess masters did not have superior memory. Chess has a structure that the experts had learned but the novice players had not learned. Similarly, English spelling of words has a structure, and sentences in a text follow grammatical patterns and rules. Through the practice of reading and learning how to spell words, the skilled readers have learned the structure of our words, whereas the beginner has not. In addition, English grammar itself has a structure, so that we are comfortable when we read "green grass" and uncomfortable if we read "grass green."

Huey described in his book an exercise in which students were shown a phrase in a book for a brief exposure period and then were asked to recreate on paper what they had seen. Or, after the brief exposure, they were asked to recite orally what they had seen. This is precisely what DeGroot did with his chess players. After a brief exposure to the pieces on the board, the players were asked to recreate their positions, whereas in reading, the students were asked to reproduce what they had seen. Huey thought this exercise might help students become fluent readers. This might well be the case, but with the advantage of a century of research on our side, it is more likely that Huey had discovered a good way to determine which students were fluent and which were not. With Huey's task, only fluent readers could perform well.

At about the same time that Huey was writing his book on reading, Bryan and Harter (1897, 1899) began their investigations of how telegraph operators became skilled at sending and receiving Morse code. In many respects, learning Morse code is like learning to read. They found that when faced with the task of receiving the code and making sense of it, beginning Morse code operators were like beginning readers in that they were slow, inaccurate, and had to place all their attention on the task at hand. In fact, beginning Morse code operators found they could only do one task at a time. First, the letters had to be received and made into a word. Second, the meanings could only be constructed after the first task was completed. One of the problems encountered was that if the code came in at a rapid pace, the student could not tell one letter from another, much less one word from another.

Bryan and Harter (1897, 1899) found that with considerable time and practice, the Morse code operators became so automatic at receiving messages that they were able to do this task quickly, accurately, and with little attention. Consequently, they were able to get the meaning of the message at the same time. In other words, they had become "fluent" at the task of reading Morse code. In a remarkable way, the stages of becoming skilled at receiving Morse code paralleled the stages of reading and fluency development described by Ehri (1991) and Chall (1983).

Tim Rasinski's (2003) excellent book on fluency has a section devoted to the history of oral reading. In this section, he describes how oral reading was as important as silent reading from the time of the birth of our nation to the beginning of the 1900s, at which time it began to decline in importance. From a historical perspective, oral reading was important, and for good reason. Before the 1900s, often only one person in a family could read, and that person had the responsibility of reading to the others. Oral reading took on the role of entertainment. So the person who did the oral reading had to do it with skill. Reading out loud had to sound natural. It had to sound like conversational speech. In order to achieve these goals, the person who read out loud had to meet the criteria we currently use as indicators of fluency; that is, the oral reading had to be accurate, reasonably fast, and it had to be done with expression. Furthermore, one of the most important reading researchers of his day, William S. Gray, developed the Gray Oral Reading Test (GORT). This test had students read orally, and, as they read, they were scored for word recognition, accuracy, and speed, but in addition, they were tested for their ability to understand what they had been reading. In essence, this test developed about 80 years ago utilized a technique that measures fluency as we would advocate that it be done today. The test, originally developed by Gray in the 1920s, has gone through four revisions and is still in use today.

Despite the important contributions made by scholars of the past on helping us to understand how fluency develops and can be measured, it did not develop as an important research topic from the 1900s until very recently. Exactly why fluency failed to become an important part of the reading curriculum is not exactly clear. One possibility is that other reading-related problems had priority over fluency. For example, the major psychological paradigm from the 1900s until the late 1950s was behaviorism. This paradigm limited what reading researchers could study to what we could classify as outside-the-head topics, such as word recognition or test development. The investigation of inside-the-head topics, such as comprehension, was discouraged during behaviorism. So when the paradigm shift from behaviorism to cognitive psychology took place during the late 1950s and early 1960s, there was a rush by some of the best minds in psychology to study the long-neglected topic of comprehension.

Like comprehension, the underlying mechanism for fluency is an inside-the-head phenomenon and, under the rules of behaviorism, fluency was neglected. It was only with the birth of the new paradigm, cognitive psychology, that the work on fluency emerged. In addition, by the mid-1960s, Professors Ken Goodman and Frank Smith had begun their attacks on the reading curriculum, and with the coming years their whole language philosophy became one of the most powerful approaches to instruction. The reading wars were on in full swing. There seemed to have been three different groups represented in the wars. There was the whole-language group, the skills-based group, and those who advocated a balanced approach. It is now apparent that the whole-language emphasis is on a downward trajectory and the balanced approach is winning favor. Those who are working on reading fluency are seeing a new interest in fluency as part of a balanced reading approach. As we see in the next section, there were new factors emerging that brought fluency to the forefront.

READING FLUENCY: 1970–PRESENT

In the mid-1960s the University of Minnesota started a research institute called the Human Learning Center, which brought together professors from related disciplines such as psychology, educational psychology, and child development, and encouraged them to collaborate on research. That was how I met Professor David LaBerge, who was in the Psychology Department. LaBerge had developed a machine that presented words on a screen, and when "Yes" or "No" buttons were pushed, the machine could measure accuracy and the reaction time of response. He thought the machine could be used in reading instruction, so we began our collaboration with discussions of the reading process.

These discussions lasted for hours each week, and at the end of the year, we realized that we had developed a theory of reading that focused upon the development of automaticity in word recognition. Our theory stated that if the student was not automatic at word recognition, the important job of reading for meaning had to be done in two stages. First, the student had to attend to the task of decoding the words in the text. Because the word recognition task was not automatic, all of the available cognitive resources were used in the decoding task. Second, the student had to switch attention to comprehension. This two-step process was relatively slow and placed heavy demands on the memory systems. However, over a period that typically lasted for two or three grades, during which time the student had practiced reading books that were in his or her zone of reading ability, the student became automatic at the decoding task. Now, the two tasks, decoding and comprehending, could be done together. We wrote up our ideas, and our article was accepted for publication in *Cognitive Psychology* (LaBerge & Samuels, 1974). Following notification that our article was accepted for publication, a most unusual thing happened. Word had apparently gone out to the research community that a new theory describing automatic information processing in reading was about to be published, and LaBerge and I began to get three, four, or five requests each week for copies of our unpublished manuscript, more requests than we had ever received before for any of our other research reports. Our theory on automaticity was readily accepted by the research and educational communities, and has been viewed as one of the harbingers of what would become a new interest in reading fluency.

There was a problem with LaBerge and Samuels's automaticity theory, however. Our article on automaticity was only a theory, with no practical suggestions in it, and I had always thought that a good theory should have some practical aspects. Following the publication of our article, I struggled for 2 years with the problem of what could be derived from our automaticity theory that would have some useful aspects to it. One day, as I was running around the city lakes near my home, I asked myself two important questions. Who are the most highly skilled people in our society, and what kind of training did they get? I came up with two categories of highly-skilled people: athletes and musicians. Alpine skiers, for example, who could ski down a mountain without killing themselves, had to be highly trained. And jazz piano players, for example, who could play a complex melodic line and hold a conversation with me at the same time, always impressed me with their skill.

What was most exciting to me was the fact that athletes and musicians usually got the same kind of training. What the athletic coach or music teacher did was take these very complex activities and break each one into subskills. For example, in music, the teacher might take a very simple song and show the student how to play it. Then the student was supposed to take the song and practice it for a week, until it could be played to the music teacher's satisfaction with accuracy, appropriate speed, and expression. In wrestling, the coach might take a move and demonstrate how to do each part in sequence. The students then practiced the move until it could be done automatically, with no thought as to its execution. A college wrestling match is like a game of chess. For each move, there is a countermove, and for each counter there is a countermove to the previous one. However, unlike chess in which there is ample time to think, the wrestling moves often take place so quickly that there is no time to think. Wrestlers who have to think about their next move usually lose the match. To reach this level of skill in wrestling, where moves have to be executed automatically with speed and accuracy, considerable time must be devoted to practicing the same moves over and over again.

When I compared the way we taught reading to the way that athletes and musicians were taught, I realized that there were some important differences. In sports and music, students practice until they "get it right." I had been a classroom teacher for 10 years and knew about the pressures placed on teachers to cover a year's work in a year's time. For most kids, the pace of instruction was fine, but for students with below-average intelligence, or those with reading disabilities, the pace of instruction was too fast. For kids with special needs, every day of school was another day of frustration and failure, because they were being pushed through the curriculum too fast and failed to master their work.

What would happen, I asked myself, if we modified reading instruction so that it resembled how we train athletes and musicians? To do this, I got permission from the Minneapolis Schools to work with mentally-challenged beginning reading students. I asked the students how one becomes good at a sport, and they all said that one had to practice to become good at it. I then explained that getting to be a good reader was like getting good at a sport, and that we were going to practice at getting good at reading stories. Before meeting with the children, I had taken a short children's story and had broken it into passages about 150 words in length. Then I made enough copies so that each student in the class had a copy of the passages that covered the short story. As the students held the copy of the beginning of the story in their hands and looked at the words, I read the 150-word passage to them. Then the students practiced at their desks, and each student read the short passage to their teacher, who recorded the word-per-minute reading rate for the story, as well as the number of word recognition errors. The students reread the 150-word passage a number of times, until each one could reach a criterion rate of 85 words a minute. When the criterion rate of reading was reached, the student was given the next passage to practice.

With each rereading of a passage, the students found they made fewer errors, and their reading rate got faster. Before long, the students realized that as they reread the same passage a number of times, they began to sound like good readers. Sounding good was an exciting realization for students who had a history of failure. We had charts for these poor readers that showed their progress, and they liked to see how they were improving. Some of the students asked their parents for stopwatches so they could practice at home on their own. I described the method of repeated reading in an article for *The Reading Teacher* (1979) and it was later reissued as a classic study in reading (1997).

This was the birth of repeated reading, an offshoot of automaticity theory, and the start of numerous studies others have done to investigate a technique that helps to build fluency. Unknown to me, work similar to my own was being done at Harvard's School of Education by Carol Chomsky. Chomsky's work was in response to teachers who wanted a new technique for helping students who failed to make adequate progress in reading. What Chomsky did that was different from my repeated reading method was to tape-record a children's story, and the students who were having trouble learning to read listened to the tape while they looked at the words in their story. When they had listened to the tape enough times that they could read the story on their own, they did so. Chomsky and I independently had come upon similar methods for helping struggling readers. After learning about her work, and the similarity to mine, I invited her to write a chapter for the first edition of *What Research Has to Say about Reading Instruction* (Chomsky, 1978).

The method of repeated reading became a popular method of instruction, especially with students who were having difficulty learning to read. Although the method was effective for helping students become more fluent in reading, there was an important problem with the method, especially as it was first introduced. It was labor intensive, requiring a teacher, or aide, to hear each student read orally to determine if the word-per-minute goal was reached. A research discovery was made, however, that overcame the need for computing reading speed. O'Shea, Sindelar, and O'Shea (1985) found four rereadings to be the most efficient number of times to read the passage, and although more rereadings led to gains, they were too small to be worth the extra time and effort. Thus, one way to do repeated readings is simply have students reread a passage four times. There are many variations of the method of repeated reading as it is now used in the classroom. Children, for example, are paired up and they read to each other, or they reread poems and plays.

The method of repeated reading has even been programmed onto computers (Renaissance Learning, 2005). Students using the fluency development program are tested by the computer to determine their zone of current reading ability; then numerous selections of graded passages at the students' zone of reading development are stored in the computer program and can be used for repeated reading practice. When the time comes for students to move to a more advanced level, there are passages that increase in difficulty, so that the students can practice rereading more difficult texts. For each passage the student selects for practice, a model teacher reads the passage to the student. Then the student reads the passage silently for 1 minute and, based on the initial reading speed for the selection, the computer automatically selects a target speed for the student. The computer even determines when the student's word-per-minute reading rate has reached the target speed. Although the computer frees up the teacher to work in other ways with students, the teacher is called upon to make the decision as to when the student is ready to advance to a higher text readability level.

There were other developments that had significant impact upon fluency. Stanley Deno, a professor of special education, had developed a method to help teachers evaluate the week-by-week rate of growth of students learning to read. His reasoning was that what is wrong with many evaluations is that they take place after months of instruction. If a student did not make progress, then months had been wasted. Deno wanted a method that would be fast and easy to use. He came up with 1-minute time samplings of student reading speed. The student was asked to read for 1 minute from a text that was typical of text used in that student's regular instruction. The number of words read in 1 minute was the test score, and that number was entered onto a chart. A week later, the student was tested again on a similar passage, and the score was entered. If progress was being made, the rate of reading should increase, and the curve should go upward. Deno called the method curriculum-based measurement (CBM). CBM has caught on as a method to evaluate progress in reading, because it is fast, easy to administer, and reliable (Deno, 1985; Deno, Mirkin, & Chang, 1985).

Still other developments helped to elevate reading fluency to the important status it enjoys today. Two highly prestigious reports emphasized fluency. The National Research Council report, *Preventing Reading Difficulties in Young Children* (Snow, Burns, & Griffin, 1998), emphasized that reading fluency should be an important goal of the reading curriculum. This was followed by the National Reading Panel report (2000). Research for the National Reading Panel report was mandated by the U.S. Congress. Congress was aware of the reading wars and wanted to know what reading practices were supported by research. The Report had an entire section on automaticity theory and repeated reading. In addition, it presented a statistical analysis of some of the best repeated reading studies in the research literature to determine whether this method was effective. The Panel concluded that repeated reading was an effective method for improving word recognition, fluency, and comprehension across grade levels.

To conclude this section on the state of reading fluency in the United States today, it is clear that more and more educators view fluency as an important goal of reading instruction. The routes to fluency development seem reasonably clear. One route is to have students get extensive practice reading books that are at their zone of reading development. By encountering high-frequency, common words in a variety of meaningful contexts, students acquire the ability to recognize the words automatically. The other route for building fluency is through using the many varieties of repeated reading. While the routes to developing fluency are clear, the routes to the measurement of fluency are in a state of flux. A commonly used method for assessing fluency is to give students a CBM test of reading speed. This method only measures one aspect of fluency, that is, the ability to read words rapidly and accurately. As reading teachers have discovered, there are students whose oral reading speed is adequate, but who have poor comprehension of what they have read. Another route to fluency measurement is to find out whether students can decode and comprehend at the same time. This is done by simply informing students at the time of testing that they will be asked to read a passage orally and, when they are finished, will be tested for comprehension with questions or by being asked to recall as much as possible about what they read. This method is a good match for the definition of fluency used in this chapter. Furthermore, one test developer already has a test on the market that can determine whether a student can simultaneously decode and comprehend, and a second company is developing a computerized version of such a test.

READING FLUENCY: ITS FUTURE

The discovery of alphabetic writing and reading, now about 4,000 years old, ranks in importance with the discovery of how to harness fire and to use the wheel. Although alphabetic reading has a solid future, many of the methods used to teach reading have a short life cycle. For example, whole language, once considered to be an important methodology, has significantly dropped in popularity. While reading fluency is now considered to be an important aspect of the reading curriculum, its future is tied to what will happen in the area of measurement of fluency. To the extent that experts in the field can design valid instruments that measure the ability of students to decode and comprehend texts simultaneously, the topic will enjoy a longer life cycle than if they cannot design such instruments. One of the attractive aspects to American reading instruction is the willingness of teachers to try different approaches. What works, they keep, and what fails to work, they discard. With regard to fluency, only time will tell.

REFERENCES

Allington, R. L. (1983). Fluency: The neglected reading goal. *Reading Teacher*, 36(6), 556 561.

Bryan, W. L., & Harter, N. (1897). Studies in the physiology and psychology of the telegraphic language. *Psychological Review*, 4, 27–53.

Bryan, W. L., & Harter, N. (1899). Studies on the telegraphic language: The acquisition of a hierarchy of habits. *Psychological Review*, 6, 345–375.

Cassidy, J., & Cassidy, D. (December 2003–January 2004). What's hot, what's not for 2004. *Reading Today*, p. 3.

Chall, J. S. (1983). *Stages in reading development*. New York: McGraw-Hill.

Chomsky, C. (1978). When you still can't read in third grade: After decoding, what? In S. J. Samuels (Ed.), *What research has to say about reading instruction* Newark, DE: International Reading Association.

De Groot, A. D. (1965). *Thought and choice in chess*. The Hague: Mouton.

Deno, S. L. (1985). Curriculum-based measurement: The emerging alternative. *Exceptional Children, 52,* 219–232.

Deno, S. L., Mirkin, P. K., & Chiang, B, (1982). Identifying valid measures of reading. *Exceptional Children, 49*(1), 36–45

Ehri, L. C. (1991). Development of the ability to read words: Update. In P. D. Pearson (Ed.), *Handbook of reading research* (Vol. 2). New York: Longman.

Huey, E. B. (1968). *The psychology and pedagogy of reading.* Cambridge, MA: MIT Press.

LaBerge, D., & Samuels, S. J. (1974). Toward a theory of automatic information processing in reading. *Cognitive Psychology, 6,* 293–323.

National Reading Panel. (2000). *Teaching children to read: An evidence-based assessment of the scientific research literature on reading and its implications for reading instruction.* Washington, DC: National Institute of Child Health and Human Development.

O'Shea, L. J., Sindelar, P. T., & O'Shea, D. J. (1985). The effects of repeated readings and attentional cues on reading fluency and comprehension. *Journal of Reading Behavior, 17,* 19–142.

Renaissance Learning Inc. (2005). *Fluent reader.* Madison, WI: Author.

Rasinski, T. (2003). *The fluent reader: Oral reading strategies for building word recognition, fluency, and comprehension.* New York: Scholastic Books.

Samuels, S. J. (1997). The method of repeated readings. *Reading Teacher, 32,* 403–408/50(5), 376–381. (Original work published 1979)

Samuels, S. J., LaBerge, D., & Bremer, C. (1978). Units of word recognition: Evidence for developmental changes. *Journal of Verbal Learning and Verbal Behavior, 17,* 715–720.

Snow, C. E., Burns, M. S., & Griffin, P. (1998). *Preventing reading difficulties in young children.* Washington, DC: National Academy Press.

CHAPTER 2

Developing Fluency
in the Context
of Effective Literacy Instruction

TIMOTHY SHANAHAN

For more than a decade, I have spent much of my time encouraging teachers to teach fluency. In this work, I employ a framework I developed to guide the improvement of pre-K–12th-grade literacy achievement, and that framework (the Chicago Reading Framework)—more than any other—places great emphasis on the teaching of fluency (Shanahan, 2001). Recently, I was director of reading for the Chicago Public Schools and, in that role, mandated that all 600 of our schools teach fluency on a daily basis. I even coauthored the fluency section of the National Reading Panel report (2000), which found that fluency could be taught, and that such teaching improved reading achievement.

Yes, my credentials on fluency instruction are impeccable. Yet my role in this volume is less to promote fluency instruction (there are more than enough excellent chapters that do that) than to put fluency into a fitting instructional context. To explain the reason for this, let me relate something from my experience as a consultant to school districts. Over the years, I gained a reputation as an effective staff developer. This meant two things: Teachers liked my presentations and often adopted the ideas I shared at the institute or workshop into their classroom routines. If I was brought in to do a workshop on vocabulary instruction, the teachers would start to teach vocabulary or would change how they were teaching it.

As good as I was at that kind of work, sadly, I rarely helped raise achievement. How could that be? I was showing teachers how to teach vocabulary—or comprehension, writing, and so on—in ways proven successful in research. The teachers were adopting these effective practices, and the results in terms of children's learning were . . . well, less than gratifying. What was happening? The scenario that played out was usually something like this: I would encourage teaching an essential part of reading in sound ways; teachers would consequently drop some of the other essentials they were already addressing in order to accommodate the new stuff that I shared, and *voilà*, no improvement in reading. I assumed they would add vocabulary to their otherwise successful teaching routine. The teachers assumed they were supposed to do vocabulary *instead* of the terrific comprehension strategies they were teaching and . . . well, you can see how the results of that would be a wash.

I stopped doing those kinds of workshops more than a decade ago, and I'm glad, because now when I work with teachers and schools, reading achievement often does rise. In Chicago, 75% of the schools—schools that serve 85% low-income students in a minority–majority district— improved in reading, and the lowest performing elementary schools in the district improved in reading as much as the higher performing schools for the first time in history. Fluency was part of that, because fluency is part of the Chicago Reading Framework, but it was not the whole story. Fluency—or any specific outcome, such as comprehension or phonics skills, that we teach in literacy instruction—is not the whole story. Fluency is essential, but it is not a magic bullet. The success of fluency instruction depends not only on the quality of the teaching, but it also depends on the degree to which that quality teaching is *embedded in a full agenda* of other sound literacy instruction. A teacher—confident that fluency is *the* key to success—who drops phonics in order to clear space for fluency in his or her daily teaching schedule is making a bad trade.

The key to adding fluency, or any other important element, to a classroom routine is to ensure that all the other essentials are addressed, too. For me, an "essential" is an aspect of instruction that has been proven to make a difference in children's reading achievement. I am talking here about "scientific reading research-based" teaching, but that term is bandied about a lot these days, and my standards are high for determining which practices fit this description (Shanahan, 2002; Shavelson & Towne, 2002). Before I'm willing to endorse a practice as essential, it must have certain kinds of evidence behind it. There must be, for instance, studies that show that kids who get this kind of teaching do better than kids who don't. There must be evidence drawn from experimental studies in which some teachers adopt the new practice in their classrooms, while other, similar teachers continue as usual. The classrooms in the study must be roughly equal in reading achievement at the start, but they have to be different in the end. There are standards of quality for such studies, and I expect this evidence to come from investigations that meet these quality standards. Finally, I don't think it is enough that a study or two support a particular finding. There should be many independent investigators that tried this practice in different places, but with consistent results.

The Chicago Reading Framework emphasizes three critical steps schools can take to improve achievement, and these steps help ensure the existence of the kind of instructional context in which fluency teaching should be embedded. These critical steps include (1) securing adequate amounts of instructional time for the teaching of reading and writing, (2) ensuring the teaching of all essential aspects of literacy, and (3) providing ongoing monitoring of student learning to allow for appropriate adjustments to teaching. Yes, fluency is an essential aspect of literacy and it should be taught, but the teaching of fluency will be most productive when there is a sufficient amount of literacy teaching, adequate attention to the other essential outcomes or components, and ongoing monitoring of student progress.

THE ROLE OF INSTRUCTIONAL TIME

If that is the standard of evidence for determining what is essential, then what meets this standard? One thing that leaps out of the literature as an essential is the amount of instructional time (Fisher & Berliner, 1985; Meyer, Linn, & Hastings, 1991; Pressley, Wharton-McDonald, Mistretta-Hapston, & Echevarria, 1998). National surveys of teaching suggest that we fail to spend sufficient time teaching kids how to read and write well (Baumann, Hoffman, Duffy-Hester, & Ro, 2000). We've allowed lots of wonderful activities that have little to do with children's learning to encroach on reading and language arts time. In my schools, I require 2–3 hours per day of reading and writing instruction. That is a lot more time for learning than most teachers provide, and increasing the amount of instruction is a proven way to enhance achievement.

ESSENTIAL CONTENT COVERAGE

Another essential is to teach the right stuff; that is, it is important to teach children to know or do those things that constitute proficiency. In large-scale analyses of educational research, content coverage or curriculum focus comes out as the second most important thing, right after amount of instruction (Walberg, 1986; Wang, Haertel, & Walberg, 1990, 1993). Reading instruction is most effective when it focuses on those skills and abilities that give kids an advantage in learning to read (Barr, Dreeben, & Wiratchai, 1983; Fry & Lagomarsino, 1982; Roehler, 1992). That might seem like a no-brainer, but far too often I visit schools that neglect or barely touch upon some of these key areas of learning.

In the Chicago Reading Framework, I organize what needs to be taught into four categories and require equal amounts of teaching for each category. The amount of teaching doesn't necessarily have to balance each day, but each element should receive roughly equal attention over a week or two. There are four areas that I am convinced require regular teaching: word knowledge, fluency, comprehension, and writing. Teachers in my schools must teach each of these for 30–45 minutes per day.

Given that the purpose of this book is to explain fluency instruction, and that the purpose of this chapter is to put fluency into the larger instructional context, I detail each of these four categories, but with greater attention to fluency (not because it is most important—they are all equally important). Before turning to each component, let me explain why these particular components merit this much concentrated and continued instructional attention. Although all four components meet the selection standards I set, all of my examples here deal with how fluency satisfies these criteria.

CRITERIA FOR INCLUSION IN THE MODEL

In order to be included in this model, a component had to meet five basic requirements. First, it had to be a learning outcome and not an instructional practice. Too many instructional schemes emphasize teaching routines over learning outcomes, and this is a big mistake. Research shows how difficult it is for teachers to keep focused on learning within the complexity of classroom life (Doyle, 1983). Good teachers manage to focus on learning, and less effective ones get wrapped up in the activities themselves. It is sort of like the old joke: When you are up to your neck in alligators, it is hard to remember that your purpose was to drain the swamp. With all the "alligators" out there in a challenging classroom, ineffective teachers often lose sight of the purpose. I don't want teachers aimed at guided reading, teacher reading, the ABC Reading Program, or at any technique, practice, program, or approach. The research is pretty clear: Methods of teaching don't make that much difference if the content covered is equivalent (Bond & Dykstra, 1967). I don't want my teachers setting aside a certain amount of time each day to do a particular *activity*. I want them to set aside a certain amount of time each day to teach children to do particular things. Learning—not teaching—is the point.

Second, to be included, research studies had to demonstrate the *teachability* of a component. This means that there had to be several research studies showing that teaching could improve performance in that outcome. For example, the National Reading Panel (2000) examined 14 independent studies in which having students practice oral rereading of a text with some kind of feedback led to improved fluency in reading those texts. Furthermore, several other studies found that this kind of teaching led students to be more fluent, that is, to read texts aloud more accurately or quickly. It only makes sense to focus our instruction upon outcomes that can actually be taught.

Third, to be included as an essential outcome, research had to reveal the *generalizability* of a component. This means that there had to be several research studies proving that if one taught this particular aspect of literacy, overall reading achievement would improve. It is not enough to teach fluency, even if that instruction would result in better fluency, if this improvement doesn't, consequently, translate into better overall reading achievement. The National Reading Panel (2000) examined 16 independent studies in which fluency instruction not only improved fluency performance but also actually translated into higher reading achievement on silent reading comprehension tests.

Fourth, in order for a learning outcome to be essential in this model, it had to fit together in a coherent manner with the other components in the model. It had to be *combinable* with the other parts of the model, so there was a chance that the combination of components would lead to even better performance than would be obtained by attending to any one of the components alone. What this means is that, statistically, each component had to correlate positively and significantly with the others and with overall reading achievement as well. Student fluency performance has just that kind of pattern of relationship with other reading achievement variables (Fuchs, Fuchs, Hosp, & Jenkins, 2001).

Fifth, despite the correlations just noted, each outcome had to be an *independent* entity to justify inclusion in the framework. Instruction in one component should not necessarily lead to growth in all of the components. Evidence for independence could include case studies of children with learning disabilities and brain injuries who may excel in one or another component, without commensurate levels of performance in the others (Coslett, 2000). In the case of fluency, many experts have assumed that it is simply the result of high-proficiency word recognition. If that were true, then the best way to teach fluency would be to put more time into teaching word recognition. In fact, research shows that though fluency is closely aligned with word recognition, it is also—at least in certain cases—a somewhat independent outcome. For instance, Carol Chomsky (1975) identified a sample of children high in decoding skills but low in fluency. Also, clinical studies have identified students who can read text fluently, but without commensurate levels of comprehension (Kennedy, 2003). Independence matters, because it argues for the value of direct teaching of a specific outcome. Since phonics instruction doesn't lead to fluency for all kids, we teach phonics and fluency. Since fluency proficiency does not result in higher comprehension for all students, we teach fluency and comprehension. The surest way to success is to leave nothing to chance in children's learning.

The four key components that satisfy all five of these requirements are word knowledge, reading comprehension, writing, and fluency. And it is to each of these that I now turn.

Word Knowledge

Word knowledge emphasizes two very different instructional goals. We need to teach children both to recognize written words and to expand their knowledge of word meanings. In most discussions of reading instruction, word meanings are categorized as part of reading comprehension, which makes sense, since both vocabulary and comprehension are focused on meaning. The reason I make such a different choice of organization is threefold. First, everything that we teach in reading, from the lowliest phonic skill to the loftiest interpretive strategy, should ultimately be connected to meaning. This suggests that there is nothing special about vocabulary in that particular regard that justifies categorizing it with reading comprehension. Second, I wanted there to be a consistent plan of instruction—in terms of amounts of time and areas of emphasis in my framework—across the grade levels. By putting word recognition together with word meaning, I have established a routine in which upper grade teachers spend similar amounts and proportions of time on word learning as primary grade teachers, albeit the emphasis of this word work does shift. Third, this plan requires a lot more vocabulary teaching than is accomplished in most instructional programs. When vocabulary is just a part of comprehension, there isn't a great deal of time devoted to its teaching. In this framework, from the time word recognition proficiency is accomplished (in second or third grade for most kids), substantial work with word meanings has to be provided.

In the primary grades, it is imperative that teachers give children substantial amounts of word recognition instruction, including phonemic awareness, phonics, and sight vocabulary teaching (National Reading Panel, 2000). Phonemic awareness instruction teaches children to hear and manipulate the separable sounds in words. Most kids benefit from approximately 20 hours of phonemic awareness instruction (about 15 minutes per day for a semester). Of course, some children don't need this much, and others need more. In any event, phonemic awareness instruction should begin by kindergarten and continue until students can fully segment simple words (e.g., dividing the word *cat* into its separate sounds: /k/ /a/ /t/). Children who can hear the sounds within words are at a great advantage in figuring out the relationship between speech and print.

In addition to phonemic awareness, children should get daily phonics instruction. Phonics teaching aims to impart three kinds of knowledge: It should help children master the letter names and sounds, including the sounds related to common letter combinations such as *sh*, *ch*, *th*, and *ng*; it should help them to recognize and pronounce common spelling patterns, such as *ain*, *tion*, and *ight*; and it should guide children to use this information to decode and spell new words (that means reading and spelling practice should be regular parts of phonics instruction).

Additionally, there needs to be an emphasis on teaching children sight vocabulary; that is, they must learn to recognize some words immediately, without sounding out or any other obvious mediation. English uses some words with great frequency (words such as *the*, *of*, *was*, *can*, *saw*, *there*, *to*, and *for*), and if children can recognize these words easily and accurately, they will be better able to focus on the meaning of text.

After about 3 years of phonics instruction and sight vocabulary instruction, word knowledge teaching should shift, for most kids, to a formal or academic emphasis on vocabulary building or word meaning

(Blachowicz & Fisher, 2000). As with phonics and phonemic awareness, many approaches to the teaching of vocabulary have proven effective. The best instructional efforts require students to use new vocabulary in a wide variety of ways (speaking, listening, reading, writing), and guide them to analyze and explore rich contextualized meanings of words and the interrelationships among words. Effective vocabulary instruction also includes small amounts of drill and practice and a considerable amount of review.

Finally, spelling instruction can be part of the word component as well. Such teaching should aim to help students spell in a conventional way, and can provide them with an opportunity to think systematically about how words are structured. Spelling instruction necessarily must be kept brief and is probably best accomplished in conjunction with the word recognition and word-meaning teaching that are the major instructional emphases within word knowledge.

Word knowledge is obviously complex. There are multiple aspects of word teaching, and the relative importance of the parts changes over time as children advance through the grades—with relatively less attention devoted to word recognition and more to word meaning over time. Word knowledge is central to reading achievement and is closely allied with fluency performance (Perfetti, Finger, & Hogaboam, 1978; Stanovich, 1981). Children who cannot recognize words quickly and easily—who lack strong decoding skills or extensive sight vocabularies—struggle when they try to read a text. They make lots of errors, and instead of moving along quickly and smoothly, they labor through a text, impelled more by their efforts to decode each word than by the flow of the author's ideas. Using the time devoted to word knowledge to develop expertise in the quick decoding and automatic recognition of words should ultimately contribute to fluency. And this appears to be a two-way street. Research shows that fluency instruction for poorer readers typically results in much improved word recognition abilities (National Reading Panel, 2000).

Vocabulary knowledge also has a role to play in fluency development. Fluency by its very nature is part rapid sequential decoding and part on-the-fly initial text interpretation. To read a text aloud successfully, a student not only has to recognize the words quickly and easily enough to be accurate but also have sufficient sense of the meaning of the message to make it sound like language. Vocabulary instruction generally helps in initial interpretation by familiarizing students with the meanings of a broad range of words, but it works, more specifically, in helping students correctly interpret homographs (words with one spelling but different pronunciations, depending on meaning) such as *read, minute, wind, bass, sow, does,* and *tear* (Plaut, 1996).

Reading Comprehension

A second instructional component in my framework is the teaching of reading comprehension. Students need to be taught to achieve a deep understanding of text on their own, and this instruction has three major goals. We need to teach students to seek particular types of information when they read a text. We need to teach them how texts are organized or structured and how to use these organizational plans to remember or understand information effectively. Last, we need to teach children a variety of thinking strategies or procedures they can use on their own before, during, and after reading to improve understanding and recall.

For young children, learning what kind of information is important—which needs to be attended to and remembered—entails some fairly general notions, such as the idea that both explicit and inferential information are important (Raphael & Wonnacott, 1985). With development, text demands become more complex and tied to the disciplines, so instruction needs to emphasize the kinds of information that are important within the various disciplinary fields (i.e., history, science, mathematics, and literature). It is not just type of information that matters, either, because these disciplines differ as to how precise or approximate a reader's understanding has to be ("gist," for instance, is not well thought of in science or math texts).

Narrative and expository texts differ greatly in their organizations, vocabulary, and even with regard to the reasons why someone might read them. Students benefit from experience and instruction in dealing with both of these text types. Some of the instruction should guide students to think about how these texts are organized. For narratives, that means teaching about plot structure (including characters, problems, solutions, outcomes, time sequencing, etc.). Students need to learn analogous information about how expository texts are structured (e.g., problem–solution, cause–effect, comparison–contrast), as well as what types of information are likely to appear in particular types of texts. Social studies books, for example, usually provide information on geography, economics, culture, and history on each major topic being discussed; knowing that allows a reader to analyze the text in those terms.

There are also a plethora of techniques or procedures that can be used by kids to guide their thinking about text more effectively on their own (National Reading Panel, 2000). Teaching students to monitor their reading (to make sure that they understand and know what to do about it when they do not), to ask their own questions, to summarize, and to translate text into graphic form are just a few of the techniques that have been found to improve reading comprehension.

It is important to remember that students benefit from comprehension instruction—not just comprehension practice. Too many teachers give assignments that require reading comprehension but do nothing to improve students' capacity to comprehend. Practice alone is insufficient. Children should be taught how to comprehend, and, in the Chicago Reading Framework, time is regularly devoted to this.

As has already been noted, fluency is closely connected to reading comprehension. Fluency instruction improves reading comprehension scores, and studies with proficient readers show that, even for them, rereading a text improves interpretation—improvement that is first obvious in the fluency changes that take place. Fluency at its base is a kind of integration of word recognition and initial sentence interpretation (Young & Bowers, 1995).

Writing

Children need to be able to write their own texts. Reading and writing depend on much of the same information (including knowledge of spelling patterns, text organization, vocabulary, etc.), and learning to read and write simultaneously can give children an advantage (Shanahan, 2005). Writing instruction should teach children to compose for a variety of purposes and audiences, using strategies that help them to solve various writing problems. The compositions that children write should make sense and be effective in communicating their ideas.

Children need to know how to retell events (narrative writing), explain and analyze information (exposition), and argue a position (persuasion), and good instruction should show them how to do these effectively. Children need to know how to adjust their voice and message to meet the needs of an audience. They need to know how to write compositions that are appropriately elaborated, focused, and organized, and that reflect proper mechanics, usage, grammar, and spelling. And students should have at their command a variety of techniques or strategies that can be used effectively and independently to prepare for writing, and to revise and edit what they have drafted.

Writing is less obviously connected to fluency. I know of no study that looks at correlations between writing achievement and reading fluency, and I know of no experimental studies that look at the effects of writing instruction on fluency or fluency instruction on writing. It is evident that spelling accuracy within writing is closely connected to fluency, but this is more likely due to connections between word knowledge and fluency rather than a more general composition–fluency connection (Zutell & Rasinski, 1986). Nevertheless, writing proficiency in composing words and sentences has been found to be connected to reading achievement generally, and this likely means that regular attention to writing instruction may benefit fluency.

Fluency

Fluency refers to the ability to read text aloud with sufficient speed, accuracy, and expression. Although fluency is important to both silent and oral reading, research suggests that oral reading practice and instruction is most effective for developing this ability (National Reading Panel, 2000). Activities such as paired or assisted reading, in which students take turns reading portions of a text aloud to each other and give each other feedback, and rereading the text multiple times until it can be done well, have been found to be effective practices from the primary grades through high school. These practices have some commonalities: They all require oral reading, provide the reader with feedback and help, and require repetition of the reading until the text can be read well.

If a student is fluent with a particular text, the teacher has two choices. First, if the teacher believes the student is placed in an appropriate level text for reading, then he or she only has to continue to monitor the child's reading (by listening), and—in my framework—the amount of fluency instruction for this student can be reduced (fluency is the only component of the framework that can be reduced in terms of time coverage—and this should only be done if the students are fluent at an appropriate level). Second, if the teacher thinks the student should be working on more difficult materials, then he or she can have the child practice fluency in more difficult texts, including social studies or science books.

Students who are fluent with a text can usually read it with only about one mistake per 100 words, and they can read the text smoothly and quickly. Young children (through second grade) should strive to read a text at about 60–80 words per minute, while for older children, reading should proceed at 100+ words per minute. Students also need to pay attention to punctuation and pause appropriately so that the text sounds like language.

What about round robin reading, in which a child reads a portion of text aloud with everyone else listening? It really has no place here. It is not that the oral reading practice provided by round robin is so bad—it is really no different than what is provided in other kinds of oral reading activity; it is that it is so brief (Stallings & Krasavage, 1986). Let's say the teacher is requiring 30 minutes per day of fluency work and has 30 children in class. Using round robin, it would only be possible to provide about 1 minute per day of reading per child under the best circumstances, and only about 3 hours of practice per child across an entire school year. That same teacher, using paired reading, in which children take turns reading and giving feedback to each other, would provide 15 times the amount of reading practice—15 minutes per day, and 45 hours of individual practice per year!

It has often been asserted that fluency develops from silent reading practice and not just the kinds of oral reading practice lauded here. Accordingly, some teachers (and programs) include sustained silent reading in place of the fluency time. It should be noted that despite the logic of having students simply reading more, research doesn't actually support it, and without a credible research base, it seems unwise to replace a procedure that we know works (oral reading practice) with one of which we are uncertain (National Reading Panel, 2000).

Some teachers, of course, are afraid to turn their classes loose with something like paired reading, afraid that the result will be mayhem rather than fluency. These teachers are correct that they should not turn their classes loose, because paired reading time is very involving for both the children and the teacher—after all, this is teaching time. If the teacher has the class organized into pairs and those pairs are all reading to each other, the teacher needs to move among the pairs giving additional guidance and feedback. In one pair, the teacher might intervene by giving one of the partners some direction ("How well did Jimmy do? Should Jimmy read it again?"). In another case, he or she may explain the meaning of a challenging word or help the children to decode a challenging word. In still another, the teacher may listen to a child's reading in order to evaluate the appropriateness of the text placement. The point is that the teacher is actively listening and interacting with the children during fluency instruction time, and that kind of active involvement helps maintain classroom order, as well as improve children's reading achievement.

As with any of the other components in the framework, the time organization can be flexible. What I mean by this is that the plan does not require block scheduling. It is not necessary to set aside 9:00–11:00 A.M. each day for reading instruction, with each component receiving 30 minutes of uninterrupted time in sequence. School days are more complex than that, and research does not support any particular organization over another. Some teachers like to have two 15-minute fluency periods rather than a single half-hour. Some prefer to use time during the afternoon for this rather than the morning. These are reasonable choices made by reasonable teachers.

Some teachers seek special materials for fluency teaching, usually opting for materials that are heavy on predictability and rhyme. There is no question that poetry can be great fun for fluency time (Shel Silverstein and Jack Prelutsky are especially popular choices). However, I recommend caution with regard to such choices and would relegate them to the "we read those occasionally" category. My reasoning is that the research on fluency was not conducted with such materials, and it is not enough that children become fluent with poetry—they must be able to read prose, with its very different rhythms and cadences, as well. A good deal of fluency practice can take place profitably using the same materials used for reading comprehension. There is one problem with this approach, however; the difficulty levels of books used to build comprehension have increased to such an extent that they may be too hard for some children to allow them the best fluency practice (Menton & Hiebert, 1999). Most authorities on reading encourage fluency practice at levels that are instructional (about 95% accuracy on a first reading), and most studies of fluency instruction used materials that were more controlled than some literature-based basals (National Reading Panel, 2000). However, it is much easier to select appropriate supplementary materials for fluency practice that are nearer to student reading levels when students are working in pairs than when the teacher is doing a whole-class or larger group activity. There may be a benefit to having everyone think about the same ideas in a particular text, but there is no analogous benefit to having everyone practice fluency at exactly the same levels.

MONITORING LEARNING

Another requirement in the Chicago Reading Framework—beyond the standards for amount of instruction and content coverage—is that teachers should monitor student learning. Successful teaching depends on not only the use of research-proven instructional techniques but also on teacher awareness of how well the children are doing. Effective teachers pay attention to their children's progress and adjust their efforts accordingly (Shepard, 2000). This is important with word knowledge, comprehension, writing, and fluency, but, again, for this discussion, my examples emphasize fluency monitoring.

Testing can play an obvious role in monitoring student progress, and there are some fine ways to assess whether students can read a text fluently, including Diagnostic Indicators of Basic Early Literacy Skills (DIBELS; Good & Kaminski, 2002), running records (Clay, 1985), and informal reading inventories (Johnson, Kress, & Pikulski, 1987). However, even these informal measures, designed to be administered and readministered, cannot be given often enough to inform instruction as frequently as would be beneficial. By all means, use tests like these early in the year to determine where to start, and give them occasionally throughout the year to check on progress. But between the administrations of these tests, I encourage my teachers to continue to examine their students' fluency development less formally.

One simple way to do this is to maintain written records of students' oral reading performances obtained during teaching. I've always done this on index cards, one per child, but it is now possible to keep such records on a personal digital assistant (PDA) or similar device, if that is easier. However the records are maintained, the teacher listens to each child reading at least once each week (and, yes, you will want to hear some kids more often than that). That means the teacher needs to listen to 5 or 6 readers during each fluency period depending on the size of the group, but that isn't too hard if there are 30–45 minutes per day devoted to fluency. Then the teacher simply makes a note of what the child was reading and how well he or she did.

How do we determine how fluently a child reads? There are really three options. One is to evaluate the accuracy of what a child reads. This means counting (or estimating, since this is an informal look) how many words the child read and how many errors were made. In a second-grade book, 100 words are equivalent to approximately 15 lines of text. I listen to a child read, keeping track of the mistakes, and when 15 lines have been completed, I tally up the mistakes and make my calculations. If the youngster made five errors in about 15 lines, that would mean that he or she read the text with 95% accuracy. That is good, but it could be better, and by monitoring the accuracy of the reading, I can see if he or she is improving.

Another possibility is to consider how fast the child is reading. I'm not talking about speed reading here, just that reading should move along like language. Hasbrouck and Tindal (1992) tested 7,000 children to develop reading speed norms, and these can be useful as well. (Using these norms, I generally shoot for getting my first graders to read at 60 words correct per minute (wcpm) by the end of the school year, my second graders at 90 wcpm, and third graders at 120 wcpm, with increases of about 10 words per year after that). I might have a child read for 1 minute, then simply count the number of words read accurately (all the words read in a minute minus the errors). Then I can record that speed and, again, keep track over several weeks to see if the child's speed and accuracy are improving.

Finally, I can look at how much the reading sounds like language. The National Assessment of Educational Progress (NAEP) put forth a plan for monitoring oral reading that allows an oral reading performance to be classified on a 4-point scale or rubric, with 1 being dysfluent and 4 being fluent and expressive (Pinnell et al., 1995). A reading performance is rated as 1 (dysfluent) if it is so choppy that the child is reading word by word. The performance is rated a 2 if the child is reading in two- or three-word phrases, but the pauses do not reflect the punctuation or the meaning. The reading is rated a 3 if the child is chunking into two-, three-, or four-word phrases, and these reflect the meaning and punctuation (i.e., it is understandable as language). Finally, a reading is rated a 4 if it has the positive pausing characteristics noted for a rate of 3 but is more expressive. The teacher can listen to an oral reading performance and rate it on this 4-point scale. The goal is to get children reading at level 3 or 4 on this scale.

By recording this kind of information once or twice per week, a teacher is at a great advantage for adjusting instruction and sharing helpful information with parents (if oral reading were monitored once per week, imagine how much information could be provide to parents on a report card or at conferences). If a child isn't making sufficient progress, this information should lead to some adjustment in instruction: an easier book; the use of an adult volunteer as a reading partner; additional fluency time at home, after school, or during another part of the school day; or greater attention to some aspect of fluency (e.g., building up sight vocabulary).

SUMMARY

Teachers who have not been teaching fluency, or have not devoted sufficient attention to it, by all means should strive to improve fluency instruction with children. However, fluency instruction works best when it is part of a more complete regimen of reading and writing instruction. Teachers should strive to teach reading and writing for 2–3 hours per day, including instruction in word knowledge (recognition and meaning), fluency, comprehension, and writing. These should receive roughly equal amounts of instructional attention, and should be taught using research-proven instructional approaches, such as those described by the National Reading Panel (Armbruster, Lehr, & Osborn, 2001). Finally, teachers need to monitor student progress toward the learning goals in fluency and the other components of reading as they teach. By bringing fluency into classroom reading programs in this way, teachers really can raise reading achievement.

REFERENCES

Armbruster, B. B., Lehr, F., & Osborn, J. (2001). *Put reading first: The research building blocks for teaching children to read.* Jessup, MD: National Institute for Literacy.

Barr, R., & Dreeben, R., with Wiratchai, N. (1983). *How schools work.* Chicago: University of Chicago Press.

Baumann, J. F., Hoffman, J. V., Duffy-Hester, A. M., & Ro, J. M. (2000). The first R yesterday and today: U.S. elementary reading instruction practices reported by teachers and administrators. *Reading Research Quarterly, 35,* 338–377.

Blachowicz, C. L. Z., & Fisher, P. (2000). Vocabulary instruction. In M. L. Kamil, P. Mosenthal, R. Barr, & P. D. Pearson (Eds.), *Handbook of reading research* (Vol. 3, pp. 503–524). New York: Longman.

Bond, G. L., & Dykstra, R. (1997). The cooperative research program in first-grade reading instruction. *Reading Research Quarterly, 32,* 345–427.

Chomsky, C. (1975). When you still can't read in third grade: After decoding, what? In S. J. Samuels (Ed.), *What research has to say about reading instruction* (pp. 13–30). Newark, DE: International Reading Association.

Clay, M. M. (1985). *The early detection of reading difficulties* (3rd ed.). Portsmouth, NH: Heinemann.

Coslett, H. B. (2000). Acquired dyslexia. *Seminars in Neurology, 20,* 419–426.

Doyle, W. (1983). Academic work. *Review of Educational Research, 53,* 159–199.

Fisher, C. W., & Berliner, D. C. (1985). *Perspectives on instructional time.* New York: Longman.

Fry, M. A., & Lagomarsino, L. (1982). Factors that influence reading: A developmental perspective. *School Psychology Review, 11,* 239–250.

Fuchs, L. S., Fuchs, D., Hosp, M. K., & Jenkins, J. R. (2001). Oral reading fluency as an indicator of reading competence: A theoretical, empirical, and historical analysis. *Scientific Studies of Reading, 5,* 239–256.

Good, R. H., & Kaminski, R. A. (2002). *DIBELS oral reading fluency passages for first through third grades* (Technical Report No. 10). Eugene: University of Oregon.

Hasbrouck, J. E., & Tindal, G. (1992). Curriculum based fluency norms for grades two through five. *Teaching Exceptional Children, 24,* 41–44.

Johnson, M. S., Kress, R. A., & Pikulski, J. J. (1987). *Informal reading inventories.* Newark, DE: International Reading Association.

Kennedy, B. (2003). Hyperlexia profiles. *Brain and Language, 84,* 204–221.

Menton, S., & Hiebert, E. H. (1999). *Literature anthologies: The task for first-grade readers.* Ann Arbor, MI: Center for the Improvement of Early Reading Achievement.

Meyer, L. A., Linn, R. A., & Hastings, C. N. (1991). Teacher stability from morning to afternoon and from year to year. *American Educational Research Journal, 28,* 825–847.

National Reading Panel. (2000). *Teaching children to read.* Washington, DC: National Institute of Child Health and Human Development.

Perfetti, C. A., Finger, E., & Hogaboam, T. W. (1978). Sources of vocalization latency differences between skilled and less skilled readers. *Journal of Educational Psychology, 70,* 730–739.

Pinnell, G. S., Pikulski, J. J., Wixson, K. K., Campbell, J. R., Gough, P. B., & Beatty, A. S. (1995). *Listening to children read aloud.* Washington, DC: U.S. Department of Education.

Plaut, D. C. (1996). Relearning after damage in connectionist networks: Toward a theory of rehabilitation. *Brain and Language, 52,* 25–82.

Pressley, M., Wharton-McDonald, R., Mistretta-Hapston, J., & Echevarria, M. (1998). Literacy instruction in 10 fourth and fifth grade classrooms in upstate New York. *Scientific Studies of Reading, 2,* 159–194.

Raphael, T. E., & Wonnacott, C. A. (1985). Heightening fourth students' sensitivity to sources of information for answering comprehension questions. *Reading Research Quarterly, 20,* 282–296.

Roehler, L. R. (1992). Embracing the instructional complexities of reading instruction. In M. Pressley, K. R. Harris, & J. Guthrie (Eds.), *Promoting academic competence and literacy in school* (pp. 427–455). San Diego, CA: Academic Press.

Shanahan, T. (2001). Improving reading education for low-income children. In G. Shiel & U. N. Dhálaigh (Eds.), *Reading matters: A fresh start* (pp. 157–165). Dublin: Reading Association of Ireland/National Reading Initiative.

Shanahan, T. (2002). What research says: The promises and limitations of applying research to reading education. In A. E. Farstrup & S. J. Samuels (Eds.), *What research has to say about reading instruction* (3rd ed., pp. 8–24). Newark, DE: International Reading Association.

Shanahan, T. (2005). Relations among oral language, reading, and writing development. In C. A. MacArthur, S. Graham, & J. Fitzgerald (Eds.), *Handbook of writing research* (pp. 171–184). New York: Guilford Press.

Shavelson, R. J., & Towne, L. (Eds.). (2002). *Scientific research in education*. Washington, DC: National Academy Press.

Shepard, L. (2000). The role of assessment in a learning culture. *Educational Researcher, 29*(7), 4–14.

Stallings, J., & Krasavage, E. M. (1986). Program implementation and student achievement in a four-year Madeline Hunter Follow-Through Project. *Elementary School Journal, 87*, 117–138.

Stanovich, K. E. (1981). Relationship between word de-cod-ing speed, general name retrieval ability, and reading progress in first-grade children. *Journal of Educational Psychology, 73*, 809–815.

Walberg, H. J. (1986). Syntheses of research on teaching. In M. J. Wittrock (Ed.), *Handbook of research on teaching* (3rd ed., pp. 214–230). New York: Macmillan.

Wang, M. C., Haertel, G. D., & Walberg, H. J. (1990). What influences learning?: A content analysis of review literature. *Journal of Educational Research, 84*, 30–43.

Wang, M. C., Haertel, G. D., & Walberg, H. J. (1993). Toward a knowledge base for school learning. *Review of Educational Research, 63*, 249–294.

Young, A., & Bowers, P. G. (1995). Individual difference and text difficulty determinants of reading fluency and expressiveness. *Journal of Experimental Child Psychology, 60*, 428–454.

Zutell, J., & Rasinski, T. (1986). Spelling ability and reading fluency. *National Reading Conference Yearbook, 35*, 109–112.

CHAPTER 3

Fluency

The Link between Decoding
and Comprehension for Struggling Readers

David J. Chard
John J. Pikulski
Sarah H. McDonagh

Fluency, which has been referred to as a "neglected" aspect of reading (National Reading Panel, 2000), is receiving substantial attention currently from both researchers and practitioners. This may be because the influential report of the National Reading Panel identifies fluency as one of only five critical components of reading: phonemic awareness, phonics, vocabulary, fluency, and comprehension. For struggling readers, fluency and its reciprocal relationship to comprehension is frequently ignored as a focus for remedial instruction, with teachers maintaining an emphasis on phonemic awareness and phonics instruction.

DEFINING READING FLUENCY

Fluency has sometimes been viewed as essentially an oral reading phenomenon. However, because most readers spend a miniscule amount of time engaged in oral reading compared to silent reading, a definition of fluency needs to encompass more than oral reading. The International Reading Association's (IRA) *The Literacy Dictionary: The Vocabulary of Reading and Writing* defines "fluency" as "freedom from word identification problems that might hinder comprehension" (Harris & Hodges, 1995, p. 85). This definition enlarges our understanding of reading fluency to include comprehension. Samuels (2002), a pioneer in research and theory in reading fluency, cites this expanded definition as a major force in elevating the importance of fluency in the field of reading.

The National Assessment of Educational Progress (NAEP) established that there is a significant and positive relationship between oral reading fluency and reading comprehension (Pinnell et al., 1995). However, the relationship between fluency and comprehension is fairly complex. This complexity is summed up well by Stecker, Roser, and Martinez (1998) in their review of fluency research: "The issue of whether fluency is an outgrowth or a contributor to comprehension is unresolved. There is empirical evidence to support both positions" (p. 300). However, in the end, they conclude: "Fluency has been shown to have a 'reciprocal relationship' with comprehension, with each fostering the other" (p. 306).

A comprehensive definition, then, would relate the centrality of fluency to reading comprehension and its established dimensions. Previously, we proposed the following synthesis of definitions:

> Reading fluency refers to efficient, effective word recognition skills that permit a reader to construct the meaning of text. Fluency is manifested in accurate, rapid, expressive oral reading and is applied during, and makes possible, silent reading comprehension. (Pikulski & Chard, 2005, p. 3)

We think that the issue of a definition is not trivial but central to making important decisions about the teaching and assessment of fluency for struggling readers. Rather than a surface view of reading fluency that might lead to the practice of telling students to read faster, our definition suggests a deep construct view of fluency, which considers fluency broadly as part of a developmental process of building oral language and decoding skills that form a bridge to reading comprehension, resulting in a reciprocal, causal relationship with reading comprehension. More specifically, we contend that this deep construct view considers four dimensions of fluency: oral reading accuracy, oral reading rate, quality of oral reading, and reading comprehension. It becomes necessary to think about fluency as part of a child's earliest experiences with print, and with the phonology that becomes associated with that print. In this view, efficient decoding is consistently related to comprehension. In the next section, we describe several theories related to reading fluency and their contribution to our understanding of how fluency develops.

HISTORICAL DEVELOPMENT OF THE CONSTRUCT OF READING FLUENCY

While an early discussion of the construct of reading fluency is found in the classic 1908 publication by Edmund Huey (1908/1968), most discussions of fluency trace their modern theoretical foundations to the 1974 seminal article by LaBerge and Samuels, who argued that human beings can attend to only one thing at a time. However, we are able to do more than one thing at a time if we alternate our attention between two or more activities, or if one of the activities is so well learned that it can be performed automatically. Reading successfully is a complex interaction of language, sensory perception, memory, and motivation. To illustrate the role of fluency, it helps to characterize this multifaceted process as including *at least* two activities: (1) word identification or decoding and (2) comprehension, or the construction of the meaning of text. In order for reading to proceed effectively, the reader cannot focus attention on both word identification and comprehension. Understanding an author's message involves making inferences, responding critically, and so on, and it *always* requires attention. The nonfluent reader can alternate attention between the two processes; however, this makes reading a laborious, often punishing process. If attention is drained by decoding words, little or no capacity is available for the attention-demanding process of comprehending. Therefore, automaticity of decoding—a critical component of fluency—is essential for high levels of reading achievement.

Perfetti (1985) applied the LaBerge and Samuels argument to an information-processing approach to understanding the importance of efficient lower level processes in fluent, connected text reading. His "verbal efficiency theory" highlights the importance of lower level lexical skills in reading and explains the impact of processing information at multiple levels of reading comprehension. He suggests that lower level processes (e.g., word identification) must reach a minimum performance level before higher level processes can be performed simultaneously during reading. When lower level processes are performed inefficiently, higher order processes will attempt to compensate. Perfetti's theory assumes that resource demands can be reduced through learning and practice, and efficiency may be enhanced through careful allocation of resources.

More recently, Logan (1988) developed a memory-based theory of fluency titled the "instance theory of automatization." Logan posits that automaticity and fluency are based on memory retrieval. Three key assumptions of Logan's memory-based theory include (1) obligatory encoding, (2) obligatory retrieval, and (3) instance representation (Logan, 1997). "Obligatory encoding" refers to focusing attention on a stimulus (e.g., a word) and storing details of that stimulus in memory. "Obligatory retrieval" suggests that merely attending to a stimulus is sufficient to retrieve previous exposures or similar stimuli from memory. "Instance representation" refers to the coding and storage of each memory trace of experiences with a stimulus in memory. Each memory trace is coded and stored separately regardless of prior experience with the stimulus. Logan contends that information recall is automatic when it relies on retrieval of "stored instances" from memory. Stored instances refer to the theoretical memory traces laid down in the brain each time a task is executed. As the number of trials on a task increases, the strength of the number of memory traces or instances also increases.

In his further refinement of the theory, Logan (1997) suggests that automaticity develops as a consequence of the "power law," which states that the reaction time to a stimulus decreases as a result of practice and repetition. The level of automaticity developed is dependent on the amount of practice, the level of consistency in the task environment, and the number of relevant instances of the task recorded in memory. As the reader's knowledge base expands and becomes accurate, performance becomes reliant on memory retrieval rather than problem solving (Logan, 1997). Based on Logan's theory, as students read words, they lay down traces for each word. If the word is read frequently enough, the cumulative practice with that word results in an increased likelihood that the word will be recognized upon further exposures, and that the speed with which it will be recognized will increase. While we are attracted to the obvious notion that frequent practice with words will speed subsequent access to those words, we believe Logan's theory alone does little to help guide fluency instruction for struggling readers.

Stanovich (1986) also contributed to the contemporary focus on reading fluency. He demonstrated a clear relationship between fluency and the amount of reading in which a reader engages. Readers who achieve some fluency are likely to be readers who read more extensively than those who lack fluency, because the latter find reading difficult.

Stanovich points out that as a result of reading more extensively, readers grow in all the skills that contribute to fluency and in fluency itself. Nonfluent readers who avoid reading fall further and further behind.

The report of the National Reading Panel (2000) significantly elevated attention to fluency. The Panel's review largely reflected the position that "fluency develops from reading practice" (p. 3-1). Therefore, they devoted much of their review to analyzing the research support that exists for two major approaches to providing students with reading practice: "first, procedures that emphasize repeated oral reading practice or guided repeated oral reading practice; and second, all formal efforts to increase the amounts of independent or recreational reading that students engage in" (p. 3-5). Basically, they concluded that there is substantial evidence to support the use of the repeated reading procedures. However, they raised questions about the evidence to support wide independent reading for promoting fluency:

> There seems little reason to reject the idea that lots of silent reading would provide students with valuable practice that would enhance fluency and, ultimately, comprehension. . . . It could be that if you read more, you will become a better reader; however, it also seems possible that better readers simply choose to read more. (p. 3-21)

In essence, they conclude that while there is very strong correlational support for independent reading contributing to fluency, there is no convincing experimental research to show that increasing independent reading will increase fluency or reading achievement.

This discussion of fluency and of the related research is certainly not a comprehensive review. Many important research findings are omitted. For more comprehensive discussions of fluency, readers are encouraged to consult reviews such as those by the National Reading Panel (2000), Reutzel (1996), Stecker and colleagues (1998), and the entire Summer 1991 (Vol. 30, No. 3) issue of the journal *Theory Into Practice*.

While the recent report of the National Reading Panel is clearly instructive for its critical review of how practice may affect fluency, the position taken here is that a much broader approach is warranted, one that addresses the need of systematic, long-term, explicit fluency instruction, along with careful monitoring and assessment for struggling readers. Rather than focus solely on how to improve fluency when it is not developing as expected, it would seem instructive to examine the elements of early literacy that contribute to fluency. For this purpose, we turn to yet another theory that attempts to explain the relation of word reading development to reading fluency.

EHRI'S STAGES OF READING DEVELOPMENT AND FLUENCY

Ehri (1995, 1998) has developed a carefully researched, elegant theory of the stages through which readers systematically progress in order to achieve fluency. Her theory is in line with a "deep" developmental construct of fluency. We review her theory because it brings coherence to much of the research on fluency, and because it offers a framework for instruction designed to promote and improve fluency. Ehri distinguished five stages of reading development.

Readers at the *prealphabetic stage* have no appreciation of the alphabetic principle—the idea that in alphabetic languages like English there is a systematic relationship between the limited number of sounds and the graphic forms (letters) of the language. At the prealphabetic stage, children attempt to translate the unfamiliar visual forms of print into familiar oral language through visual clues in the print. Children might remember the word *monkey* by associating the descending shape of the last letter with a monkey's tail. Obviously this is not a productive approach, and it quickly leads to confusion, since *my*, *pony*, and many other words would also be read as *monkey*. It would also not be productive in an alphabetic language (e.g., English, Spanish) to pursue an instructional approach that emphasizes word shape rather than a more generalizable approach to word recognition.

At the *partial alphabetic stage*, readers have learned that letters and sounds are related. However, they are not able to deal with the full complexity of the sounds in words, and are unable to make complete use of the letter–sound relationships. Therefore, children focus on the most salient parts of a word and consequently use initial and, later, final letters as the clues to a printed word's pronunciation. If readers at this stage learn that the letter sequence *g-e-t* is *get*, they may focus just on the *g* and the sound it represents to identify the word. However, using this strategy of focusing on the first letter, the letter sequences *give*, *go*, and *gorilla* might also be identified as *get*. While children at this stage of development will make errors in identifying words, they can make progress toward becoming fluent, since they have developed the insight that the letters of a word are clues to the sounds of the word.

As children become more familiar with letters and sounds, they move into the *fully alphabetic stage*. Now, even though they may never have seen it in print before, if they know the sounds commonly associated with the letters *b-u-g*, they can think about the sounds for each of the letters and blend them together to arrive at the pronunciation of the word. As a result of encountering the printed word *bug* several times, as few as four according to a widely cited study (Reitsma, 1983), they come to accurately and instantly identify the word *bug* without attending to the individual letters, sounds, or letter–sound associations. Ehri (1998) describes skilled reading in the following way: "Most of the words are known by sight. Sight reading is a fast-acting process. The term *sight* indicates that sight of the word activates that word in memory including information about its spelling, pronunciation, typical role in sentences, and meaning" (pp. 11–12). This instant, accurate, and automatic access *to all these dimensions* of a printed word is the needed *fluency* that will allow readers to focus their attention on comprehension rather than on decoding. It is important to note that Ehri's theory and research incorporates Logan's "power law" but goes further to indicate that it is the careful processing of print in the fully alphabetic stage that leads to this rapid, instant recognition. Partial alphabetic readers store incomplete representations of words and, therefore, confuse similar words such as *were*, *where*, *wire*, and *wore*. However, once the word form is fully processed, with repeated encounters of the word, it is recognized instantly.

Readers who recognize whole words instantly have reached the *consolidated alphabetic stage*. They also develop another valuable, attention-saving decoding skill. In addition to storing words as units, repeated encounters with words allow a reader to store letter patterns across different words. A multiletter unit, *-ent*, will be stored as a unit as a result of reading the words *went*, *sent*, and *bent*. Upon encountering the word *dent* for the first time, a consolidated alphabetic reader would need to connect only two units, *d* and *-ent*, rather than the four units that the fully alphabetic reader would need to combine. While this approach to reading a word is faster than blending the individual phonemes, it is not as fast and efficient as sight recognition of the word. Readers who have reached the consolidated stage of reading development are in a good position to progress toward increasingly efficient fluency; however, in addition to these advanced word identification skills, they also need to increase their language vocabulary development in order to reach advanced levels of fluent reading.

The final *automatic stage* is characterized by instant recognition of words and the ability to apply advanced decoding strategies with competence and automaticity. Readers in the automatic stage unconsciously apply multiple strategies to decode and confirm unfamiliar words, resulting in accurate, fluent reading (Ehri & McCormick, 1998). This stage is characteristic of mature readers.

The previous research focuses singularly on the reader's development. However, fluency and fluency difficulties are influenced by both learner factors and other factors. In the following section, we review a range of factors that contribute to fluency difficulties and discuss how to use this information when working to improve fluency for struggling readers.

FACTORS CONTRIBUTING TO FLUENCY DIFFICULTIES FOR STRUGGLING READERS

To best understand an instructional program based on a deep construct of fluency for struggling readers, it is helpful to understand the etiology of individual differences in reading fluency. Torgesen, Rashotte, and Alexander (2001) identified the following five factors that impact a child's ability to read fluently:

1. The proportion of words in text that are recognized as orthographic.
2. Variations in speed with which sight words are processed.
3. Speed of processes that are used to identify novel words.
4. Use of context to increase word identification.
5. Speed with which word meanings are identified.

Below we describe each factor within the context of our definition of fluency, highlighting the reciprocal relationship between fluency and comprehension.

The ability to read words as orthographic chunks or units increases speed of word recognition. This speed in word recognition enables readers to focus on constructing meaning from text. Torgesen, Rashotte, and colleagues (2001) found that the ability to identify words by sight is the variable most strongly related to connected text reading rate both in students with and without reading disabilities.

Individuals vary in the speed with which sight words are processed based on the number and quality of exposures to the word (Ehri, 1997; Logan, 1988) or on differences in processing speed (Wolf, Bowers, & Biddle, 2000). If words are not effectively assimilated into a child's sight word repertoire, speed of word identification will be reduced as the child attempts to decode the word. Bower and Wolf (cited in Levy, 2001) hypothesize that slow processing speed is related to slow letter processing. Difficulties with word identification, peripheral processing, and letter processing result in inhibited processing of larger orthographic units and dysfluent reading. This hypothesis supports a focus on a deeper construct of fluency with a focus on providing instruction that encompasses a broader range of reading skills and behaviors to support reading comprehension.

Speed of processing novel words is reduced when words are not recognized as orthographic chunks (i.e., spelling patterns) or morphemes. Reading novel words requires conscious analysis, including phonetic decoding, recognition by analogy to known words, and guessing from the context or meaning of the passage (Torgesen, Rashotte, et al., 2001). If processing at the subskill level is not automatic and requires conscious analysis, reading comprehension will be compromised.

Evidence indicates that while fluent readers do not rely on passage context for word identification, struggling readers and beginning readers do (Ben Dror, Pollatsek, & Scarpati, 1991, cited in Torgesen, Rashotte, et al., 2001; Pring & Snowling, 1986, cited in Torgesen, Rashotte, et al., 2001). Although the role of context for beginning and poor readers in reading fluency is unclear, Torgesen, Rashotte, and colleagues (2001) suggest that combining the use of vocabulary and background knowledge with passage context during reading may be a contributing factor in accurate, fluent word recognition. Struggling readers with limited vocabulary and background knowledge may be less able to construct meaning from a passage, resulting in slow, effortful reading. This assertion is supported by the theories of fluency development proposed by Ehri (1997), LaBerge and Samuels (1974), and Perfetti (1985), and further supports the adoption of a deeper construct of fluency.

Torgesen, Rashotte, and colleagues (2001) posit that the ability to identify rapidly the meaning of words while reading connected text has the potential to affect oral reading fluency. If students are able to decode accurately and identify the meaning of a word while reading connected text, speed can be maintained and comprehension can occur. If students are unable to recognize the meaning of a word rapidly and must actively reflect on word meanings while reading, both fluency and comprehension will decline. There is evidence to indicate that differences in the ability to recognize the meaning of words (vocabulary growth) result in differences in developing sight word vocabularies in favor of students who understand the meaning of words (Cunningham & Stanovich, 1998; Torgesen, Alexander, et al., 2001).

Each of the five factors that Torgesen, Rashotte, and colleagues (2001) identified as contributing to fluency difficulties for struggling readers provides additional support for a deeper construct of fluency. It is evident from an analysis of these factors that the development of fluency for struggling readers should encompass instruction in multiple skills, including phonemic awareness, decoding, vocabulary, oral language, and connected text reading. Instruction across multiple skills has the potential to impact positively both independent text reading fluency and comprehension, and should be considered when planning and providing instruction to struggling readers.

AN INSTRUCTIONAL PROGRAM FOR STRUGGLING READERS BASED ON A DEEP CONSTRUCT OF FLUENCY

Our perception is that until recently, some, though certainly not all, educators took a rather simplistic approach to developing fluency that is summed up in the phrase: "Read, read, read." The expectation was that if students read more, they would achieve fluency. However, research and theory suggest that at least some students will need expert instruction and teacher guidance in order to progress efficiently through the stages of reading development. We propose an eight-step program for developing fluency. Some of the steps, such as building the graphophonic foundation for fluency or high-frequency vocabulary, are usually accomplished in a relatively short period of time (e.g., often 1 or 2 years), while others, such as building oral language skills, are unending. Our goal in this chapter is to outline the rationale and the breadth of instruction needed for developing a deep construct of fluency with struggling readers. We give some references that offer suggestions for instructional strategies and materials, but space limitations preclude treating each of these areas in depth. The eight-step program for struggling readers should include explicit and systematic instruction that

1. Builds the graphophonic foundations for fluency, including phonological awareness, letter familiarity, and phonics.
2. Builds and extends vocabulary and oral language skills.
3. Provides expert instruction and practice in the recognition of
   high-frequency vocabulary.
4. Teaches common word parts and spelling patterns.
5. Teaches, models, and provides practice in the application of a decoding strategy.
6. Uses appropriate texts to coach strategic behaviors and to build
   reading speed.
7. Uses repeated reading procedures as an intervention approach for
   struggling readers.
8. Monitors fluency development through appropriate assessment
   procedures.

BUILDING THE GRAPHOPHONIC FOUNDATIONS FOR FLUENCY

Ehri (1998) lists three prerequisite "graphophonic" capabilities as foundations for fluency: (1) letter familiarity; (2) phonemic awareness; and (3)
knowledge of how graphemes typically represent phonemes in words.

A new publication from the International Reading Association
(Strickland & Schickendanz, 2004) offers practical, research-based approaches to developing graphophonic skills, including letter familiarity, in
emergent readers. Instruction in the area of phonological awareness has
been addressed widely (e.g., Adams, Foorman, Lundberg, & Beeler, 1998;
O'Connor, Notari-Syverson, & Vadasy, 1998).

The importance of the three graphophonic factors is fully docu-
mented in numerous research reports (e.g., Adams, 1990; National Reading Panel, 2000). In order to move from the prealphabetic stage to the
partial and fully alphabetic stages, students need to grasp the alphabetic
principle and to apply efficiently information about the relationship
between the letters and sounds (phonics) to recognize words. This clearly
requires a high level of familiarity with letter forms, as well as the ability
to segment and blend the smallest units of spoken language, phonemes.

To build these foundations for struggling readers requires moving systematically from simpler to more complex tasks. For example, for phonemic awareness, instruction should progress on a continuum from simple
tasks, such as rhyming, to more complex tasks, such as blending and seg-

menting. For alphabetic principle instruction, begin with simple skills such as letter-sound identification and work to more advanced skills, such as reading multisyllabic words and more complex sentences. Phonemic awareness and alphabetic principle instruction should occur in concert. Activities to build the graphophonic foundations for fluency that can occur in addition to a commercially produced core reading program might include reading poetry that focuses on target sounds and words, matching pictures to word types, and manipulating letter tiles to spell words using known letter sounds.

ORAL LANGUAGE FOUNDATIONS FOR FLUENCY

In addition to the graphophonic skills, Ehri's (1995) theory requires a foundation in language skills, so that students are familiar with the meanings of words and phrases, as well as with their syntactical or grammatical function.

We know that the relationship between reading comprehension and vocabulary knowledge is strong and unequivocal (Baumann & Kame'enui, 2004; Stanovich, 1986). However, developing the oral language and vocabulary skills of children is one of the greatest challenges facing us as educators, particularly for those children who are learning English as a second language or who spend their preschool years in language-restricted environments. Many excellent resources exist for meeting this challenge. Recent examples include texts by Beck, McKeown, and Kucan (2002), Blachowicz and Fisher (2002), and the highly regarded IRA publication by Nagy (1988).

Ehri (1995) shows that progress in reading beyond the beginning stages is dependent on oral language development, pointing out that reading words, particularly reading them fluently, is dependent on familiarity with them in their oral form. If the syntactic and meaning aspects of the word are to be activated, they must be part of what the reader knows through oral language development. For the word recognition process as proposed in Ehri's theory to be complete, it must connect with meaning that has been developed as another aspect of language development. Consider the following words: *zigzags* and *onychophagia*. Mature readers have no trouble rapidly decoding the first word, even though it is one of the least frequent words in *printed* English. However, it takes mature readers much longer to arrive at a pronunciation of the second word, because it not only infrequently appears in print but is also very infrequently used in speech and is therefore not likely to be a word in a mature reader's mental lexicon. Unless a printed word can connect with both the phonological memory for the word and with the syntactical and meaning aspects of the word, it cannot be fluently decoded or read. It seems unfortunate that many surface discussions of fluency fail to make the point that fluency is dependent on the reader's vocabulary, as well as on his or her decoding skills.

To facilitate oral language and vocabulary growth for struggling readers, explicit and systematic instruction is required. Instructional approaches might include preteaching unknown high-utility vocabulary and vocabulary essential to the meaning of a passage using a picture, synonym, or concise definition prior to read-alouds. Instruction can occur in whole-class or small groups. Vocabulary instruction in small groups should be heterogeneous to enable students with more limited vocabularies to dialogue with students with rich vocabularies. Opportunities for additional practice and review of taught words can be provided using strategies such as word walls in which high-frequency vocabulary is posted and practiced, semantic mapping, questioning to promote deep processing, and relating new vocabulary to meaningful experience.

TEACHING HIGH-FREQUENCY VOCABULARY

High-frequency words are those words that appear over and over again in our language—words such as the, of, and, at, and to. If developing readers cannot instantly identify these words, they are unlikely to become fluent.

One approach to building fluent recognition of high-frequency vocabulary that is exceedingly popular with primary grade teachers is the use of word walls (Cunningham, 2000). A second approach is to prepare a 5 × 5 grid in which students practice high frequency words to the level of fluency by placing one new word and four review words randomly in each row. Students are provided an untimed practice, and then do a timed recall of the words, working toward a desired criterion rate (e.g., one word per second). Cunningham also offers a variety of other methods for teaching high-frequency words, as do Bear, Invernizzi, Templeton, and Johnston (1996).

Ehri's theory and research also offer important, practical teaching suggestions. High-frequency words often have been seen as a serious challenge, because many of them don't lend themselves to straightforward application of decoding skills; they are, in the jargon of reading instruction, phonically irregular—words such as *the, of, was,* and *have.* Teaching high-frequency words can be difficult. This difficulty may very well be a contributor to the periodic abandonment of phonics approaches and the rise of whole-word approaches to teaching beginning reading skills, with accompanying emphasis on drill using flash cards to force children to read the words as a whole. Ehri's (2005) work suggests that they also contain many letter–sound regularities and that these regularities are the best mnemonics for developing accurate, instant recognition. For example, while the word *have* does not follow the generalization about the effect of a final *e* on a preceding vowel sound, the *h, v,* and *e* all behave as they should, and the *a* does represent a sound that it often represents. Ehri suggests that we should point out the regular elements of "irregular" words in order to help children gain instant recognition of them. This is a practice rarely mentioned by "experts" or used by teachers, but it might play a very important role in avoiding difficulty with such words and thus promoting the development of fluency.

RECOGNIZING WORD PARTS
AND SPELLING PATTERNS

Word parts and spelling patterns are combinations of letters such as *at, ell, ick, op* that are found as units in many words that appear in beginning reading texts. Like Ehri (1997, 1998), Samuels (1999, 2002) maintains that the size of the unit a child recognizes during reading varies between beginning and experienced readers. Beginning readers rely on cues at the single letter-sound level and integrate the use of word parts, spelling patterns and word reading as they become more capable. Proficient readers are able to identify word parts, spelling patterns and whole words as units automatically. Differences in strategy use between beginning and proficient readers suggest a differential reliance on word parts and spelling patterns which depends on the individual stage of reading development. Here again, Cunningham (2000) and Bear and colleagues (1996) are among the many resources that offer many practical teaching suggestions, including a list of the most common word parts found in beginning reading materials. Lovett and colleagues (2000) provide additional validated instructional approaches to teaching word parts.

Introducing multiple-letter units clearly moves students from the fully alphabetic to the consolidated alphabetic stage. However, Ehri's research and theory offer an important instructional generalization: Students should first be introduced to and made cognizant of the individual letters and sounds that constitute the rime (a fully alphabetic approach) in order to recall and identify better the unit that they constitute. In addition, Torgesen, Wagner, Rashotte, Alexander, and Conway (1997) offer a further caution. They assert that isolated instruction in word parts and spelling patterns alone is not sufficient to develop reading fluency for struggling readers. Word parts and spelling patterns will only enable children to reach satisfactory levels of oral reading fluency if they are routinely used and practiced in reading connected text, and if the amount of connected text reading is sufficient to maintain growth.

TEACHING A DECODING STRATEGY

There are several major ways in which words can be recognized or identified in print: instantly as units; through recognition of and blending of phonic elements; through the context in which they appear, including language–sentence context and picture clues; and by checking the phonetic respellings of a dictionary or glossary. Ehri's theory is clear: The best way to recognize words is through instant recognition that does not drain attention. All other approaches require attention. However, when a word is not instantly recognized, it is useful for readers to be strategic. Struggling readers frequently experience difficulty in being strategic during reading.

In kindergarten and the beginning of first grade, emphasis is on moving young readers from the partial to the fully alphabetic stages of reading, with an emphasis on careful attention to the graphophonic characteristics of the word. By mid first grade, the goal is to move students increasingly into the consolidated alphabetic stage. The italicized portion of the strategy is recommended as young readers and struggling readers become familiar with word parts:

1. Look at the letters from left to right.
2. As you look at the letters, think about the sounds for the letters.
3. Blend the sounds together *and look for word parts you know* to read the word.

4. Ask yourself: Is this a word I know? Does it make sense in what I am reading?
5. If it doesn't make sense, try other strategies (e.g., pronouncing the word another way, reading on).

Readers at the partial and fully alphabetic stages will need to look carefully at the word they are trying to identify and think about the sounds the letters are likely to represent, then use the skill of phoneme blending to try to arrive at the correct decoding or pronunciation of the word. Because some words are not completely phonically regular, students should then be encouraged to ask themselves if their use of phonics results in the identification of a word that makes sense—that it is a word they have heard before and that it fits the context of what they are reading. As children begin to move from the fully alphabetic to the consolidated alphabetic stage of development, in addition to using phonic elements, they should also be encouraged to look for word parts (chunks) and spelling patterns that they know, such as phonograms. The order of phonics and word parts, *followed by* use of context, appears to be by far the best order.

Use of context as the primary approach to identifying words has serious limitations. First, if the context is highly predictive of a word, it is likely that students will not pay attention to the graphic information of the word. Careful processing of the printed form is what eventually enables a reader to recognize that word instantly. This is a major limitation of the predictable texts that use very heavy, artificial context to allow word identification. Second, context rarely leads to the correct identification of a specific word. Ehri reviewed research that suggests that the words in a text that carry the most meaning can be correctly identified by context only about 10% of the time. However, context and the other approaches to decoding words do play an important role in decoding— that of confirming the identification of words. As Ehri puts it:

> As each sight word is fixated, its meaning and pronunciation are triggered in memory quickly and automatically. However, the other word reading processes do not lie dormant; their contribution is not to identify words in text but to *confirm* the identity already determined. Knowledge of the graphophonic system confirms that the word's pronunciation fits the spelling on the page. Knowledge of syntax confirms that the word fits into the structure of the sentence. Word knowledge and text memory confirm that the word's meaning is consistent with the text's meaning up to that point. (1998, p. 11, emphasis added)

USING APPROPRIATE TEXTS TO PROMOTE FLUENCY

In order to make progress in fluency, students need to engage in the practice and application of their growing word identification skills to appropriate texts. Appropriate texts are particularly critical for students having difficulty with word identification skills. Guided reading has once again emerged as a useful way to match students and texts. Resources such as the work of Fountas and Pinnell (1996) offer guidance in selecting texts and providing appropriate instruction with those texts.

Hiebert and Fisher (2002) studied fluency development as it relates to the features of the texts used for promoting fluency. Specifically, they were interested in examining the effects of texts in which particular text features were carefully controlled. The treatment texts that Hiebert and Fisher designed had the following key features: a small number of unique words, a high percentage of most frequently used words, and often repeated critical words (those words that influence the meaning of the text most). Students in the comparison group read from texts typically associated with commercial reading programs. Students reading in the treatment texts made significant gains in fluency over their peers in the comparison condition. There also seemed to be an effect for comprehension for second language learners (Taguchi & Gorsuch, 2002). These findings suggest that the features of the texts used to promote fluency should be carefully considered.

USING REPEATED READING PROCEDURES

As noted earlier, the report of the National Reading Panel was unequivocal in its support of repeated reading procedures. The references describe a range of procedures in sufficient detail to allow teachers to employ them with students who need extra support in developing fluency. These procedures include repeated reading (Samuels, 1979), neurological impress (Heckelman, 1969), radio reading (Greene, 1979), paired reading (Topping, 1987), "and a variety of similar techniques" (National Reading Panel, 2000, p. 3-1). A review of these approaches suggests substantial differences in the procedures used and the amount of teacher guidance offered (Chard, Vaughn, & Tyler, 2002; Kuhn & Stahl, 2000). However, all appear to have merit. Features of effective procedures for struggling readers consisted of (1) brief daily practice, (2) repeated oral reading of passages, (3) overlap of shared words across passages, (4) consistency in text context, (5) controlled text difficulty, (6) provision of corrective feedback, (7) teacher-modeled text reading, (8) audiotaped modeled reading, (9) repeated reading with a partner, (10) cross-age tutoring with a partner, and (11) specified performance criterion levels of fluency (Chard et al., 2002; Kuhn & Stahl, 2000; National Reading Panel, 2000).

THE ASSESSMENT OF FLUENCY
FOR STRUGGLING READERS

As noted at the beginning of this chapter, fluency has been referred to as the "neglected aspect" of reading. The assessment of fluency, in particular, appears to have received very limited attention. Few research studies have investigated how fluency should be assessed or what criteria should be applied to determine whether a reader has achieved fluency. The reader may want to review research by Deno (1985), Fuchs, Fuchs, Hamlett, Walz, and Germann (1993), Hasbrouck and Tindal (1992), and Shinn, Good, Tilly, Knutson, and Collins (1992) as examples of work in the area of fluency assessment. The National Reading Panel (2000) concludes: "A number of informal procedures can be used in the classroom to assess fluency: informal reading inventories, miscue analysis, pausing indices, and reading speed calculations. All these assessment procedures require oral reading of text, and all can provide an adequate index of fluency" (p. 3-9). While few experimental studies have been conducted using these informal procedures, it may very well have been that the Panel's recognition of the very practical need for classroom assessment led it to endorse procedures that may not have the strong research support typically required in other parts of the report.

To meet this practical need are many published informal inventories that can be practically used to assess periodically the four dimensions of fluency that are necessary for a full, deep, developmental construct of fluency: oral reading accuracy, oral reading rate, quality of oral reading, and reading comprehension. Teachers who want to assess selective aspects of fluency can use guidelines suggested for assessing oral reading rate and accuracy (e.g., Hasbrouck & Tindal, 1992; Rasinski, 2003). Likewise, procedures have been established for assessing the quality of oral reading using standardized rubrics that go beyond rate and accuracy, such as that based on NAEP data (Pinnell et al., 1995).

We recommend that teachers take measures of fluency beginning in the middle of first grade. At second grade and beyond, assessment should occur at least at the beginning, middle, and end of a school year to gauge progress in this important area and to check periodically through the year any students who are making doubtful progress. A more comprehensive review of the research related to fluency assessment is beyond the scope of this chapter.

CONCLUSIONS

While the construct of fluency may have been neglected in the past, it is receiving much deserved attention presently. A very strong research and theoretical base indicates that while fluency in and of itself is not sufficient to ensure high levels of reading achievement, fluency is absolutely necessary for that achievement, because it depends on and typically reflects comprehension. If a reader has not developed fluency, the process of decoding words drains attention, and insufficient attention is available for constructing the meaning of texts.

Fluency builds on a foundation of oral language skills, phonemic awareness, familiarity with letter forms, and efficient decoding skills. Ehri's description of the stages of word recognition explains how readers come to recognize words by sight through careful processing of print.

Substantial research has also been conducted on how best to develop fluency in students who do not yet have it. While there is a dearth of experimental research studies on developing fluency through increasing the amount of independent reading in which students engage, substantial correlational evidence shows a clear relationship between the amount students read, their reading fluency, and their reading comprehension. However, students who are struggling with reading are not in a position to engage in wide reading, and they may need more guidance and support in order to develop fluency. Research shows that a variety of procedures based on repeated readings can help struggling readers to improve their fluency.

While more research is needed on the issues of adequate rates of fluency at various grade levels and for judging the quality of oral reading, there is agreement that the comprehensive assessment of fluency must include measures of oral reading accuracy, rate, and quality. There is also growing agreement that these dimensions of fluency must be assessed within the context of reading comprehension. Fluency, with accompanying high levels of reading comprehension, is of ultimate advantage to readers. By defining fluency as a deep construct, we seek to articulate carefully the features of reading development and their role in the reciprocal relationship between fluency and comprehension. Moreover, a deeper construct of fluency provides a clearer focus for systematic intervention, remediation, and assessment for struggling readers.

REFERENCES

Adams, M. J. (1990). *Beginning to read: Thinking and learning about print.* Cambridge, MA: MIT Press.

Adams, M. J., Foorman, B. R., Lundberg, I., & Beeler, T. (1998). *Phonemic awareness in young children.* Baltimore: Brookes.

Baumann, J. F., & Kame'enui, E. J. (Eds.). (2004). *Vocabulary instruction: Research to practice.* New York: Guilford Press.

Bear, D. R., Invernizzi, M., Templeton, S., & Johnston, F. (1996). *Words their way.* Columbus, OH: Merrill.

Beck, I. L., McKeown, M. G., & Kucan, L. (2002). *Bringing words to life: Robust vocabulary instruction.* New York: Guilford Press.

Blachowicz, C., & Fisher, P. J. (2002). *Teaching vocabulary in all classrooms.* Columbus, OH: Merrill.

Chard, D. J., Vaughn, S., & Tyler, B. J. (2002). A synthesis of research on effective interventions for building fluency with elementary students with learning disabilities. *Journal of Learning Disabilities, 35,* 386–406.

Cunningham, A. E., & Stanovich, K. E. (1998, Spring/Summer). What reading does for the mind. *American Educator,* pp. 8–15.

Cunningham, P. M. (2000). *Phonics they use.* New York: Longman.

Deno, S. (1985). Curriculum based measurement: An emerging alternative. *Exceptional Children, 52,* 219–232.

Ehri, L. C. (1995). Stages of development in learning to read words by sight. *Journal of Research in Reading, 18,* 116–125.

Ehri, L. C. (1997). Sight word learning in normal readers and dyslexics. In B. Blachman (Ed.), *Foundations of reading acquisition and dyslexia* (pp. 163–189). Mahwah, NJ: Erlbaum.

Ehri, L. C. (1998). Grapheme–phoneme knowledge is essential for learning to read words in English. In J. L. Metsala & L. C. Ehri (Eds.), *Word recognition in beginning literacy* (pp. 3–40). Mahwah, NJ: Erlbaum.

Ehri, L. C. (2005). Learning to read words: Theory, findings, and issues. *Scientific Studies of Reading, 9*(2), 167–188.

Ehri, L. C., & McCormick, S. (1998). Phases of word learning: Implications for instruction with delayed and disabled readers. *Reading and Writing Quarterly, 14*(2), 135–163.

Fountas, I. C., & Pinnell, G. S. (1996). *Guided reading: Good first teaching for all children.* Portsmouth, NH: Heinemann.

Fuchs, L. S., Fuchs, D., Hamlett, C. L., Walz, L., & Germann, G. (1993). Formative evaluation of academic progress: How much growth can we expect? *School Psychology Review, 22,* 27–48.

Greene, F. P. (1979). Radio reading. In C. Pennock (Ed.), *Reading comprehension at four linguistic levels* (pp. 104–107). Newark, DE: International Reading Association.

Harris, T. L., & Hodges, R. E. (1995). *The literacy dictionary: The vocabulary of reading and writing.* Newark, DE: International Reading Association.

Hasbrouck, J. E., & Tindal, G. (1992). Curriculum based fluency norms for grades two through five. *Teaching Exceptional Children, 24,* 41–44.

Heckelman, R. G. (1969). A neurological impress method of remedial reading instruction. *Academic Therapy, 4,* 277–282.

Hiebert, E. H., & Fisher, C. W. (2002). *Text matters in developing fluent reading.* Unpublished manuscript.

Huey, E. B. (1968) *The psychology and pedagogy of reading: With a review of the history of reading and writing and of methods, texts, and hygiene in reading.* Cambridge, MA: MIT Press. (Original work published 1908)

Kuhn, M. R., & Stahl, S. A. (2000). *Fluency: A review of developmental and remedial practices.* Ann Arbor, MI: Center for the Improvement of Early Reading Achievement.

LaBerge, D., & Samuels, S. J. (1974). Towards a theory of automatic information processing in reading. *Cognitive Psychology, 6,* 293–323.

Levy, B. A. (2001). Moving the bottom: Improving reading fluency. In M. Wolf (Ed.), *Dyslexia, fluency, and the brain* (pp. 307–331). Timonium, MD. York Press.

Logan, G. D. (1988). Toward an instance theory of automatization. *Psychological Review, 95*(4), 492–527.

Logan, G. D. (1997). Automaticity and reading: Perspectives from the instance theory of automatization. *Reading and Writing Quarterly, 13*(2), 123–146.

Lovett, M., Borden, S. L., Lacerenza, L., Frijters, J. C., Steinbach, K. A., & DePalma, M. (2000). Components of effective remediation for developmental reading disabilities: Combining phonological and strategy based instruction to improve outcomes. *Journal of Educational Psychology, 92*(2), 263 283.

Nagy, W. E. (1988). *Teaching vocabulary to improve reading comprehension.* Newark, DE: International Reading Association.

National Reading Panel. (2000). *Teaching children to read: An evidence-based assessment of the scientific research literature on reading and its implications for reading instruction.* Washington, DC: National Institute of Child Health and Human Development.

O'Connor, R. E., Notari-Syverson, A., & Vadasy, P. F. (1998). *Ladders to literacy: A kindergarten activity book.* Baltimore: Brookes.

Perfetti, C. A. (1985). *Reading ability.* New York: Oxford University Press.

Pikulski, J. J., & Chard, D. J. (2005). Fluency: Bridge between decoding and reading comprehension. *Reading Teacher, 58,* 510–519.

Pinnell, G. S., Pikulski, J. J., Wixson, K. K., Campbell, J. R., Gough, P. B., & Beatty, A. S. (1995). *Listening to children read aloud.* Washington, DC: Office of Educational Research and Improvement, U. S. Department of Education.

Rasinski, T. V. (2003). *The fluent reader.* New York: Scholastic.

Reitsma, P. (1983). Printed word learning in beginning readers. *Journal of Experimental Child Psychology, 75,* 321–339.

Reutzel, D. R. (1996). Developing at-risk readers' oral reading fluency. In L. Putnam (Ed.), *How to become a better reader: Strategies for assessment and intervention* (pp. 241–254). Englewood Cliffs, NJ: Merrill.

Samuels, S. J. (1979). The method of repeated readings. *Reading Teacher, 32,* 403–408.

Samuels, S. J. (1999). Developing reading fluency in learning disabled students. In R. J. Sternberg & L. Spear-Swerling (Eds.), *Perspectives on learning disabilities: Biological, cognitive, contextual* (pp. 176–189). Boulder, CO: Westview Press.

Samuels, S. J. (2002). Reading fluency: Its development and assessment. In A. E. Farstrup & S. J. Samuels (Eds.), *What research has to say about reading instruction* (3rd ed., pp. 166–183). Newark, DE: International Reading Association.

Shinn, M. R., Good, R. H., Knutson, N., Tilly, D., & Collins, V. (1992). Curriculum based measurement of oral reading fluency: A confirmatory analysis of its relation to reading. *School Psychology Review, 21*(3), 459–479.

Stanovich, K. E. (1986). Matthew effects in reading: Some consequences in individual differences in the acquisition of literacy. *Reading Research Quarterly, 21,* 360–407.

Stecker, S. K., Roser, N. L., & Martinez, M. G. (1998). Understanding oral reading fluency. In T. Shanahan & F. V. Rodriguez-Brown (Eds.), *47th yearbook of the National Reading Conference* (pp. 295–310). Chicago: National Reading Conference.

Strickland, D. S., & Schickendanz, J. (2004). *Learning about print in preschool: Working with letters, words and links with phonemic awareness.* Newark, DE: International Reading Association.

Taguchi, E., & Gorsuch, G. J. (2002). Transfer effects of repeated EFL reading on reading new passages: A preliminary investigation. *Reading in a Foreign Language, 14*(1), 43–65.

Topping, K. (1987). Paired reading: A powerful technique for parent use. *Reading Teacher, 40,* 608–614.

Torgesen, J. K., Alexander, A. W., Wagner, R. K., Rashotte, C. A., Voeller, K., Conway, T., & Rose, E. (2001). Intensive remedial instruction for children with severe reading disabilities: Immediate and long-term outcomes from two instructional approaches. *Journal of Learning Disabilities, 34*(1), 33–58, 78.

Torgesen, J. K., Rashotte, C. A., & Alexander, A. W. (2001). Principles of fluency instruction in reading: Relationships with established empirical outcomes. In M. Wolf (Ed.), *Dyslexia, fluency, and the brain* (pp. 307–331). Timonium, MD: York Press.

Torgesen, J. K., Wagner, R. K., Rashotte, C. A., Alexander, A. W., & Conway, T. (1997). Preventive and remedial interventions for children with severe reading disabilities. *Learning Disabilities: An Interdisciplinary Journal, 8*(1), 51–62.

Wolf, M., Bowers, P. G., & Biddle, K. (2000). Naming speed processes, timing, and reading: A conceptual review. *Journal of Learning Disabilities, 33*(4), 387–407.

CHAPTER 4

"Hey, Teacher, When You Say 'Fluency,' What Do You Mean?"

Developing Fluency in Elementary Classrooms

D. RAY REUTZEL

Fluent reading, like the thread of life itself (Kendrew, 1966), is intrinsically elegant in both form and cadence. . . . We certainly know it when we see it, and we are quick to celebrate it, along with the trajectory of success it portends.

—KAME'ENUI AND SIMMONS (2001, p. 203)

It was a hot, dry, dusty spring morning at Eagle Rock Cliffs (pseudonym) Elementary School on a Native American reservation in the desert southwestern United States. Over a 3-year period, the teachers in this school had received copious amounts of professional development as a part of their involvement with a Federal Reading Excellence Act grant competitively awarded to high-poverty, low-performing schools. After several years of learning, applying, and refining, the teachers felt relatively confident about their ability to provide systematic, explicit, and effective phonemic awareness, phonics, vocabulary, and comprehension instruction.

But when it came to providing similar systematic, explicit, and effective fluency instruction, teachers expressed concern and frustration.

These teachers had tried for several months to incorporate daily fluency work into their classroom literacy instructional routines but had been unable to do so with a sense of accomplishment and satisfaction. On this particular day, two literacy professors, a school-based reading coach, and the district literacy coordinator, had been asked to observe two individual teachers' fluency instruction—Mrs. Lonetree, a third-grade teacher, and Ms. Bearclaw, a fourth-grade teacher.

We began our observations in Mrs. Lonetree's third-grade classroom. The children were seated on the floor around an overhead projector. Mrs. Lonetree displayed a copy of the text from the Caldecott Medal book *Drummer Hoff* (Emberley, 1967). She informed the children that she was going to model fluent oral reading of this cumulative poetic text. She read the text aloud, evidencing appropriate pauses, expression, and a conversational reading rate. Upon completion, she asked the children to indicate whether they felt she had read the text fluently by giving her thumbs up or thumbs down. Most of these third-grade children gave their teacher thumbs up. Two children gave her oral performance of *Drummer Hoff* thumbs down. When Mrs. Lonetree questioned these children about why they gave her thumbs down, they replied, "You didn't sound right when you read it. You sounded funny." Mrs. Lonetree commented that these were good observations and briskly moved on in the lesson. Next, she invited the children to read the text with her in choral unison. She reminded them to use "good expression" as they read with her, while she pointed to the words on the overhead. We came away reflecting on how this lesson lacked the systematic, explicit, and effective explanation, modeling, feedback, guided practice, and monitoring we saw with the instruction typically provided by this teacher in other essential elements of reading instruction.

Next we walked across the school building to a fourth-grade classroom to observe another fluency lesson taught by Ms. Bearclaw. She had her desks arranged in a U shape facing the chalkboard, where she had carefully written the lyrics to the Shel Silverstein poem "There's Too Many Kids in This Tub." Ms. Bearclaw had also prepared a poster displaying the elements of fluent oral reading—accuracy, rate, and expression. Before reading the poem aloud, Ms. Bearclaw discussed each of these elements of fluent oral reading with the group. Next, she indicated that she would read the poem aloud. The children were to listen carefully and be prepared to comment on her oral reading of the poem relative to each of the elements of fluent reading displayed on the poster—accuracy, rate, and expression.

Following a brief explanation, as described in the previous paragraph, of the elements of fluent reading, Ms. Bearclaw read the poem aloud, modeling hesitant, mostly accurate reading with a few inaccuracies dispersed throughout the oral reading, and in a monotone voice. The children giggled as she modeled this oral reading. After her oral reading concluded, children's hands shot into the air. "I know what you did wrong," one round-faced, brown-eyed little girl blurted out. "You sounded like you were a machine, sort of like a computer reading aloud; you didn't have expression." Ms. Bearclaw encouraged more observations and evaluations of her reading from the children, and then she replied, "Oh, so you think you could do better, do you?" They all responded in a choral "Yes." "Okay," she said, "I want you to pair up with a partner and practice this poem together. At first, one of you is to be the listener and one of you is to be the reader. The reader is to practice the poem until the listener says it is a good example of fluent reading. Then, you are to exchange the roles of reader and listener. And when you are finished, I will select several readers to come up and read the poem aloud to the whole class. We will then give feedback to each reader using our fluency poster. Any questions?" She pauses. "Okay, then start working. We have about 10 minutes."

During the practice time, Ms. Bearclaw moved around the pairs of practicing children, listening and providing feedback. The children were all very much engaged. After the practice time concluded, Ms. Bearclaw invited three children to read the poem aloud and receive feedback from their peers. As we exited the classroom, we expressed greater satisfaction with this lesson, but we still had a nagging sense that something was missing.

Later that same day, we met with the two teachers we had observed, as well as the other teachers in the building. We complimented the two teachers on the strong points of their lessons, such as their efforts to (1) model, (2) explicitly teach the elements of fluency, (3) provide guided practice, and (4) offer constructive and informative feedback. Next, we expressed our nagging concerns that even with many elements of effective instruction in place to one degree or another, the fluency instruction we observed was unlikely to develop children's ability and disposition to monitor and adjust their own reading fluency. As we continued our conversations about fluency, we came to a consensus that the ultimate goal of fluency instruction was to lead children to independence in fluency—the ability to self-monitor their fluent reading of texts and to know what they needed to do to "fix up" their fluency across a range of text difficulty levels and text types.

We determined that what children needed was a daily routine in which they received explicit instruction and systematic practice for developing fluency and metafluency ability—the ability to self-monitor and self-adjust oral reading processes to produce fluent oral renditions of texts. To accomplish this aim, we undertook an in-depth study of the research and professional literature on fluency in weekly afterschool and monthly Saturday study group meetings. The information we gleaned from our reading and study formed the basis for the creation of what would later become known as the Fluency Development Workshop.

UNDERSTANDING READING FLUENCY: "YOU CAN'T TEACH WHAT YOU DON'T KNOW"

As we began our study of fluency, we found that there wasn't a single, agreed upon definition. For example, we found that Harris and Hodges (1981) defined "fluency" as the ability to read smoothly, easily, and readily with freedom from word recognition problems. Some years later, Harris and Hodges (1995) modified their fluency definition to suggest that "fluency" is "the clear, easy, written or spoken expression of ideas" (p. 85). S. J. Samuels (1979) defined a "lack of fluency" as characterized by a slow, halting pace; frequent mistakes; poor phrasing; and inadequate expression. Taken together, these various definitions distill down to *three* major elements clearly associated with the concept and definition of fluency as best expressed in the report of the National Reading Panel: "Fluent readers can read text with 1) speed, 2) accuracy, and 3) proper expression" (p. 3-1).

Our continuing study of fluency led us to reconsider the place and importance of oral versus silent reading, levels of text difficulty, text genres, and varying forms of reading fluency practices found in the elementary classroom. The history of oral and silent reading, much like the field of reading generally, is characterized by the swinging of the pendulum of fashion. Prior to and during the early part of the 20th century, oral reading ability and performance were highly valued as a cultural asset (Rasinski, 2003; Smith, 2002). However, with the advance of research, it was demonstrated that reading silently seemed to hold an advantage for readers in terms of both reading rate and comprehension (Huey, 1908).

Moreover, the utility and superiority of silent reading seemed apparent, since most adult readers engaged almost exclusively in silent reading as compared with oral reading (Rasinski, 2003). Coupling this with the rise of "round robin" or "barbershop" reading practices in elementary classrooms, which led to the ritualistic routine of having one reader read aloud while others passively listened in until it was their turn, culminated in the general elevation of silent reading practice over oral reading practice in schools. But now, due to the analyses and findings of the National Reading Panel (2000) about effective fluency practice, this report has once again reenthroned the importance of oral reading practice versus silent reading practice, at least in the earliest stages of reading development.

The National Reading Panel's (2000) meta-analysis of fluency studies showed that fluency practice is most effective when the reading practice is oral versus silent; when it involves repeated readings of a text (more than twice); and when students receive guidance or feedback from teachers, parents, volunteers, and peers (p. 3-11). We also noted that the National Reading Panel was unable to locate sufficient evidence showing a significantly positive impact for silent reading practice on students' reading fluency acquisition. Of the 14 studies that met the National Reading Panel's selection criteria dealing with silent reading practice, only three studies showed any evidence of gains in reading achievement from more time spent in silent reading practice, and the size of the gains were so small so as to be "of questionable educational value" (p. 3-26). And the National Reading Panel further noted that none of the 14 silent reading studies even attempted to measure the impact of increased amounts of silent reading on children's development of reading fluency. From these findings, we concluded that our students would likely benefit far more from oral, repeated reading practice, with feedback during the early stages of reading fluency acquisition, instruction, and practice.

More recently, Stahl (2004) reported an investigation of the effects of FORI (fluency-oriented reading instruction) using two variations of practice: monitored, wide silent reading practice compared with oral repeated readings with feedback. He also used a control group to examine whether either form of reading practice was superior to a control group on the fluency acquisition of second-grade readers. He found that repeated oral readings with feedback and wide silent readings with monitoring were both superior to the control group performance. On the other hand, the two variations, oral readings with feedback and wide silent readings with monitoring, were roughly equivalent to one another, suggesting that "the increased amount of reading and the support given during the reading are what underlie the success of the two approaches" (p. 205).

As we continued our study, we found that there exists some confusion around the idea of "automaticity" in reading as this concept relates to the development of fluency in elementary-age children. "Automaticity," a term coined by reading theorists LaBerge and Samuels (1974), indicates that the ability to decode words has become so well developed, even automatic, that little or no cognitive attention is needed or used. We have found that some authors in the professional literature (Blevins, 2001; Wolf & Katzir-Cohen, 2001) advocate timed practice on word patterns and high-frequency word list drills. Although such a practice may be useful in developing "automatic" decoding of words, it leaves unaddressed matters of phrasing and expression. In fairness, none of these authors recommended developing fluency from timed word list drills alone, but there are classrooms in which such word list drills occupy an inordinate amount of time and significance.

We found also that a number of authors and researchers have developed, through a variety of processes, guidelines for appropriate reading rates by grade level. For example, the work of Hasbrouck and Tindal (1992, 2005), Germann (2001), and Howe and Shinn (2001) provides a listing of appropriate reading rates that span grades 1–8. Most of these reading rate norms adjust reading rate for accuracy using a metric called words correct per minute (wcpm). We also noted that fluency rate norms seem to begin with second-grade readers, which implies that a focus on fluency development in first-grade classrooms ought to be delayed until decoding processes have been well taught and students are approaching proficiency or automaticity with word-level decoding. Recent research on reading rate norms suggests that first-grade readers ought to be able to read about 53 wcpm by the end of first grade (Hasbrouck & Tindal, 2005).

We found little information about how expression and intonation affect fluency (Dowhower, 1991). We did, however, find that most measures of expression in the reading literature make use of informal scales (Zutell & Rasinski, 1991) that ask teachers to make judgments about the prosodic features of oral reading rather than use more exacting prosodic measures similar to those used by speech–language pathologists.

We also found that fluency, much like reading comprehension, needs to be developed across text types and levels of text difficulty. The RAND Reading Study Group (2002) described how the reader, the text, the task, and the context all work together in unique ways to affect reading comprehension performance. This also seems to be true with respect to fluency development (National Reading Panel, 2000). Because a student can read narrative or poetry texts fluently does not necessarily imply a concurrent ability to read information or expository texts with similar facility. We found from our study of fluency research that when levels of text difficulty increase, most students' fluency levels decrease. Researchers are at present unclear about which levels of text to use for fluency practice and instruction. In answer to this continuing dilemma, Kuhn and Stahl (2000) recommended the use of instructional-level text for fluency instruction and practice in their review of fluency developmental and remedial practices. These findings suggest that fluency when reading different text genres and difficulty levels is not a perfectable process—at least not in the primary-grade elementary school years.

Finally, we determined from our studies that while fluency practice and instruction are an essential component of high-quality reading instruction in the elementary years (Stahl, 2004), too much of a good thing can be a bad thing! In one short-term study, Anderson, Wilkinson, and Mason (1991) reported that too much attention and time spent on developing fluency within a reading lesson may detract from students' ability to comprehend the text. Thus, the National Reading Panel (2000) found in its review of fluency instruction that fluency lessons ranging in length between 15 and 30 minutes showed positive effects on students' fluency development.

From our study of the fluency literature, we came to agree with Wolf and Katzir-Cohen (2001, p. 211) when they wrote, "The history of fluency research in the field of reading might be characterized as intellectually spasmodic: There are periods of great effort and creativity, followed by fallow periods of relative disinterest. In 1983 fluency was described as the 'most neglected' reading skill" (Allington, 1983).

Although fluency has recently assumed a central position in the discourse about effective classroom literacy instruction, many classroom teachers remain somewhat bewildered about how to teach and practice fluency effectively in the classroom with children of differing reading levels. On the other hand, we believe that a bright future likely awaits fluency research, instruction, and classroom practice in the years that lie ahead. We, like many of our colleagues, realize that Allington was right in 1983, and that fluency instruction must no longer be a neglected goal of reading instruction. This was particularly indicated in a large-scale study of fluency achievement in U.S. education, in which the NAEP found that "44% of fourth-grade students tested were dysfluent *even with grade-level stories that the student read under supportive testing conditions*" (National Reading Panel, 2000, p. 3-1, emphasis added).

METAFLUENCY INSTRUCTION: A MISSING PIECE
OF EFFECTIVE FLUENCY INSTRUCTION

J. V. Hoffman (2003) rightfully points out that the "interface between fluency and comprehension is quite tight" (p. 5). High-quality fluency instruction, similar to high-quality comprehension instruction, is largely permeated with understanding and constructing meaning. An instructional focus on developing only the observable performances of reading fluency—accuracy, rate, and expression—is insufficient to produce the desired outcomes in both comprehension and in fluent oral renditions.

Since fluency and comprehension are so tightly connected, many aspects of high-quality comprehension instruction also pertain to providing high-quality fluency instruction. For example, comprehension monitoring is a critical part of self-regulation of the comprehension process, leading to students' increased understanding and independence as a reader. It is not enough for students to be taught comprehension strategies or processes; they must also become aware of when reading processes are going along as they should (Pressley, 2002). The same can be said of fluency development. For children to become self-regulating, fluent readers, they must become aware of what fluency is, whether or not it is going along as it should, and what can be done about it if it is not! To begin this process, children must learn what fluency is—not just how it sounds. They must understand the elements and concepts associated with fluency, and the language necessary for talking and thinking about fluency, and become aware of what fluency should sound like in oral reading.

To further drive home this important point, Hoffman (2003) asserts, "Work to develop the meta-language of fluency with your students, which includes concepts of expression, word stress, and phrasing. It will serve you well in explicit instruction" (p. 6). Students need to know that fluency is an important goal of reading instruction. They need to know what fluency is, and they need to have the language, so that teachers and students can talk specifically about fluency as a concept and as a performance to be examined and developed. They must develop an awareness of fluency in order to monitor it, fix it, and improve it. Students must own the concepts, elements, and language; have an awareness of and know how to use fix-up strategies; and understand the varying purposes of fluency in order to self-regulate and improve it. We must not only facilitate reading fluency practice but also cultivate a deeper appreciation among students of the importance of fluency as a personal goal of reading improvement. Equally important, we need to develop students' understanding of what we mean when we say that reading is fluent and that they can go about fixing fluency up when it isn't going along as it should.

What Is Meant by "Metafluency"?

Because comprehension and fluency processes are so integrally intertwined, we reviewed research around the concept of metacomprehension or metacognitive monitoring (Good, Simmons, & Kame'enui, 2001; Pinnell et al., 1995; Rasinski, 2003). Vygotsky (1962) described the acquisition of knowledge in two distinct phases (1) through automatic, unconscious acquisition processes, followed by (2) gradual increases in active, conscious control over the acquisition of knowledge. According to Brown (1980), "metacognition" is defined as "the deliberate conscious control of one's own cognitive actions" (p. 453). Readers who are aware of their own cognitive processes are aware of what they need to know, as well as how and when to actively intervene to ensure that the acquisition of knowledge is proceeding as it should.

From Brown's (1980) review of comprehension-monitoring research, we reasoned that because metacomprehension or comprehension monitoring is fundamental to the improvement of comprehension, so then metafluency, or fluency monitoring, is fundamental to the improvement of fluency. Explicitly teaching children the metalanguage of fluency (accuracy, rate, and speed; reader's purpose; text difficulty; and expression, phrasing, smoothness, stress, pitch, and volume, etc.) is important in developing children's ability to think and talk about fluency as an object that they can consciously monitor and control. Along with explicitly teaching children the concepts and language associated with fluency, we believe that teachers need to build into children's emerging reading strategy repertoire a propensity to monitor the status of their own reading fluency. Children also need to know how to take steps to "fix up" ineffective or inefficient fluency behaviors.

Next, we examined what constitutes high-quality comprehension instruction to understand further this concept of *metafluency*. We found from our examination of the research that high-quality comprehension instruction is characterized by explicit explanations, modeling, descriptions, and demonstrations, followed by guided practice, both in groups and individually, that gradually transfers the responsibility for comprehension strategy use from the teacher to the students. As a result, we reasoned that high-quality fluency instruction would likely, in this respect, once again look very similar to high-quality comprehension instruction. From these studies and our own discussions of fluency and comprehension-monitoring research, we coined the term "metafluency." And as a result of coining this term, we created and refined a fluency instructional framework supported by the findings of the scientific reading research that extend fluency instruction further into the somewhat less well-understood domain of developing children's metafluency ability—the knowledge and the language to talk about what fluency is; the propensity or inclination to self-monitor one's own fluency, then learning how to take conscious, strategically selected steps to increase one's own reading fluency. Our collective efforts culminated in what we termed the Fluency Development Workshop (FDW)—an instructional framework created to help children develop fluency and metafluency across a wide variety of texts and levels of text difficulty.

THE FLUENCY DEVELOPMENT WORKSHOP: HELPING ALL CHILDREN BECOME FLUENT READERS

The design of FDW was created to provide optimally effective fluency instruction for elementary-age children. The fluency and comprehension instructional research suggests that children need:

- Explicit, systematic explanation and instruction about the elements of reading fluency.
- Rich and varied modeling and demonstrations of fluent reading.
- Guided oral reading practice with appropriately challenging and varied texts on a regular basis.
- Guided repeated or multiple rereadings of the same text.
- Assessment and self-monitoring of oral reading fluency progress.
- Information on how to "fix up" faltering reading fluency.
- Genuine audiences and opportunities for oral reading performance.

Using the guidelines from the National Reading Panel (2000), we also determined that fluency instruction needs to be happening on a daily basis for 15–30 minutes as an essential part of the daily reading instructional routine or schedule. An occasional flirtation with fluency instruction would not provide the systematic instruction and regular practice necessary to achieve fluency for many children.

The Fluency Development Workshop Daily Routine

The FDW daily routine is organized around three major time periods. The first time period is intended for teacher explanation, modeling, demonstrations, description, and definition of the elements of fluent oral reading and takes about 5–7 minutes. The second time period of the FDW continues for about 10–15 minutes and is designed to provide children with guided group and individual repeated oral reading practice using a variety of practice formats and approaches. The third and final time period of the FDW is for assessment and monitoring, and takes about 5–7 minutes. The daily routine of the FDW is summarized in Figure 4.1.

A Daily Lesson Framework

A daily lesson framework was developed as a part of the overall design of the FDW. It was designed to maintain a rapid pace, moving the lesson along from high teacher input and responsibility to high student activity and responsibility. The design of the lesson was built around the comprehension instructional model of *gradual release of responsibility* (Pearson &

I. Teacher explanation and modeling of the elements and nature of fluent oral reading

5–7 Minutes

II. Guided group or individual repeated oral reading practice

10–15 Minutes

III. Group and/or individual assessment and progress monitoring

5–7 Minutes

Total Maximum Daily Scheduled Time: 25–30 Minutes

FIGURE 4.1. The Fluency Development Workshop daily routine.

Gallagher, 1984). How this model works in practice is described later in this chapter.

Explicit Explanation

The FDW lesson framework begins with an explicit explanation, description, or definition of the importance of reading fluency and the elements, terms, and metalanguage of fluent oral reading as defined in the research and professional literature: (1) accuracy, (2) rate, and (3) expression. For example, the teachers in this project develop a classroom poster where the elements of fluency are defined and described in "kid-friendly" language. This poster is displayed and referred to frequently as teachers explicitly, intentionally, and systematically teach and model for children the concepts, terms, and elements of fluent oral reading. The underlying thinking behind the explicit explanation part of the lesson framework is that children need to clearly understand what oral reading fluency is in order to produce, monitor, or increase it, either with guidance or independently. In Figure 4.2, text from a typical classroom poster used in the explicit explanation part of the FDW lesson framework is shown.

Teacher Monitoring and Clarification

Of course, explicit explanation, description, or definition of the elements of fluent oral reading are insufficient to make the point with most young readers. They need to see and hear models of what one means as well. So, the next part of the FDW lesson framework involved teacher modeling, think-alouds, and demonstration of the elements of fluent oral reading,

---

Becoming a fluent reader is an important part of becoming a good reader. In order to become a fluent reader, you need to

- Read accurately, or without mistakes, what is on the page.
- Vary the speed of reading according to your purpose(s) and how difficult the text is for you.
- Read with appropriate volume, expression, phrasing, and smoothness.
- Remember the important ideas from your reading.

FIGURE 4.2. Classroom poster of essential elements of fluent oral reading.

including examples and intentional miscues. Teachers selected one of the essential elements of oral reading fluency for each lesson (i.e., accuracy). For example, the teacher might have selected the poem "You Need to Have an Iron Rear" by Jack Prelutsky (1984, p. 15) for this lesson.

> You need to have an iron rear
> To sit upon a cactus,
> Or otherwise, at least a year
> Of very painful practice.

After reading this poem aloud to the group of children with accuracy, the teacher reminded the children that accurate oral reading is *reading what is on the page, without making mistakes*. Next, the teacher performed an inaccurate oral reading of the same poem. For example, the teacher might have read the poem as follows:

> You need to *wear* an iron *tear*
> To *look* upon a cactus,
> Or otherwise, at least a *spear*
> Of very painful practice.

Once the inaccurate oral reading of this poem was complete, the teacher once again reminded the children that accurate oral reading is *reading what is on the page, without making mistakes*. Next, the teacher invited the children, usually amid snickering and giggles, to comment on the accuracy of the "inaccurate" modeling of oral reading. We noticed that greater discussion and attention flowed from the inaccurate reading than from accurate renditions of text. When we asked children why this was the case, they indicated that the miscues tended to reveal the characteristics of fluent reading more obviously than did examples of fluent reading. As a result, children became very active in attempting to "detect" the teacher's inaccuracies or other fluency flaws.

Group-Guided Repeated-Reading Practice and Monitoring

After explaining, defining, describing, modeling, demonstrating, and discussing, the teacher involved the children in repeated, group-guided oral rereadings of the text, poem, or story that had been previously modeled. During this part of the FDW lesson, teachers used various formats for choral reading, such as echoic, unison, popcorn, antiphonal, mumble, line-a-child, and so on. For those who are unfamiliar with these choral reading variations, we recommend reading Opitz and Rasinski's *Good-Bye Round Robin* (1998), or Rasinski's *The Fluent Reader* (2003). After the first reading of the text as a group, teachers stopped and asked children to assess the fluency of the group reading using an informal fluency-monitoring rubric that highlighted the elements of fluent reading that the teacher had previously explicitly explained. This informal fluency-monitoring rubric made use of a simple dichotomous rating scale of "yes" or "no," and for the younger children, a display of smiling or frowning faces (see Figure 4.3). Teachers usually produced this rubric in a variety of sizes. One version of the fluency-monitoring rubric was enlarged and laminated as a classroom poster. Laminating the fluency monitoring rubric poster allowed teachers to use water-based markers or dry-erase markers to mark the oral reading fluency items, yet be able to erase these marks easily for later reuse of the poster.

Teachers also often used a "think-aloud" process to show *how* they would rate the group's oral reading fluency on each of the three elements of oral reading fluency. They also explained *why* they gave the ratings they did on each item. After modeling this process a few times, teachers would *share and gradually release* the fluency-monitoring process to the children through three phases. In the first phase of the release of responsibility for fluency monitoring, the teachers shared the task of monitoring fluency by asking the children to rate the group's fluency on each element displayed in the rubric, and then explained why they, the teachers, thought the children gave the rating they did. Of course, children cor-

FIGURE 4.3. Informal assessment rubric of the elements of oral reading fluency.

rected the teachers if they did not give the right reasons! In phase two of the release, the teachers continued sharing the responsibility for completing the task of rating the group's oral reading fluency by rating each oral reading fluency item, then asking the children to explain why the teachers rated the group's oral reading fluency as they did. And finally, the teachers fully released the task of rating the group's oral reading fluency by asking the children both to rate and to explain the ratings on the informal fluency assessment poster.

Children were also taught how to "fix up" specific fluency problems through teacher explanation, modeling, and group or individual practice. Teachers explained specific types of fluency problems and "fix-up" steps for each type of fluency problem displayed in a classroom poster. Teachers modeled specific fluency problems and then how to use the poster to get ideas about how to "fix up" fluency. Children were then encouraged to use these fix-up strategies with other classmates and by themselves during group and individual oral reading practice each day. The fix-up strategies used are shown in Figure 4.4.

Accuracy
1. Slow your reading speed down.
2. Look carefully at the words and the letters in the words you didn't read on the page.
3. Think about whether you know this word or parts of this word. Try saying the word or word parts.
4. Make the sound of each letter from left to right and blend the sounds together quickly to say the word.
5. Listen carefully to see whether the word you said makes sense.
6. Try rereading the sentence again.
7. If the word still doesn't make sense, then ask someone to help you.

Rate
1. Adjust your reading speed to go slower when the text is difficult or unfamiliar.
2. Adjust your reading speed to go faster when the text is easy or familiar.

Expression
1. Try to read three or more words together before pausing, stopping, or taking a breath.
2. Take a big breath and try to read to the comma or end punctuation, without stopping for another breath.
3. Read so that you sound like "someone talking."

FIGURE 4.4, Fluency fix-up strategies for major fluency elements.

Individual Guided Repeated-Reading Practice

Next in the FDW lesson framework, children were involved in individual guided practice and repeated readings of the text, poem, or story previously modeled. Unlike classroom practices such as independent reading, where children may or may not be reading and receive no guidance or feedback, or round robin reading, where only one child at a time gets to read a part of the text aloud only once and receive feedback, teachers used paired reading approaches, such as buddy, peer, or dyad reading, to optimize each student's practice time and the oral reading feedback each student received.

Pairs of readers were either same-age peers or older peers from another age- or grade-level classroom. Each pair of children alternated roles of reader and listener. As pairs of children practiced, they were reminded to consult the fluency-monitoring scoring rubric poster as well as the "fix-up" poster for offering feedback to their peers during individual oral reading practice (see Figure 4.4). After each oral reading by the reader, the listener provided feedback using the same fluency-monitoring rubric printed on a small, wallet-size paper. Guided, oral, repeated reading practice with feedback was one of the practices that produced the largest effect sizes and student gains for fluency in the studies analyzed by the National Reading Panel (2000).

Oral Reading Performance

Once children, especially the younger ones, sensed their emerging fluency, they wanted to demonstrate it for others. To provide an alternative approach and purpose for fluency practice, the teachers in our project arranged for children to perform their practiced oral reading for an audience of either parents or other students in the school building. When preparing an oral reading performance, teachers used one of three well-known oral reading instructional approaches: (1) Readers Theatre, (2) radio reading, and (3) read around (Opitz & Rasinski, 1998). Each of these oral reading performance approaches was used to perform specific text types. For children who wanted to share a favorite poem read aloud to the group, we used the "read around" process, where each student, in turn, identifies and rehearses a passage, poem, or story text to share (Tompkins, 1998). For performing information texts, we used "radio readings" as described by Greene (1979), Rasinski (2003), and Searfoss (1975). The idea for radio readings is to perform a text well enough that the listener can picture the events. As a consequence, we divided information texts into four parts for a group of readers. Then, each reader, with feedback from a peer, practiced his or her part of the information book. Then, students read their part of the book as if they were broadcasting a news flash on the radio. For practicing and performing stories or plays, teachers turned to Readers Theatre. We found, like many teachers had already discovered, that many Readers Theatre scripts are readily available over the Internet. Some of our favorite web addresses for obtaining copies of Readers Theatre scripts are www.geocities.com/EnchantedForest/Tower/3235 and www.readers-theatre.com.

In addition to these more formal opportunities to perform oral readings for other audiences, teachers also provided a daily closing session where children could share their oral readings with their classmates using a practice called "reading corners." In reading corners, four children were selected on a daily basis to (1) give a book, text, poem, or story talk in which the reader tells the other children briefly about the text they have been reading, and (2) orally read a selected passage or paragraph from their selected text to a small group of class members—usually six to eight peers. Peers listen to each text talk and select which of the reading corner texts they would most like to hear. We found that the "reading corners" approach also encouraged children to learn the art of book selling or promotion, as well as to develop their fluent oral reading performance skills. In any case, this part of the FDW lesson was brief, usually about 5 minutes or less.

Although the explanation of the FDW offered here is lengthy and detailed, the actual flow of the FDW lesson each day was briskly paced and, as we said earlier, lasted for only 20–25 minutes total. In fact, keeping the pace brisk, moving through the parts of the FDW lesson quickly, and varying the text difficulty levels and types of texts kept the lessons from becoming either boring or repetitive.

As expected, we observed that fluency achieved with one type of task or text was insufficient, and that children required instruction and practice with a variety of reading fluency tasks, and a variety of text types and levels of challenge. Since many of our teachers were familiar with and used leveled readers for providing daily guided reading groups as in Fountas and Pinnell (1996), we relied heavily upon A–Z book levels to help us provide texts of appropriate levels of challenge. We also felt that at each grade level, children should practice oral reading fluency with a variety of text types, including stories, poems, journal entries, jokes, articles, and information books as well. In grades 2–6, we found that we needed to provide new, fresh, or novel short, high-interest texts for fluency practice nearly every day. In grades K–1, we found that multiple days of fluency practice with the same texts were often needed to move the oral reading of a text to fluency.

Fluency Instruction Scope and Sequence

As we worked together to develop the FDW schedule and lesson framework, we also found that teachers wanted and needed guidance on a scope and sequence of fluency-related skills, tasks, and texts. To meet this need, we developed and used the scope and sequence of fluency concepts, skills, and so on, in Figure 4.5 in our project classrooms.

Fluency Concepts
- ☐ Accuracy: (1) reading accurately, and (2) reading inaccurately.
- ☐ Rate: (1) reading too fast, (2) reading too slow, and (3) reading at "just the right rate" for the text or task.
- ☐ Phrasing: (1) reading with appropriate phrasing, (2) reading with two- or three-word phrasing, and (3) word-by-word reading.
- ☐ Expression: (1) reading with appropriate pitch, stress, and intonation, and (2) reading in a monotone style.

Fluency Texts
- ☐ Poetry
- ☐ Song lyrics
- ☐ Stories
- ☐ Plays
- ☐ Jokes, riddles, and comics
- ☐ Information books
- ☐ Newspapers
- ☐ Magazines
- ☐ Directions or instructions

Student Fluency Tasks
- ☐ Word part and word recognition drills
- ☐ Oral reading practice—group and individual
- ☐ Monitoring and fix up
- ☐ Performance
- ☐ Assessment

FIGURE 4.5. Fluency instruction scope and sequence chart.

ASSESSING FLUENCY AND METAFLUENCY GROWTH

According to the definition of the National Reading Panel, "fluent readers" can read text with speed, accuracy, and proper expression (p. 3-1). With this definition in mind, we determined that adequate assessment of fluency would involve periodically sampling children's reading rate, decoding accuracy, and expression. Our fluency assessment model is shown in Figure 4.6. In this model, we used a 1-minute reading sample to examine students' decoding accuracy and reading rate. To assess expressive reading, we used the Zutell and Rasinski (1991) Multidimensional Fluency Scale (MFS; see Appendix at the end of the book). By using these simple assessments, a comprehensive assessment of reading fluency can be acquired within roughly 1.5 minutes of teacher time per student, or about 4.5 minutes per day.

To accomplish this aim, we determined that children's fluency would be sampled every 2 weeks using the 1-minute reading sample (Rasinski, 2003). This was done by giving every child in the class a preselected grade-level passage to read aloud. To save time during the instructional day, the teacher asked three students to go to a fluency recording station to read the passage. Each student had his or her own audiocassette tape. They put the audiocassette tape into the machine, pushed record, and turned on a 1-minute egg timer. When the timer sounded, they were to stop reading, turn off the recorder, and place the audiocassette tape into a tray on the teacher's desk. The teacher listened to three to four tapes

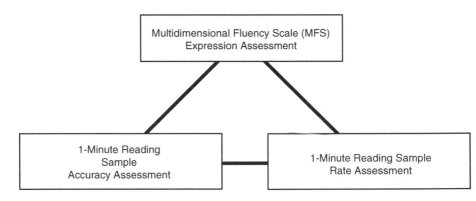

FIGURE 4.6. Fluency Development Workshop assessment model.

each evening or 15–20 tapes per week, or about 15 minutes of assessment time. The teacher marked any errors on a copy of the passage and recorded the total number of words read correctly and the number of errors. Reading accuracy was judged as adequate if the students achieved 95% accuracy or higher on the passage, using the criteria of Howe and Shinn (2001).

Once every 2 weeks, using the information from the 1-minute reading samples that were audiotaped and scored by the teacher, children recorded their rate and accuracy using charts kept in private folders, as shown in Figure 4.7 (Reutzel & Cooter, 2003).

Children were taught that fluency progress is being made when the reading rate line is going up and when the error line is going down. Along with this measurement of fluency, teachers also asked children to record an oral retelling of the passage to rate for comprehension assessment purposes. Although quite simple, the 1-minute assessment model has been validated in recent research by Good and colleagues (2001), showing that fluency measures are comprehensive measures of reading progress and accurately predict students' comprehension as measured by standardized reading comprehension subtests. This very simple, yet comprehensive, ongoing measurement of fluency and comprehension informed teachers,

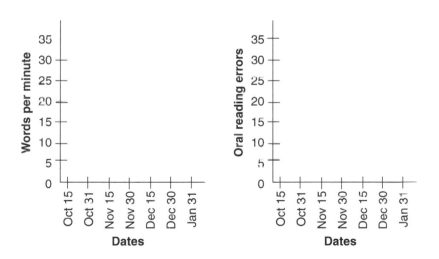

FIGURE 4.7. Rate and accuracy charts. From Reutzel and Cooter (2003). Copyright 2003 by Pearson Education. Reprinted by permission.

parents, and children on a regular basis about individual students' reading development.

FUTURE DIRECTIONS IN FLUENCY RESEARCH

We have begun a randomized experimental exploration of the value of the FDW on third-grade students' acquisition of fluency and metafluency. Because of the way we have designed this study, we will be able to examine the unique contributions of each aspect the FDW: explicit instruction, fluency monitoring, and performance/practice, as well as the total instructional approach taken. Our initial observations of the effects of the FDW in informal trials during a pilot session give us a fair degree of optimism. We also want to examine how the FDW may or may not differentially impact above-average, average, and below-average achieving readers at the third-grade level.

We chose third-grade level because most current national and state standards, as well as laws, mandate grade-level reading by the end of the third-grade year. If students are going to be able to read on grade level, teachers and students must give increased and sustained attention to the development of fluency in young readers. And, to our knowledge, no extant research has directly investigated teaching students to attend to their own fluency. In conclusion, there exists a clear need to investigate the effects of fluency instruction over longer periods of time, with differing text types, and varying the tasks attached to demonstrating fluency. For example, we need to know:

1. How does fluency instruction affect children reading poetry, narrative, or information texts?
2. How does fluency instruction affect students of differing reading abilities?
3. How does fluency instruction affect the development of individual readers as they progress throughout a year of instruction or over multiple years of instruction?

Answers to these questions and others await the work of future research studies and investigation. For now, we believe the elements of effective fluency instruction are becoming more widely understood. How to package the multiple elements of effective fluency instruction to obtain the optimal benefit for all children also awaits the incremental but steady march of research progress.

REFERENCES

Allington, R. L. (1983). Fluency: The neglected goal of reading. *The Reading Teacher, 36*, 556–561.

Anderson, R. C., Wilkinson, I. A. G., & Mason, J. M. (1991). A microanalysis of the small-group, guided reading lesson: Effects of an emphasis on global story meaning. *Reading Research Quarterly, 26*, 417–441.

Blevins, W. (2001). *Building fluency: Lessons and strategies for reading success.* New York: Scholastic.

Brown, A. L. (1980). Meta-cognitive development and reading. In R. J. Spiro, B. C. Bruce, & W. F. Brewer (Eds.), *Theoretical issues in reading comprehension: Perspectives from cognitive psychology, linguistics, artificial intelligence, and education* (453–481). Hillsdale, NJ: Erlbaum.

Dowhower, S. L. (1991). Speaking of prosody: Fluency's unattended bedfellow. *Theory Into Practice, 30*(3), 158–164.

Emberley, B. (1967). *Drummer Hoff.* New York: Simon & Shuster Books for Children.

Fountas, I. C., & Pinnell, G. S. (1996). *Guided reading instruction: Good first teaching for all children.* Portsmouth, NH: Heinemann.

Germann, G. (2001). Fluency norms. Eden Prarie, MN: Edformations. Retrieved June 2, 2003, from www.edformation.com

Good, R. H., Simmons, D. C., & Kame'enui, E. J. (2001). The importance and decision-making utility of a continuum of fluency-based indicators of foundational reading skills for third-grade high-stakes outcomes. *Scientific Studies in Reading, 5*(3), 257–288.

Greene, F. (1979). Radio reading. In C. Pennock (Ed.), *Reading comprehension at four linguistic levels* (pp. 104–107). Newark, DE: International Reading Association.

Harris, T. L., & Hodges, R. E. (Eds.). (1981). *The dictionary of reading.* Newark, DE: International Reading Association.

Harris, T. L., & Hodges, R. E. (Eds.). (1995). *The literacy dictionary: The vocabulary or reading and writing.* Newark, DE: International Reading Association.

Hasbrouck, J. E., & Tindal, G. (1992). Curriculum-based oral reading fluency norms for students in grades 2 through 5. *Teaching Exceptional Children, 24*, 41–44.

Hasbrouck, J. E., & Tindal, G. (2005). *Oral reading fluency norms, grades 1–8.* Personal communication, retrievable at www.jhasbrouck.com and Fluency Q&A.

Hoffman, J. V. (2003). Foreword. In T. V. Rasinski, *The fluent reader: Oral reading strategies for building word recognition, fluency, and comprehension* (pp. 5–6). New York: Scholastic.

Howe, K. B., & Shinn, M. M. (2001). *Standard reading assessment passages (RAPS) for use in general outcome measurements: A manual describing development and technical features.* Eden Prarie, MN: Edformations.

Huey, E. B. (1908). *The psychology and pedagogy of reading.* New York: Macmillan.

Kame'enui, E. J., & Simmons, D. C. (2001). The DNA of reading fluency. *Scientific Studies of Reading, 5*(3), 203–210.

Kuhn, M. R., & Stahl, S. A. (2000). *Fluency: A review of developmental and remedial practices* (Center for the Improvement of Early Reading Achievement Report No. 2-008). Ann Arbor: University of Michigan.

LaBerge, D., & Samuels, S. J. (1974). Toward a theory of automatic information processing in reading. *Cognitive Psychology, 6,* 293–323.

National Reading Report. (2000). *Teaching children to read: An evidence-based assessment of the scientific research literature in reading and its implications for reading instruction.* Washington, DC: National Institute of Child Health and Human Development.

Opitz, M. F., & Rasinski, T. V. (1998). *Good-bye round robin: 25 effective oral reading strategies.* Portsmouth, NH: Heinemann Educational Books.

Pearson, P. D., & Gallagher, M. C. (1983). The instruction of reading comprehension. *Contemporary Educational Psychology, 8*(3), 317–344.

Pinnell, G. S., Pikulski, J. J., Wixson, K. K., Campbell, J. R., Gough, P. B., & Beatty, A. S. (1995). *Listening to children read aloud: Oral fluency.* Washington, DC: National Center for Educational Statistics, U.S. Department of Education.

Prelutsky, J. (1984). You need to have an iron rear. In *The new kid on the block* (p. 15). New York: Greenwillow Books.

Pressley, M. (2002). Improving comprehension instruction: A path for the future. In C. Collins-Block, L. B. Gambrell, & M. Pressley (Eds.), *Improving comprehension instruction: Rethinking research, theory, and classroom practice* (pp. 385–399). San Francisco: Jossey-Bass.

RAND Reading Study Group. (2002). *Reading for understanding: Toward an R&D program in reading comprehension.* Santa Monica, CA: Science and Technology Policy Institute, RAND Education.

Rasinski, T. V. (2003). *The fluent reader: Oral reading strategies for building word recognition, fluency, and comprehension.* New York: Scholastic.

Reutzel, D. R., & Cooter, R. B. (2003). *Strategies for reading assessment and instruction: Helping every child succeed.* Upper Saddle River, NJ: Merrill/Prentice-Hall.

Samuels, S. J. (1979). The method of repeated readings. *Reading Teacher, 32*(4), 403–408.

Searfoss, L. W. (1975). Radio reading. *Reading Teacher, 29,* 295–296.

Smith, N. B. (2002). *American reading instruction*. Newark, DE: International Reading Association.

Stahl, S. (2004). What do we know about fluency? In P. McCardle & V. Chhabra (Eds.), *The voice of evidence in reading research* (pp. 187–211). Baltimore: Brookes.

Tompkins, G. E. (1998). *Fifty reading strategies step by step*. Upper Saddle River, NJ: Merrill/Prentice-Hall.

Vygotsky, L. S. (1962). *Thought and language*. Cambridge, MA: MIT Press.

Wolf, M., & Katzir-Cohen, T. (2001). Reading fluency and its intervention. *Scientific Studies in Reading, 5*(3), 211–238.

Zutell, J., & Rasinski, T. V. (1991). Training teachers to attend to their students' oral reading fluency. *Theory Into Practice, 30*, 211–217.

CHAPTER 5

Reading Fluency

More Than Fast and Accurate Reading

Barbara J. Walker
Kouider Mokhtari
Stephan Sargent

Reading fluency is an integral part of the complex reading process. As such, it requires the simultaneous, thoughtful coordination of various cognitive, linguistic, and affective competencies. Readers characteristically develop knowledge and skill in orchestrating these competencies gradually over the primary to elementary school years. As they advance in reading development, most of them learn to recognize words more rapidly and with greater accuracy. Others, for various reasons, find it hard to develop such facility with word decoding. Common sense, supported by much credible research and theorizing (e.g., Samuels, 2002, 2004; Samuels & Flor, 1997), indicates that automatic word reading is unquestionably crucial for reading fluency and comprehension, because it allows the mind to have more capacity for thinking when less attention is devoted to word identification.

However, a critical question posed by many researchers and practitioners is whether rapid and accurate reading, while necessary, is sufficient for fluent reading. A part of the answer to this important question originated in a research report entitled *Listening to Children Read Aloud* (Pinnell et al., 1995), which has shown that highly accurate decoding performance did not necessarily guarantee highly fluent reading. This finding has been supported by other researchers, who have argued that while

> fluency is dependent on adequate word recognition, proficiency in word recognition does not always result in fluent reading. Proficient word recognition may be sufficient to read accurately, but it is not sufficient to read faster with proper expression. In order to have proper expression (i.e., know which words to emphasize and when to pause), there must be some sensitivity to grammatical units (syntax) and punctuation cues. (Kamhi, Allen, & Catts, 2001, p. 176)

In other words, a developing reader must be able to attend not simply to the sound–symbol relationships of words but also to the morphological and syntactic layers of language that govern how words and sentences are formed. In addition, the development of such skills and competencies is influenced by the reader's exposure to and experiences in the act of reading.

Indeed, when thinking of reading fluency as an interpretation of printed text, which includes text understanding and appreciation, we have reason to believe that reading fluency involves more than fast and accurate reading. We see the act of reading as a multifaceted process of interconnected relationships among aspects of reading, involving, among other things, cognitive, linguistic, and affective aspects. Thus, we submit what we believe is a preliminary attempt at building the ingredients of a conceptual framework that can be used to explain what might be involved in fluent reading. Our proposed preliminary framework is influenced by current research and theorizing relative to reading fluency and, more importantly, by the role of language in learning to read, the reader, and the context in which reading takes place (Kuhn & Stahl, 2003). Our goal is to invite much extended dialogue and discussion about reading fluency far beyond the speed and accuracy of word reading. Because the proposed sketch of our reading fluency framework is "under construction," we can only begin to lay out what we consider to be key ingredients of what constitutes the act of fluent reading. In the following sections, we provide a skeletal outline of our proposed conceptual framework and use the elements of the framework as a structure for making suggestions relative to the assessment and instruction of reading fluency.

CONCEPTUAL FRAMEWORK FOR READING FLUENCY

While long-established interpretations of reading fluency have generally emphasized *performance attributes* of (oral) reading fluency (what readers can do), recent research on the interface of language and literacy (e.g., Allington, 2001; Biemiller, 1999; Mahony, Singson, & Mann, 2002; Menyuk, 1999; Mokhtari & Thompson, in press) has underscored important *competence attributes* (what readers know about language and its functions) and what influences the acquisition of the knowledge and skills involved in becoming fluent readers—both of which have been shown to contribute significantly to the acquisition of fluent oral *and* silent reading. Reading fluency in this sense refers to the ease with which a person reads within the constraints of certain cognitive, linguistic, and affective aspects of reading development. Reading fluency is further influenced by what we like to call *disposition attributes* (or tendencies toward reading), which include, among other things, attitudes toward reading, perceptions of self as reader, and reading habits—having to do with whether one engages in any reading activity at all.

The conceptual framework we propose is depicted in Figure 5.1, which illustrates the interrelationships among the key components involved in the development of fluent reading. These components involve *performance attributes*, including decoding accuracy (reading with minimal or no errors), reading rate (reading at a pace permitting understanding of what is read), and expression (reading naturally and effortlessly adhering to prosodic features of language, such as stress and intonation patterns). The acquisition of these performance prerequisites is interrelated with *competence attributes* having to do with one's awareness of how words are formed (morphological awareness), how phrases and sentences are structured (syntactic or grammatical awareness), how information is organized in texts (discourse structure awareness), and how one navigates texts (metacognitive reading awareness). The performance and competence attributes are in turn influenced by the third facet of this framework, *disposition attributes*, which have some to do with whether one wants to read (attitudes towards reading), how one views oneself as a reader (perceptions of self as reader), and whether one engages in reading (reading habits).

Each of the three foundational attributes depicted in this framework consists of multifaceted but interrelated features. Performance attributes are supported by an array of competency attributes, such as phonological, morphological, syntactic, and discourse awareness structures. The disposi-

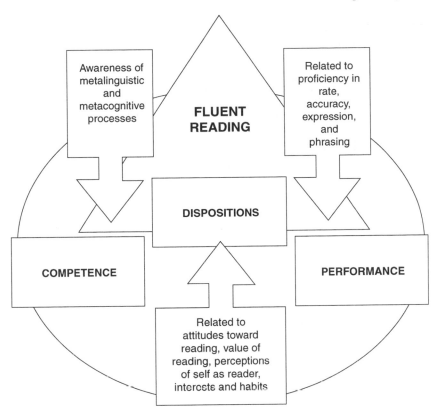

FIGURE 5.1. Components of fluent reading.

tion attributes support the performance attributes, because they maintain engagement in reading. These aspects are part of the larger picture of reading, which is represented by the circle. A key aspect within the circle is constructing meaning or reader comprehension. Fluency, another key aspect, is represented by the triangle. We now discuss each of the three components that constitute fluency.

Performance Attributes

The first major component of the proposed conceptual framework for fluent reading relates to reader performance abilities. These abilities relate to quantitative aspects of reading fluency (decoding accuracy and reading rate), as well as qualitative features (expression and appropriate phrasing) that can describe performance and also indicate progress in reading development. The ability to read naturally and effortlessly involves decoding words automatically, accurately, and with appropriate speed; using prosodic cues or text signals, such as punctuation marks and other writing conventions; and chunking information in meaningful syntactic units indicated by pauses while reading. Researchers concur (1) that reading rate is an essential component of proficient reading and is significantly correlated with word accuracy (Rasinski, 2000), and (2) that reading fluency and comprehension are closely associated with one another (Kuhn & Stahl, 2003). For instance, Fuchs, Fuchs, Hosp, and Jenkins (2001) reported a correlation between oral reading fluency and reading comprehension of .91. The high correlation for oral reading fluency measured by words correct per minute (wcpm) does corroborate the theoretically driven hypotheses about the potential of oral reading fluency as an indicator of overall reading performance.

Expression or prosodic reading—also described as reading with appropriate phrasing—is considered a sign that an individual has become a fluent reader (Dowhower, 1991; Rasinski & Zutell, 1990). "Expression" refers to the way oral reading sounds and silent reading feels. It has to do with the "music" that accompanies fluent reading, which includes inflection, pitch, and stress patterns, all of which make reading sound smooth and natural. When one reads with expression or appropriate phrasing, he or she is able to chunk groups of words into meaningful units, indicating sensitivity to the word, syntactic, and text structures. All of these skills are reliable indicators of competence attributes that are important for fluent reading.

Aspects of expression cover a range of interrelated linguistic and paralinguistic attributes: rises and falls in intonation patterns and fluctuations in articulation rates, pitch, and duration. These elements can signal or mark discourse units and syntactic boundaries. They play a significant role in managing and controlling the flow of reading. Thus, a reader can deliberately include fluctuations in intonation, for instance, to achieve rhetorical effect, particularly in reading dramatic plays or poems. A fluent reader is one who clusters text into morphologically and syntactically appropriate phrases and sentences. The parsing of text signifies that the reader has an understanding of how meaning is encoded in the text being read. For example, many times, pauses and/or hesitations or false starts can save time while thoughts are gathered and so occur at points at which planning and decision making are taking place. Pauses tell us much about what goes on in reading; for instance, they can permit error correction in sentences not yet vocalized, and generally point to the reader's struggles to maintain control of the act of reading.

Competence Attributes

The second major component of the proposed conceptual framework for fluent reading relates to the competence attributes. Several competencies, metalinguistic and metacognitive, underlie the knowledge base that influences fluency. Recent research has shown that the processes of decoding accuracy (phonemic awareness, etc.) and rapid word identification, while important prerequisite reading skills, are a necessary but may not be sufficient for fluent reading development (Pinnell et al., 1995). Several researchers have found that some developing readers (estimates vary from 10 to 15%) turn out to be poor comprehenders despite their performance on phonological awareness tasks and their demonstrated ability to read words with appropriate speed and accuracy (Nation, Clark, & Snowling, 2002; Nation & Snowling, 2000; Snow, Burns, & Griffin, 1998). We have known for some time now that phonological awareness may indeed be a necessary but not sufficient condition for fluent reading development. Indeed, efficient word recognition processes are necessary, because they allow the reader to allocate optimal attention to the interpretation of meanings communicated in the text. They are not sufficient, because text comprehension comprises other components as well, such as word and topic knowledge, knowledge of conceptual schemas (e.g., meaning relationships), and metacognitive strategies.

The importance of (phonological) awareness—the ability to recognize, segment, and manipulate sounds—has been highlighted in a growing body of research on learning to read (Snow et al., 1998). This competence influences the development of word reading accuracy, but not necessarily reading rate (Pinnell et al., 1995). However, other critical aspects that have been found to influence reading fluency include sensitivity to the morphological, syntactic, and discourse structures of reading. Some researchers (e.g., Gough & Tunmer, 1986; Tunmer & Bowey, 1984) have shown that knowledge of language components such as morphology (word formation) and syntax (grammatical structure) contribute significantly to fluent reading. A small but growing number of studies (e.g., Gottardo, Stanovich, & Siegel, 1996; Leikin, 2002; Mahony et al., 2002; Mokhtari & Thompson, in press) have shown that children's ability to read is greatly influenced by their degree of sensitivity to word formation (morphological awareness), sentence structure (syntactic or grammatical awareness), and discourse structure (textual awareness). For instance, both morphology and syntax are major sources of information when the reader comes across a new or unknown information in text. Some words are identified by their morphological structure; that is, word formation processes have an impact on printed word identification (e.g., Feldman, 1995). While it is unclear how readers actually use morphology, the structure of words provides a grammatical foundation for linking forms and meanings in a systematic way. According to Snow and colleagues (1998), morphology is important, because it connects word forms and meanings within the structure of sentences; for example, "children learn that events that have already occurred are marked by morphological inflections such as 'ed' " (p. 74). Research on the interface between reading and language development has shown that such metalinguistic awareness is crucial for reading fluency development (e.g., Biemiller, 1999; Menyuk, 1999).

Discourse and syntactic awareness involve use of printed signals, such as text structure, and written conventions that provide a pattern of how information is organized in text, as well as how sentences are formed (Allington, 2001; Biemiller, 1999). In a recent study, Mokhtari and Thompson (in press) investigated the influence of fifth-grade students' awareness of the structure of written language (syntactic awareness) on their ability to read fluently and to comprehend what they read. The results indicated that students' levels of syntactic awareness were significantly related to their reading fluency ($r = .625$) and reading comprehension ($r = .816$). These relationships suggest that lower levels of syntactic awareness can correspond to poor reading fluency and comprehension among fifth graders.

Metacognitive strategy awareness and use are other competencies that have been shown to influence fluent reading. Although fluency has been shown to improve reading comprehension (Kuhn & Stahl, 2003), being aware of the metacognitive strategies involved in reading, and gaining practice in using these strategies while reading, influences fluent reading (Mokhtari & Reichard, 2002; Pressley, 2002). For example, students who are able to predict meaning at both the discourse and syntax levels are likely to read more fluently, because of their ability to anticipate what comes next in text. This process shows how text comprehension can be greatly facilitated by metacognitive strategy awareness and use. Research indicates that metacomprehension and reading performance are often correlated constructs (Baker & Brown, 1984), and that young, developing readers and adult, poor readers have less understanding than good readers about the cognitive, linguistic, and contextual complexities and parameters involved in reading that facilitate comprehension (Paris, Lipson, & Wixon, 1994; Pressley, 2002).

Disposition Attributes

The third important aspect of the conceptual framework that, we believe, influences the acquisition of reading fluency is the reader's disposition relative to the act of reading. This component includes, but is not necessarily limited to, the reader's attitude toward reading, perceptions of self as a reader, and reading habits. In order to understand learning and development, we must take into account the intricate relationships between cognition and motivation. Alexander and Jetton (2000, p. 296) argued that "learning from text is inevitably a synthesis of *skill*, *will*, and *thrill*," and that it "cannot take place in any meaningful fashion without the learner's commitment (i.e., will). Nor will the pursuit of knowledge continue unless the reader realizes some personal gratification or internal reward from this engagement (i.e., thrill)."

Reading, which happens both in and out of school, is evidently influenced by the beliefs, attitudes, and values that students place on reading. Readers who value reading and have a positive attitude toward it are more likely to engage in reading for longer periods of time. Research has shown that helping children to develop an interest in books and reading is not only enjoyable for adults and children alike but also has an important positive influence on reading achievement. In addition, extensive reading done outside of school and reading books in school contribute to children's ability to become fluent readers (Allington, 2001). In a study of fourth graders' oral reading abilities conducted for National Assessment of Educational Progress (NAEP), Pinnell and colleagues (1995) found that fluent reading ability was associated with extensive opportunities for reading practice outside of school (Krashen, 1993). Fluent readers reported spending more time reading outside of school than did nonfluent ones. Reading fluency appears to be positively influenced by a wide variety of literacy experiences, including the use of libraries and other activities outside of school, such as frequent practice in reading (Anderson, Wilson, & Fielding, 1988; Pinnell et al., 1995). When reading extensively, readers have an opportunity to experience language use in context, and thereby deepen their knowledge of word formation, sentence structure, and textual organization.

Likewise, reader self-perceptions can influence engagement in reading. Self-perceptions related to reading can have a strong impact on students' decisions to engage in reading (Henk & Melnick, 1992; Wigfield & Guthrie, 1997) . Reader self-perception is, in turn, influenced by reader self-efficacy, which refers to beliefs about personal competence in relation to specific tasks, such as reading a book or writing a paper (Henk & Melnick, 1992). Readers who perceive themselves as good readers are more likely to achieve success in reading than those who do not embrace such beliefs. Walker (2003) argues that succeeding encourages all readers to engage in literacy activities that in turn increase the amount of text they read, ultimately having an impact on fluent reading and comprehension. On the other hand, students who perceive themselves as poor at reading usually have not experienced successful reading. As a consequence, their disengagement from reading results in less reading activity, which clearly affects fluent reading ability.

In attempting to develop an initial framework with the goal of explaining what fluent reading involves, we have learned a great deal from the research referenced earlier regarding reading fluency development and what makes it possible. We have pointed to some of the research whose findings provide interesting avenues for viewing fluent reading and comprehension. We therefore attempted to suggest, with some support, that the ability to read fluently and with adequate comprehension requires more than reading rate and accuracy. Such ability is influenced by the metalinguistic knowledge and skills that readers bring to the process of reading, namely, phonological, morphological, syntactic, and discourse awareness; the metacomprehension processes, which emphasize meaning-making strategies, also influence fluent reading and the dispositional attributes having to do with the context in which readers function. These attributes can and should be assessed using fairly common assessment strategies. The information obtained can then be used to develop instructional strategies for addressing students' reading fluency and comprehension needs. In the following section, we present some of these assessment and instructional strategies.

ASSESSMENT AND INSTRUCTION OF READING FLUENCY

In this section, we discuss how to relate assessment and instruction to the conceptualization of fluency that we explained previously. The challenge is how to assess fluency in ways that help develop instructional implications that will advance fluent reading. Assessing fluency in based on the performance aspects of fluency, while instruction encompasses all three attributes. In the case of assessing fluency, decoding accuracy (the number of words read correctly) and rate (the number of words read in a given time) can easily be measured using quantitative methods. However, expression and phrasing are qualitative judgments, often based upon sub-jective evaluation using fluency scales depicting specific oral reading behaviors. Nonetheless, these means of evaluation can offer teachers' insights into instruction.

Rate and Accuracy

When measuring only rate and accuracy, we suggest using curriculum-based measurement (CBM) of oral reading fluency, which are based on the number of words read aloud correctly in 1 minute from passages ran-domly selected from a constant level of the curriculum, thus focusing on the performance attributes of accuracy and rate of reading (Deno, 1985). The student reads orally for 1 minute from a textbook currently used in the school curriculum. Reading aloud from curriculum materials demon-strates the "strongest relation with socially important, widely used crite-rion measures of reading" (Fuchs & Deno, 1992, p. 233). These assess-ment measures have been found to have adequate reliability and validity as measures of reading fluency (Deno, 1985; Fuchs & Deno, 1992; Shinn, 1989).

Other persuasive arguments exist for use of 1-minute timed readings. Reading researchers generally agree that "scores from the oral passage reading test appear to be a feasible and psychometrically useful method for assessing reading ability" (Fuchs, Fuchs, & Maxwell, 1988, p. 27). More-over, correlations between CBM measures of oral fluency and tests of reading comprehension are quite high (Fuchs & Deno, 1992). Finally, results of 1-minute timed readings also correlate highly with standardized tests of reading achievement (Fuchs et al., 2001; Stage & Jacobsen, 2001).

If reading rate and accuracy are a concern, a program of repeated reading is ideal (Samuels, 2002). In this technique, the teacher explains that rereading the text is like practicing a musical instrument or practic-ing a football play. The rereading helps improve reading fluency. In this procedure, a student reads aloud, while the teacher marks miscues and measures rate. Both reading rate and miscues are charted on a graph to illustrate growth for each reading. Between the oral readings with the teacher, the student practices reading the passage silently. This is often called "unassisted" repeated reading, because the teacher does not directly demonstrate fluent reading. Samuels suggests that the selection be reread orally no more than three or four times. In four readings, the benefits of the rereading are realized.

To evaluate the repeated reading technique, Dahl (1979) designed a study to evaluate three reading strategies. The study looked at training in the (1) use of context to predict the identity of unknown words, (2) repeated reading, and (3) isolated word recognition. Struggling second-grade readers were randomly assigned to treatment groups. Dahl reported that both the words in context and the repeated reading conditions produced significant gains on a measure of reading rate and on a cloze test. These two conditions together also produced significant gains; however, the repeated reading condition significantly reduced the number of miscues the students made. Dahl and Samuels (2002) led the way to further study of repeated reading variations (see Dowhower, 1994). These studies have indicated that repeated readings do improve reading rate and decrease miscues.

Expression and Phrasing

The Commission on Reading (Anderson, Hiebert, Scott, & Wilkinson, 1985) published *Becoming a Nation of Readers*, stating that current standardized tests should be supplemented with periodic observations of reading fluency. Since that time, various scales and assessment instruments have been devised to measure reading fluency. To this end, the NAEP added a measure of reading fluency to its fourth-grade assessment of reading in 1992. The NAEP assessment of reading used a four-tier fluency scale that combines the performance attributes of phrasing (based on syntax) and expression (based on features of prosody). The pupils read a passage orally that was recorded, and later the reading was rated based on a predetermined scale (see Table 5.1).

Using this rating scale, a teacher can decide whether students need to learn better expression or more appropriate phrasing. If students lack expression, Readers Theatre is a way to develop prosody. Readers Theatre is the reading of a play script with expression. The play lines are not memorized; rather, the oral reading should interpret the meaning through intonation, inflection, and pitch, so that an audience would understand the meaning of the play without action. The emphasis on expression helps the students become more fluent. When conducting Readers Theatre, teachers select an appropriate script by thinking about the reading level of

TABLE 5.1. NAEP Oral Reading Fluency Scale

Level 4

Reads primarily in larger, meaningful phrase groups. Although some regressions, repetitions, and deviations from text may be present, those do not appear to detract from the overall structure of the story. Preservation of the author's syntax is consistent. Some or most of the story is read with expressive interpretation.

Level 3

Reads primarily in three- or four-word phrase groups. Some smaller groupings may be present. However, the majority of phrasing seems appropriate and preserves the syntax of the author. Little or no expressive interpretation is present.

Level 2

Reads primarily in two-word phrases with some three- or four-word groupings. Some word-by-word reading may be present. Word groupings may seem awkward and unrelated to larger context of sentence or passage.

Level 1

Reads primarily word by word. Occasional two- or three-word phrases may occur, but these are infrequent and/or they do not preserve meaningful syntax.

Note. From National Center for Education Statistics, U.S. Department of Education, Washington, DC.

their students. Initially, the teacher discusses the selection by describing the characters and the story. Then students read the script silently, so that meaning precedes oral reading. At this time, students become aware of the meaning (comprehension), the words (morphological awareness), and the structure of the text (discourse awareness). The teacher carefully selects parts for students, so that each can demonstrate his or her strength with oral reading. In other words, struggling readers might initially need parts that are shorter, with fewer challenging words. In this way, they can participate in the reading, demonstrating their oral reading along with the more proficient peers. The script is practiced chorally several times to encourage more expression. Finally, the students stand or sit in front of the class and read the selection, conveying meaning through their intonation and inflection.

   If students parse sentences at awkward places, they often have a fuzzy notion about the meaning, which slows their reading fluency. Thus, phrasing, which is based on syntax awareness, can be addressed through chunking, a technique that teaches students to read in phrases of language, emphasizing how syntax and discourse affect reading (Walker,

2004). In this technique, the teacher selects a short passage that takes about 3 minutes to read. First, the teacher reads several sentences, modeling phrasing and marking slashes between meaningful phrases. The student then tries to imitate the teacher's model. The student reads the same sentences, while the teacher marks his/her phrasing with slashes to represent where the student pauses in the sentences. The teacher and student talk about the chunks of language they use.

Dispositions

Evaluating reader dispositions related to fluent reading has received little attention in the research literature. However, there are two ways to assess this in an indirect manner. One way, we propose, is to assess and encourage positive reader dispositions by evaluating and encouraging extensive reading. The more students read easy text, the more they will increase their fluent reading (Allington, 2001; Walker, 2003). The second way, we propose, is by evaluating reader self-perceptions and creating opportunities for students to evaluate their own successes. Increasing reader self-perceptions enhances positive dispositions toward reading, which augments the amount of reading students do, thus improving reading fluency.

As we have proposed, reading is influenced by the beliefs, attitudes, and values that students place on reading, thus affecting the amount of text they read on a daily basis. Through observations, teachers can evaluate how much reading children do in their classrooms. Inventories for outside of class reading have also been fairly good indicators of wide reading, which in turn, increases engagement and value of reading (Anderson et al., 1988). To encourage extensive reading in the classroom, teachers can create daily opportunities to read for enjoyment as part of their classroom routines and have a wide variety of books, magazines, etc. readily available. By giving book and magazine talks, teachers can demonstrate how they value reading in their personal lives and their enthusiasm about sharing their love of reading. This encourages reading inside and outside of class (Mazzoni & Gambrell, 2003).

Another indirect way to evaluate dispositions toward reading fluency is by using the Reader Self-Perception Scale (RSPS; Henk & Melinick, 1995), which was developed to use with intermediate-level students. A major component of reader self-perceptions involves self-efficacy. Self-efficacy involves beliefs we have that we can do something like read fluently and take tests. Focusing on these aspect of reading, the RSPS has four subscales, Progress (growth–self-comparison), Observational Comparison (comparing one's reading to others' speed is one comparison criterion), Social Feedback (how others respond to one's reading), and Physiological States (emotional reactions like stress, sweating, etc.). These aspects of reader self-perception or efficacy have a great deal to do with reader engagement (Wigfield & Guthrie, 1997). The scores from the RSPS indicate how readers feel about themselves as readers, thus influencing whether or not they engage in reading, as well as the amount of effort they expend when reading (Henk & Melinick, 1995). This instrument gives a good indication of positive dispositions toward reading, which increases the amount of reading, and, in turn, reading fluency.

Therefore, one way to increase positive dispositions toward reading fluency is by having students *evaluate their success* (Walker, 2003), an important aspect of reader self-perception. Paired repeated reading is an instructional technique in which students evaluate their own and their partner's success. Critical to paired repeated reading (Koskinen & Blum, 1986) is providing positive feedback to a partner on the performance aspects of fluency, as well as assessing one's own performance using a self-evaluation sheet.

Paired repeated reading is the joint reading of a text between two people. The teacher explains how to provide positive feedback for each other on the performance aspects of fluency. Initially, both students read silently to become familiar with the passage. The first student reads the passage three times. After the second and third readings, the partner comments on the improvement the student has shown in word recognition, expression, and phrasing. When both students have read their passages, the students assess their own performance using a self-evaluation sheet. These self-evaluations help students realize their progress and success in reading more fluently. In a study with intermediate readers, Koskinen and Blum (1984) had two instructional conditions: the paired repeated-reading condition and the study activities condition. They found significant results in favor of the paired repeated-reading group in fluency. This group also made fewer semantically inappropriate miscues. Thus, completing self-evaluation sheets and partner evaluation sheets along with paired repeated readings not only improves fluency but also improves students' self-perceptions as readers, thus increasing positive dispositions toward reading.

Focusing on Multiple Aspects

Combining research of rate, accuracy, expression, and phrasing, Zutell and Rasinski (1991) propose an even more detailed three-dimensional scale based on phrasing, smoothness, and pace, the Multidimensional Fluency Scale (see Appendix at the end of the book) with four levels for each of the three dimensions. Students read a passage of text orally as the instructor evaluates the reading based on the multiple dimensions of this scale. Once administration is completed, the teacher has access to the results from the distinct scales for phrasing, smoothness, and pace. First, phrasing is assessed. The teacher rates whether a student's reading is well-phrased and mostly in clauses/sentence units or whether reading is monotonic, with little sense of phrase boundaries. Also, the teacher notes smoothness of reading. As the child reads, the teacher considers whether reading is generally smooth or whether there are frequent extended pauses, "sound outs," and repetitions. Finally, the teacher rates the student's pace of reading. The teacher observes whether reading is consistently conversational or whether it is slow and laborious.

Individually, these ratings provide a tremendous amount of diagnostic data. However, the practitioner can also combine the scores for an overall examination of reading fluency. Zutell and Rasinski (1991) claim that teachers can use this measure and feel confident in its validity and reliability. Reliability has been demonstrated in preservice teachers, with coefficients as high as .99. Also, these researchers found moderately strong correlations between this measure and standardized reading test scores at the third- and fifth-grade levels.

An approach to repeated reading of text has been modified to attend to the multiple aspects of reading fluency. This procedure, responsive repeated reading (R3; Walker, 2005) has combined the procedures from repeated reading (Samuels, 1979) and retrospective miscue analysis (RMA; Goodman & Marek, 1996) to create a technique that addresses the complex nature of reading fluency. The technique uses Samuels's (1979) procedures of repeatedly reading a passage, counting miscues, and charting them. As recommended, only three readings are employed. In this procedure, after the first reading, the miscues are counted and placed on a graph. However, the procedures of RMA have been adapted for the next step. The student and the teacher have a conversation about the expectation or thinking behind the miscue (see Goodman & Marek, 1996, for questions to facilitate conversation). For all miscues, the student and teacher discuss why the student made the miscue, as well as whether the miscue affected understanding. Contrary to RMA, the teacher selects miscues that carry textual meaning and discusses them on the basis of the cuing system. The teacher prompts students to review their use of graphophonic knowledge, syntax knowledge, and semantic understanding. The teacher or tutor asks the reader questions such as "Does that miscue make sense in the sentence?" (syntactic cue), "Does it fit with overall meaning?" (semantic cue), and so on. These discussion prompts can be based on the competencies of morphological awareness, syntax awareness, and discourse awareness. Thus, the procedure helps students explain the thinking behind their miscues and alternatives for monitoring reading. Additionally, the teacher often models fluent reading, particularly using meaningful phrases within sentences containing multiple miscues. The student repeats the sentence, and the teacher and student discuss phrasing, smoothness, and pace, as well as accuracy, needed for fluent reading. This discussion includes the strategies the student is using and how to adapt those to predict readily and monitor oral reading by using the overall meaning (discourse awareness and comprehension strategies), the sentence (syntax awareness), and selected parts of words (morphological awareness).

The procedure begins with the student reading a short section of an on-level text aloud, while the teacher marks miscues. After the first reading, the teacher and student discuss key miscues and the thinking that might have precluded the miscue. Their conversations focus on the context of the sentence (syntax awareness) and the passage meaning (comprehension), as well as strategies for correcting miscues such as reading ahead and self-correcting. The overt modeling and discussion help students think about how to anticipate meaning in order to read text fluently. The graphing helps students recognize their success, but more importantly, the conversation the student and teacher have focuses on strategy deployment rather than failure. The growing improvement students see on the graph focuses on success. This increases students' motivation to continue to practice their reading, because their improvement was visually demonstrated and a conversation about growth and strategy use has ensued. Using concrete forms such as graphs and charts can help students evaluate their success and attribute that success to their own strategy use. This improves self-efficacy and self-perceptions as readers, and in turn improves dispositions toward reading, increasing engagement. Extensive engagement increases volume of reading and in turn leads to more fluent reading.

SUMMARY

In conclusion, we have described fluent reading as a multifaceted process that requires the careful orchestration of several interrelated skills and competencies. Each of the components of fluency is built upon other complex competencies, performances, and dispositions. We have proposed a tentative conceptualization of the process of fluent reading, with the goal of clarifying this complex activity and inviting discussion and debate about this important component of the reading process.

These facets involve *performance attributes* that include decoding accuracy, reading rate, expression, and appropriate phrasing. The acquisition of these performance aspects is interrelated with *competence attributes* having to do with morphological awareness, syntactic awareness, discourse awareness, and comprehension strategy awareness. Finally, the third facet of this framework includes *reader dispositions* toward reading, which include readers' attitudes, their perceptions of themselves as readers, and their reading habits. Using the performance attributes, we have suggested assessments that are currently available for evaluating various aspects of reading fluency and have recommended instructional practices that promote fluency development for all students, especially those who find reading difficult.

REFERENCES

Alexander, P. A., & Jetton, T. L. (2000). Learning from text: A multidimensional and developmental perspective. In M. Kamil, P. Mosenthal, P. D. Pearson, & R. Barr (Eds.), *Handbook of reading research* (Vol. III, pp. 285–310). Mahwah, NJ: Erlbaum.

Allington, R. L. (2001). *What really matters for struggling readers: designing research-based programs.* New York: Longman.

Anderson, R. C., Hiebert, E. H., Scott, J. A., & Wilkinson, I. A. G. (1985). *Becoming a Nation of Readers: The report of the Commission on Reading.* Washington, DC: National Institute of Education.

Anderson, R. C., Wilson, P., & Fielding, L. G. (1988). Growth in reading and how children spend their time outside of school. *Reading Research Quarterly, 23,* 285–303.

Baker, L., & Brown, A. L. (1984). Metacognitive skills and reading. In R. Barr, M. Kamil, P. Mosenthal, & P. Pearson (Eds.), *Handbook of reading research* (Vol. 2, pp. 353–394). White Plains, NY: Longman.

Biemiller, A. (1999). *Language reading and success.* Cambridge, MA: Brookline.

Dahl, P. R. (1979). An experimental program for teaching high speed word recognition and comprehension skills. In J. E. Button, T. Lovitt, & T. Rowland (Eds.), *Communications research in learning disabilities and mental retardation* (pp. 33–65). Baltimore: University Park Press.

Deno, S. L. (1985). Curriculum-based measurement: The emerging alternative. *Exceptional Children, 52*(3), 219–232.

Dowhower, S. (1994). Repeated reading revisited: Research into practice. *Reading and Writing Quarterly* 10, 343–358.

Dowhower, S. L. (1991). Speaking of prosody: Fluency's unattended bedfellow. *Theory Into Practice*, 30, 158–164.

Feldman, L. B. (1995). *Morphological aspects of language processing*. Hillsdale, NJ: Erlbaum.

Fuchs, L., & Deno, S. L. (1992). Effects of curriculum within Curriculum Based measurement. *Exceptional Children*, 58 (3), 232–242.

Fuchs, L., Fuchs, D., & Maxwell, L. (1988). The validity of informal reading comprehension measures. *Remedial and Special Education*, 9(2), 20–28.

Fuchs, L. S., Fuchs, D., Hosp, M. K., & Jenkins, J. R. (2001). Oral reading fluency as an indicator of reading competence: A theoretical, empirical, and historical analysis. *Scientific Studies of Reading*, 5(3), 239–257.

Goodman, Y., & Marek, A. (1996). Retrospective miscue analysis. In Y. Goodman & A. Marek (Eds.), *Retrospective miscue analysis: Revaluing readers and reading* (pp. 13–21). Katonah, NY: Richard C. Owen.

Gottardo, A., Stanovich, K. E., & Siegel, L. S. (1996). The relationship between phonological sensitivity, syntactic processing, and verbal working memory in the reading performance of third grade children. *Journal of Experimental Child Psychology*, 63, 563–582.

Henk, W. A., & Melnick, S. A. (1992). The initial development of a scale to measure "perception of self as reader." In C. Kinzer & D. Leu (Eds.), *Literacy research, theory, and practice: Views from many perspectives: 41st yearbook of the National Reading Conference* (pp. 111–117). Chicago: National Reading Conference.

Henk, W. A., & Melnick, S. A. (1995). The Reader Self-Perception Scale (RSPS): A new tool for measuring how children feel about themselves as readers. *Reading Teacher*, 48, 470–482.

Kamhi, A., Allen, M., & Catts, H. (2001). The role of the SLP in improving decoding skills. *Seminars in Speech and Language*, 22, 175–185.

Koskinen, P. S., & Blum, I. H. (1984). Repeated oral reading and the acquisition of fluency. In J. A. Niles & L. A. Harris (Eds.), *Changing perspectives on research in reading/language processing and instruction: 33rd yearbook of the National Reading Conference* (pp. 183–187). Rochester, NY: National Reading Conference.

Koskinen, P. S., & Blum, I. H. (1986). Paired repeated reading: A classroom strategy for developing fluent reading. *Reading Teacher*, 40, 70–75.

Krashen, S. (1993). *The power of reading: Insights from the research*. Englewood, CO: Libraries Unlimited.

Kuhn, M. R., & Stahl, S. A. (2003). Fluency: A review of developmental and remedial practices. *Journal of Educational Psychology*, 95(1), 3–21.

Leikin, M. (2002). Processing syntactic functions of words in normal and dyslexic readers. *Journal of Psycholinguistic Research*, 31(2), 145–163.

Mahony, D., Singson, M., & Mann, V. (2002). Reading ability and sensitivity to morphological relations. *Reading and Writing: An Interdisciplinary Journal, 12*, 191–218.

Mazzoni, S. A., & Gambrell, L. B. (2003). Principles of best practice: Finding the common ground. In L. M. Morrow, L. B. Gambrell, & M. Pressley (Eds.), *Best practices in literacy instruction* (2nd ed., pp. 9–22). New York: Guilford Press.

Menyuk, P. (1999). *Reading and linguistic development*. Cambridge, MA: Brookline Books.

Mokhtari, K., & Reichard, C. (2002). Assessing students' metacognitive awareness of reading strategies. *Journal of Educational Psychology, 94*(2), 249–259.

Mokhtari, K., & Thompson, B. (in press). The influence of syntactic awareness on fifth graders' reading fluency and comprehension. *Journal of Research in Reading*.

Nation, K., Clark, P., & Snowling, M. (2002). General cognitive ability in children with reading comprehension difficulties. *British Journal of Educational Psychology, 72*, 549–559.

Nation, K., & Snowling, M. (2000). Factors influencing syntactic awareness in normal readers and poor comprehenders. *Applied Psycholinguistics, 21*, 229–241.

Paris, S. G., Lipson, M. Y., & Wixon, K. K. (1994). Becoming a strategic reader. In R. B. Ruddell, M. R. Ruddell, & H. Singer (Eds.), *Theoretical models and processes of reading* (4th ed., pp. 788–811). Newark, DE: International Reading Association.

Pinnell, G. S., Pikulski, J. J., Wixon, K. K., Campbell, J. R., Gough, P. B., & Beatty, A. S. (1995). *Listening to children read aloud* (Report No. 23-FR-04). Prepared by the Educational Testing Service under contract with the National Center for Education Statistics, Washington, DC.

Pressley, M. (2002). *Reading instruction that works: The case for balanced teaching* (2nd ed.). New York: Guilford Press.

Rasinski, T. (2000). Speed does matter in reading. *Reading Teacher, 52*, 146–151.

Rasinski, T. V., & Zutell, J. B. (1990). Making a place for fluency instruction in the regular reading curriculum. *Reading Research and Instruction, 29*(2), 85–91.

Samuels, S. J. (1979). The method of repeated readings. *Reading Teacher, 32*, 403–408.

Samuels, S. J. (2002). Reading fluency: Its development and assessment. In A. Farstrup & S. Samuels (Eds.), *What research has to say about reading instruction* (2nd ed., pp. 166–183). Newark, DE: International Reading Association.

Samuels, S. J. (2004). Toward a theory of automatic information processing in reading, revisited. In R. Ruddell & N. Unrau (Eds.), *Theoretical models and processes of reading* (5th ed., pp. 1127–1148). Newark, DE: International Reading Association.

Samuels, S. J., & Flor, R. (1997). The importance of automaticity for developing expertise in reading. *Reading and Writing Quarterly, 13*(2), 107–122.

Shinn, M. R. (Ed.). (1989). *Curriculum-based measurement: Assessing special children.* New York: Guilford Press.

Snow, C. E., Burns, M. S., & Griffin, P. (1998). *Preventing reading difficulties in young children.* Washington, DC: National Academy Press.

Stage, S. A., & Jacobsen, M. D. (2001). Predicting student success on a state-mandated performance-based assessment using oral reading fluency. *School Psychology Review, 30*(3), 407–420.

Tunmer, W. E., & Bowey, J. (1984). Metalinguistic awareness and reading acquisition. In W. E. Tunmer, C. Pratt, & M. L. Herriman (Eds.), *Metalinguistic awareness in children: Theory, research, and implications* (pp. 144–168). Berlin: Springer-Verlag.

Walker, B. J. (2003). The cultivation of student self-efficacy in reading and writing. *Reading and Writing Quarterly, 19*, 173–187.

Walker, B. J. (2004). *Diagnostic teaching of reading: Techniques for instruction and assessment* (5th ed.) Upper Saddle River, NJ: Merrill/Prentice-Hall.

Walker, B. J. (2005). *Responsive repeated reading (R3).* Unpublished manuscript, Oklahoma State University Reading and Math Center, Tulsa.

Wigfield, A., & Guthrie, J. (1997). Relations of children's motivation for reading to the amount and breadth of their reading. *Journal of Educational Psychology, 89*, 420–432.

Zutell, J., & Rasinski, T. V. (1991). Training teachers to attend to their students' oral reading fluency. *Theory Into Practice, 30*(3), 211–217.

CHAPTER 6

Hijacking Fluency and Instructionally Informative Assessments

DANIELLE V. MATHSON
RICHARD L. ALLINGTON
KATHRYN L. SOLIC

At some point over the past decade or so, the definition of "fluency" has changed to become widely viewed as a measure of rate and accuracy (Dowhower, 1991; Nathan & Stanovich, 1991; Rasinski & Hoffman, 2003). Overlooking the role of prosodic features in oral reading fluency has led to an onslaught of standardized assessments of fluency such as Diagnostic Indicators of Basic Early Literacy Skills (DIBELS; Good, Wallin, Simmons, Kame'enui, & Kaminski, 2002) or Test of Word Reading Efficiency (TOWRE; Torgesen, Wagner, & Rashotte, 1997). These assessments are being used in classrooms across the country to determine the reading rates of students, but they are ignoring phrasing and intonation, ignoring fluency. Thus, "reading automaticity" may be a better term to describe what these standardized assessments are actually measuring. Nathan and Stanovich (1991) suggest that this shift is a result of the work of cognitive psychologists who study reading. Matching this assertion with the historical interpretation of reading research presented by Alexander and Fox (2004), who propose that 1976–1985 encompassed the "Era of Information Processing," perhaps we can begin to determine a precise time period for the exchange of definitions, as well as the influx of standardized assessments. This would also account for the role played by the LaBerge and Samuels (1974) model of automatic information processing in reading, which suggests that we have a limited capacity for storing information. When we read, the goal is to use little attention for decoding words—to be automatic—so attention may be used for comprehension of text.

Despite efforts to popularize curriculum-based measurement (Deno, 1985), which are designed to use oral reading of passages from classroom texts to provide teachers with fluency data to monitor growth in reading, the newer, decontextualized standardized assessments seem more commonly used today even though they provide more generalized data. What does this mean for students in today's classrooms? If assessment drives instruction, and results of decontextualized assessments of fluency are used to determine achievement levels, then is it fair to assume that instruction is also becoming more generalized and less in tune with what individual students need?

In this chapter we discuss several key points relating to the re/conceptualization of fluency. Though we ask the following questions, they are designed to provoke thought and further research into the concept of fluency rather than to provide definitive answers:

- What does a more comprehensive definition of fluency bring to the table?
- Do standardized measures of reading fluency provide teachers with enough information to make sound instructional decisions?
- Is assessing fluency as a curriculum-based measurement important?
- What is the role of prosody in reading fluency?
- Volume or frequency? Selecting interventions that work in training readers to be fluent.

WHAT DOES A MORE COMPREHENSIVE DEFINITION OF FLUENCY BRING TO THE TABLE?

The most widely used definition of fluency is that represented by the automatic information processing in reading presented by LaBerge and Samuels (1974). While Samuels (1987, 1994) considers prosody a component of automaticity, prosodic features are rarely acknowledged in work citing the LaBerge–Samuels model. Automaticity is an important feature of skilled reading; however, we agree with Kuhn and Stahl (2003) that fluency includes accuracy, automaticity, and prosodic features as a separate element. Each of these factors works in conjunction with the others. Without one, a reader does not display fluency. Because fluency is not meant to be the end goal in reading (Allington, 1983), it must be recognized as the bridge between decoding and comprehension. However, many schools are treating fluency as a race to read the most words in the shortest amount of time (Rasinski, 2004). In order to create meaningful fluency instruction, this view of fluency as automaticity alone must become more comprehensive: It must include accuracy and prosody as well. In other words, simply using one component of fluency—or even two—to determine what makes a reader "good" detracts from fluency and curricular decision making as a whole.

For example, accuracy is one component of reading fluency. Many readers are able to decode accurately, but the process they use is extremely slow and demands capacity that leads to the breakdown of comprehension (Nathan & Stanovich, 1991; Samuels, 1979). However, a reader who is both accurate and automatic increases the information-processing capacity available while reading and allows more attentional capacity to be allocated to comprehension. Furthermore, a reader capable of incorporating prosodic features in an oral reading of text indicates that he or she comprehends the meaning of the text through correct placement of phrasing, pitch, stress, and tone.

Importantly, by providing a definition of fluency that includes these three factors, teachers may rethink their instructional methods for increasing fluency. Currently, in some schools, teachers concerned about standardized fluency assessment are having their students read timed word lists or decontextualized passages. After practicing the text, students are then asked to reread orally. Typically, teachers time the student and count the errors made during the reading of the text. Zutell and Rasinski (1991) suggest that these practices develop students into readers who are less aware of the meaning of text, because their sole concern becomes increasing the rate at which they read. Is this the goal of their teacher? We think not. However, a misunderstanding of the definition of fluency, or a lack of knowledge regarding all components related to it, may lead teachers to believe that by increasing automaticity, they are working to enhance the comprehension capabilities of their students. Moreover, by embracing a more comprehensive definition of fluency, researchers may focus on

methods for training and encouraging teachers to attend to prosodic factors in their students' oral reading fluency.

DO STANDARDIZED MEASURES PROVIDE TEACHERS WITH ENOUGH INFORMATION TO MAKE SOUND INSTRUCTIONAL DECISIONS?

Fuchs, Fuchs, and Deno (1982) consider standardized assessments reliable
and robust when comparing individual student performance to that of a
group of students. However, they suggest that standardized assessments are
not valid measures for designing instruction or placing students in special
programs. This is due to the limited content validity of standardized
assessments. Caldwell (2002) contends that it is dangerous to compare
the reading rates of different students due to the variability inherent in
rate measures. Variability can occur for many reasons, including interest,
familiarity with a passage or subject, text structure, or the purpose of the
reader (Caldwell, 2002). Instead, Caldwell suggests that teachers assess
student reading fluency through informal interactions and by using their
own judgment to gain insight into development (Flurkey, 1998). Similarly, Rasinski (1999) proposed that there is not a "right" reading rate for
students. Instead, he developed prediction equations that provided a
method for estimating target reading rates at varying levels of development. This allows teachers to gauge growth of their students' reading rate
over time, using contextualized readings. These suggestions, however, are
not congruent with the nature of standardized assessments of fluency.
   DIBELS, for example, is standardized to identify students who are
reading below grade level and are considered at risk (Hintze, Ryan, &
Stoner, 2003). Hintze and colleagues cite DIBELS as an effective measurement for determining individual progress, as well as "grade level feedback toward validated instructional objectives" (p. 543). The four subtests
of DIBELS include Letter-Naming Fluency, Initial Sound Fluency, Phonemic Segmentation Fluency, and Passage Reading. Results from these
subtests would suggest that struggling readers are lacking skills in one or
more of the areas. Thus, instruction is linked to the teaching of isolated
skills, including phonemic awareness and word recognition—something
Allington (1983) cautioned against. Other researchers also warn of such
practices, arguing there is no evidence suggesting that this type of instruction improves fluency or comprehension (Ivey & Baker, 2004;
Schwanenflugel, Hamilton, Melanie, Wisenbaker, & Stahl, 2004). We

believe the evidence indicates that young children become better readers by reading, and that early literacy skills are best taught in the context of reading connected text (Dahl & Freppon,1995; Sacks & Mergendoller, 1997). A decontextualized instructional focus on exact word recognition may lead students further from literacy, because their motivation becomes correct word calling rather than making sense of what they read (Allington, 1983; Zutell & Rasinski, 1991). Despite the claims that DIBELS is a reliable measure of reading fluency, our data tell a different story.

Our DIBELS Story

In Florida, and many other states, DIBELS is mandated assessment in schools receiving funding under the federal Reading First program. We present DIBELS data from two third-grade classrooms in a Florida Reading First school. The data were from the third DIBELS assessment in the spring of the year. Our purpose for compiling the data was to determine how well the readability of the passages correlated with students' performance. Elliott and Tollefson (2001) argue that results from DIBELS assessments are both reliable and valid, and should be used more frequently by teachers to determine appropriate skills to teach individual students. Our results indicate something quite different.

The question we asked was how well the students' (n = 39) DIBELS scores correlated across the three passages they read. These standardized passages were presented by the publisher as equivalent in difficulty (using readability analyses). We found that individual student scores varied substantially from passage to passage. Several sets of student scores are presented below (the scores represent words correct per minute [wcpm], the number of words in each passage the child read correctly in the standard 1-minute period).

	Passage			Variability in wcpm
	1	2	3	
S4	118	81	71	71
S13	66	38	46	28
S14	92	60	69	32
S25	90	73	54	36
S30	94	79	45	49
S31	165	128	109	56
S32	97	64	69	33
S34	80	66	47	33

| S35 | 74 | 44 | 35 | 39 |
| S38 | 81 | 52 | 58 | 29 |

Remember that these passages are supposedly of equivalent difficulty. Nonetheless, as shown here, lots of variability in reading automaticity is evident in these data from 25% of the participants.

There were students who exhibited little variability, but these children were typically the slowest readers, a result also reported by Flurkey (1998) in his analysis of reading rates of good and poor readers. For example:

S8	48	37	41	11
S9	30	28	25	5
S17	26	13	21	13
S27	34	31	25	9
S33	36	32	36	4

These children seem not to have developed automaticity of word recognition, at least when reading these passages that were difficult for them. But the DIBELS passages were not the texts these children were reading every day, so it remains unclear where their teachers might begin with an instructional plan. Generalized findings of nonautomatic and, perhaps, inaccurate reading of standard passages may reliably indicate that these children are struggling with reading acquisition, but the performances offer little useful information that a teacher might use in planning next week's lessons.

We also calculated the correlation between passage difficulty and DIBELS performance as another way to examine the consistency of reading rate and accuracy from passage to passage. Overall, the student performances on DIBELS fell into one of three ranges. For the first group ($n = 11$) of students, the correlation of performances across the three passages was below .25. For the second group ($n = 16$), the correlation was between .26 and .50. The third group ($n = 12$) had correlation coefficients above .50. All this indicates that Caldwell's (2002) concern about variability needs serious consideration. Passages obviously vary, even passages the test publisher suggests are of equivalent difficulty.

So how might such data be useful for instructional planning? This is difficult to say. The consistently slow readers are obviously in big trouble, but it seems likely that this would be obvious without DIBELS testing, or any other sort of standardized testing. But the most useful information one might gather from children reading aloud would be unavailable from a standardized test. What we might learn from a curriculum-based measurement, something like a running record (Johnston, 2000) of oral reading of classroom texts, is whether the child is reading with sufficient accuracy that the text is an appropriate level of difficulty for that child. We could also use a fluency rubric (Rasinski, 2004; Zutell & Rasinski, 1991) to evaluate whether the child can read the classroom text with prosody, which would suggest both automaticity and the roots of understanding. None of this is available from the standardized tests. But it is standardized tests of automaticity that are now widely used.

WHAT IS THE ROLE OF PROSODY IN READING FLUENCY?

Researchers agree that fluent readers, following a specific order, demonstrate prosodic features (Dowhower, 1991; Schreiber, 1991; Schwanenflugel et al., 2004). While the three components of fluency—accuracy, automaticity, and prosody—are equally important, readers first exhibit accurate reading, then reading with automaticity, and finally use of prosodic features. The question of prosody as it is related to comprehension is that of the chicken and the egg. There is limited research suggesting that comprehension is obtained once a reader is able to utilize appropriate suprasegmental cues. However, Schwanenflugel and colleagues (2004) suggest that prosody is a result of reading with comprehension. Does prosody then become the end goal in reading? Is it important for readers to use such intonation, pitch, and stress in order to be considered proficient readers?

Furthermore, in the information-processing model, attention, or pattern recognition, involves the question of how we recognize environmental stimuli as exemplars of concepts already in memory (Leahey & Harris, 2001). In order for information to move from the sensory memory to the working memory, pattern recognition must be activated. One example of pattern recognition is speech perception—more specifically, phonemes and suprasegmental cues. Comprehension, however, occurs further along in the information-processing model, when information is encoded from the working memory to long-term memory. According to the information-processing model, then, suprasegmental cues would be necessary prior to the comprehension of text.

Obviously, more research must be conducted to determine the precise role prosody plays in reading fluency. Our assertion, however, is that prosody's role—whether the chicken or the egg—is a necessary component to oral reading fluency, and must be a goal of reading instruction and a feature of fluency assessment.

There are problems with including prosody in classroom assessments of fluency. The first is the type of measurements used. Rubrics have been devised that allow teachers to rate students on prosodic features (Caldwell, 2002; Pinnell et al., 1995; Rasinski, 2004; Zutell & Rasinski, 1991). However, research in using rubrics in assessing reading fluency has been limited at best (Dowhower, 1991; Schreiber, 1991; Schwanenflugel, 2004). There is evidence that teachers can use rubrics to provide reliable information about reading and writing development (Koretz, Stecher, Klein, & McCaffrey, 1994). However, we feel that lack of training in fluency assessment and instruction, as well as the focus on currently popular standardized assessments, limits the use of such rubrics in today's classrooms.

Educators, however, must recognize that prosody has a role in reading fluency. Caldwell (2002) suggests that teachers utilize a fluency rubric during classroom silent reading time to measure student reading fluency. This is a time when teachers can sit next to individual students and have them read aloud quietly from a text the students selected. Often the books being read during this period are the most appropriate for fluency assessment. This is due to the fact that during silent reading, students generally choose books at their independent level, which allows for a more accurate assessment of all components of fluency—including prosody. We can induce word-by-word reading in almost any subject by providing them with difficult text. It is, then, critical that fluency data be collected from texts that students can read accurately. In other words, we should not be surprised if a first grader fails to exhibit fluency if given a junior novel, such as a Harry Potter book (Rowling, 1998). Likewise, a struggling fifth-grade reader might also be unable to read a junior novel with fluency, but might demonstrate fluency when reading an early chapter book, such as the Junie B. Jones series (Park, 1992).

It is when a student exhibits accurate but dysfluent reading in independent-level texts that it is time to provide appropriate instruction. Schreiber (1991) maintains that instruction in fluency is often ignored, because it is assumed that once students are able to decode automatically, they will recognize the syntactic cues and demonstrate prosodic features while reading orally. In making such an assumption, teachers overlook one of the three components of fluency and, we contend, leave out a key factor of reading instruction. However, this may be rectified through the use of teacher modeling of fluent reading, paired reading by students (Caldwell, 2002), and the use of books on tape.

IS ASSESSING FLUENCY AS A CURRICULUM-BASED MEASUREMENT IMPORTANT?

Although Elliott and Tollefson (2001) suggest, "the DIBELS measure represents many of the best features of alternative assessments" (p. 46), we believe measuring fluency in context leads to a more accurate oral reading fluency level. In fact, Fuchs, Fuchs, and Compton (2004) caution practitioners against the use of measures of nonsense word fluency—expressly DIBELS—in favor of the curriculum-based measurement word identification fluency measure. Words in the context of stories or informational texts are typically read more accurately and at a faster rate than the same words presented in lists. Passage reading, then, provides a more accurate rendering of an individual student's oral reading fluency (Jenkins, Fuchs, van den Broek, Espin, & Deno, 2003).

Deno (1985) defines a "curriculum-based measurement" as a repeated measure of performance being drawn from one curriculum. It is both valid and reliable (Deno, 1992; Fuchs et al., 2004), and provides information that allows teachers to gauge reading fluency growth over time. Because the readings are drawn from classroom texts, they tend to be of comparable difficulty, and repeated administrations of the curriculum-based measurement depict students' short- and long-term growth (Markell & Deno, 1997). Unlike standardized assessments, curriculum-based measurements are successful because they provide classroom-based results related to an individual student. Teachers can use curriculum-based measurement fluency data to make judgments about placement in appropriate texts, as well as fluency development.

It is important to note that while school psychologists or trained measurement specialists typically administer standardized assessments (Hintze et al., 2003), classroom teachers are better served when they administer curriculum-based measurements, which afford teachers the opportunity to be involved in the process and allow for insight into individual students that is not provided by percentile rankings or grade equivalency scores. Teacher training in the proper use of curriculum-based measurement is vital, because assessments that are conducted correctly provide teachers with valuable information for making curricular decisions (Fuchs, Deno, & Mirkin, 1984). The goal for the use of curriculum-based measurements is for teachers to develop a database for each student to determine how effective the individual instructional plan is for that student (Deno, 1992).

VOLUME OR FREQUENCY?

In order to become more fluent readers, students must have ample time to practice reading, both in and out of school (Allington, 1977, 1983). If we want our struggling readers to become fluent, we must provide them with text that they can read accurately (Allington, 2002). When the texts students read from allow them to read with accuracy and automaticity, they are provided opportunities to practice using prosodic features. What interventions are successful for increasing oral reading fluency?

Perhaps the most widely known method for developing reading fluency is that of repeated readings (Allington, 1983; Kuhn & Stahl, 2003; Samuels, 1979). Samuels (1979, 1987, 1994) describes "repeated readings" as a process in which students read and reread a passage until they can do so with accuracy and fluency. Kuhn and Stahl (2003) reviewed 100+ studies of fluency training of various sorts. Using a vote-counting method, the authors found that fluency training is typically effective, although it is unclear whether this is a result of specific instructional features or simply greater volume of reading. They also found that assisted approaches seem to have an advantage over unassisted approaches, and repetitive approaches do not seem to have a clear advantage over nonrepetitive approaches. Finally, they argue that effective fluency instruction moves beyond a focus on improving automatic word recognition to include a focus on rhythm and expression, or prosodic features of language.

The National Reading Panel (2000) found that repeated reading worked better for improving word-reading accuracy on the target passages than for improving fluency. Rashotte and Torgesen (1985) compared repeated reading with simply allowing students to read independently for a comparable period of time. There were no differences in outcomes between the repeated and extended reading interventions, with both producing improved fluency. Unfortunately, few studies have contrasted fluency interventions with extended independent reading interventions.

This led the National Reading Panel to recommend that future instructional studies compare instructional interventions and extended reading activity, and that the evidence require that instructional interventions work better than just providing more reading opportunity.

SUMMARY

Current standardized assessments and instructional programs seem to focus more on reading automaticity than on reading fluency. We believe there must be a shift back to a focus on reading fluency if we expect to impact positively students' reading abilities. Definitions of oral reading fluency must include three components—accuracy, automaticity, and prosody. Without focus on and instruction of each of these elements, students will simply be word callers, without the capability to transfer to reading comprehension.

With the increased popularity of standardized tests of reading automaticity, we worry that instruction for individual students is becoming more generalized. As evidenced in "Our DIBELS Story," administrators and teachers should not rely on claims made by publishers regarding the reliability and validity of data from standardized measures of reading automaticity. With an abundance of standardized assessments set to measure isolated aspects of literacy, our fear is that instruction and assessment are becoming too compartmentalized.

Placing each facet of literacy into a separate box, teachers and students are inundated with multiple programs that "are proven to teach" each individual skill. This is a dangerous aspect of standardized testing and standardized programmatic decision making. Why would students see reading as one connected piece, when instruction separates all the elements of reading?

We must arm our teachers with expert training on the components of reading fluency, as well as on how those components are linked to other elements of reading, such as comprehension. With this training, teachers will be able to make informed decisions regarding instruction and will have the capability of assessing students using their own judgment rather than that of a test publisher.

This restored confidence will allow teachers to utilize assessments such as curriculum-based measurement (Deno, 1985), and rubrics designed to measure all components of reading fluency (Caldwell, 2002; Rasinski, 2004; Zutell & Rasinski, 1991). Through the use of contextualized measurements, teachers will also ensure that students are reading a high volume of materials rather than focusing on word lists and isolated word skills.

While standardized assessments are useful in comparing a student to a group of his or her peers (Markell & Deno, 1997), such tests do not offer teachers sufficiently reliable and valid information to provide meaningful instruction to students. The lack of training available to teachers to understand what the results of such tests represent is another issue relating to standardized assessments, but we save that discussion for another time.

REFERENCES

Alexander, P., & Fox, E. (2004). A historical perspective on reading research and practice. In R. Ruddell & N. Unrau (Eds.), *Theoretical models and processes of reading* (5th ed., pp. 33–68). Newark, DE: International Reading Association.

Allington, R. L. (1977). If they don't read much, how they ever gonna get good? *Journal of Reading, 21*, 57–61.

Allington, R. L. (1983). Fluency: The neglected reading goal. *Reading Teacher, 36*(6), 556–561

Allington, R. L. (2002). You can't learn much from books you can't read. *Educational Leadership, 60*(3), 16–19.

Caldwell, J. S. (2002). *Reading assessment: A primer for teachers and tutors.* New York: Guilford Press.

Dahl, K. L., & Freppon, P. A. (1995). A comparison of inner-city children's interpretations of reading and writing instruction in skills-based and whole language classrooms. *Reading Research Quarterly, 30*, 50–74.

Deno, S. (1985). Curriculum-based measurement: The emerging alternative. *Exceptional Children, 52*, 219–232

Deno, S. (1992). The nature and development of curriculum-based measurement. *Preventing School Failure, 36*(2), 5–11.

Dowhower, S. (1991). Speaking of prosody: Fluency's unattended bedfellow. *Theory Into Practice, 30*(3), 165–175.

Elliott, J., & Tollefson, N. (2001). A reliability and validity study of the dynamic indicators of basic early literacy skills—modified. *School Psychology Review, 30*(1), 33–50.

Flurkey, A. D. (1998). *Reading as flow: A linguistic alternative to fluency.* Research monograph, Hofstra University, Hempstead, NY.

Fuchs, L., Deno, S., & Mirkin, P. (1984). The effects of frequent curriculum-based measurement and evaluation on pedagogy, student achievment, and student awareness of learning. *American Educational Research Journal, 21*(2), 449–460.

Fuchs, L., Fuchs, D., & Compton, D. (2004). Monitoring early reading development in first grade: Word identification fluency versus nonsense word fluency. *Exceptional Children, 71*(1), 7–21.

Fuchs, L., Fuchs, D., & Deno, S. (1982). Reliability and validity of curriculum-based informal reading inventories. *Reading Research Quarterly, 18*(1), 6–26.

Good, R. H., Wallin, J. U., Simmons, D. C., Kame'enui, E. J., & Kaminski, R. A. (2002). *System-wide percentile ranks for DIBELS benchmark assessment* (Technical Report 9). Eugene: University of Oregon.

Hintze, J., Ryan, A., & Stoner, G. (2003). Concurrent validity and diagnostic accuracy of the dynamic indicators of basic early literacy skills and the comprehensive test of phonological processing. *School Psychology Review, 32*(4), 541–556.

Ivey, G., & Baker, M. (2004). Phonics instruction for older students?: Just say no. *Educational Leadership, 61*(6), 35–39.

Jenkins, J., Fuchs, L., van den Broek, P., Espin, C., & Deno, S. (2003). Accuracy and fluency in list and context reading of skilled and RD groups: Absolute and relative performance levels. *Learning Disabilities Research and Practice, 18*(4), 237–245.

Johnston, P. (2000). *Running records.* York, ME: Stenhouse.

Koretz, D., Stecher, B., Klein, S., & McCaffrey, D. (1994). The Vermont Portfolio Assessment program: Findings and implications. *Educational Measurement, 13*(3), 5–16.

Kuhn, M., & Stahl, S. (2003). Fluency: A review of developmental and remedial practices. In R. Ruddell & N. Unrau (Eds.), *Theoretical models and processes of reading* (5th ed., pp. 412–453). Newark, DE: International Reading Association.

LaBerge, D., & Samuels, S. J. (1974). Toward a theory of automatic processing in reading. *Cognitive Psychology, 6,* 293–323.

Leahey, T., & Harris, R. (2001). *Learning and cognition.* Upper Saddle River, NJ: Prentice-Hall.

Markell, M., & Deno, S. (1997). Effects of increasing oral reading: Generalization across reading tasks. *Journal of Special Education, 31*(2), 233–250.

Nathan, R., & Stanovich, K. (1991). The causes and consequences of differences in reading fluency. *Theory Into Practice, 30*(3), 177–184.

National Reading Panel. (2000). *Teaching children to read: An evidence-based assessment of the scientific research literature on reading and its implications for reading instruction.* Washington, DC: National Institute of Child Health and Human Development.

Park, B. (1992). *Junie B. Jones and the stupid smelly bus.* New York: Scholastic.

Pinnell, G. S., Pikulski, J., Wixon, K. K., Campbell, J. R., Gough, P. B., & Beatty,

A. S. (1995). *Listening to children read aloud* (Research Report No. ED 378550). Washington, DC: National Center for Educational Statistics.

Rashotte, C., & Torgesen, J. (1985). Repeated reading fluency in learning disabled children. *Reading Research Quarterly, 20,* 180–189.

Rasinski, T. (1999). Exploring a method for estimating independent, instructional, and frustration reading rates. *Journal of Reading Psychology, 20,* 61–99.

Rasinski, T. (2004). Creating fluent readers. *Educational Leadership, 61*(6), 46–51.

Rasinski, T., & Hoffman, J. (2003). Oral reading in the school literacy curriculum. *Reading Research Quarterly, 38*(4), 510–522.

Rowling, J. K. (1998). *Harry Potter and the sorcerer's stone.* New York: Arthur Levine.

Sacks, C. H., & Mergendoller, J. R. (1997). The relationship between teachers' theoretical orientation toward reading and students outcomes in kindergarten children with different initial reading abilities. *American Education Research Journal, 34*(4), 721–740.

Samuels, S. J. (1979). The method of repeated reading. *Reading Teacher, 32,* 403–408.

Samuels, S. J. (1987). Information processing abilities and reading. *Journal of Learning Disabilities, 20,* 18–22.

Samuels, S. J. (1994). Toward a theory of automatic information processing in reading, revised. In R. Ruddell & N. Unrau (Eds.), *Theoretical models and processes of reading* (pp. 1127–1148). Newark, DE: International Reading Association.

Schreiber, P. (1991). Understanding prosody's role in reading acquisition. *Theory Into Practice, 30*(3), 158–164.

Schwanenflugel, P., Hamilton, A., Melanie, K., Wisenbaker, J., & Stahl, S. (2004). Becoming a fluent reader: Reading skill and prosodic features in the oral reading of young readers. *Journal of Educational Psychology, 96*(1), 119–129.

Torgesen, J., Wagner, R., & Rashotte, C. (1997). *Test of Word Reading Efficiency (TOWRE).* Austin, TX: Pro-Ed.

Zutell, J., & Rasinski, T. (1991). Training teachers to attend to their students' oral reading fluency. *Theory Into Practice, 30*(3), 211–217.

PART II

Best Programs, Best Practices

CHAPTER 7

The Fluency Assessment System©

Improving Oral Reading Fluency with Technology

SUSAN JOHNSTON

At the beginning of the year I didn't really like reading, but when I started reading into the computer I started to like reading. If you can read you have choices to do whatever you want.

—JEREMY, GRADE 5

"**W***hat if?*" That question was posed at Educational Service Unit #3 in Omaha, Nebraska, when faced with the need to support 19 school districts as they faced increasing demands for accountability. In 1998, the Nebraska State Standards became mandatory, but districts were given autonomy with the way in which those standards would be assessed. Our Educational Service Unit had been scoring student writing samples for 13 years, but reading was another matter. Most schools were using norm-referenced tests to assess comprehension or some other form of a "text and question–answer" combination. At best, the documentation of reading ability was a mere echo of what was really happening inside the students' heads. One district, however, was doing something different: Gretna Public Schools. The district had been working on a way to assess oral reading samples, based on the research that links oral reading fluency and comprehension. Timothy Rasinski's work out of Kent State underscored their rationale. This idea seemed worth merit, so more information was gathered. The question became: *What if* we could do what Gretna was doing, on a larger scale? *What if* we were to make a service available to our school districts in much the same way that we have offered our writing service? Furthermore, *what if* students were to record themselves reading aloud into a computer? *What if* that computer sample could provide immediate feedback to the student on specific indicators, so that he or she could practice again within minutes of the first sample? *What if* we could archive those samples and play them for the student, teacher, and parents to show progress over time? Furthermore, *what if* each student could send an electronic sample to a central technology server that could be accessed by a group of trained teachers who could rate the samples using a valid and reliable rubric? Finally, *what if* those scores were easily translated the next day in the form of reports for the entire district, for each building and for each student, *and*, *what if* the entire system were Web-based, so it could be done anywhere, anytime and be used by thousands of students?

Over the next 4 years those "what ifs" became reality. To date, trained raters via a Web-based system have scored more than 20,000 oral reading samples. More importantly, impressive gains are being made in comprehension for students involved in the project, and students and teachers are reporting enthusiastic results. Gains in confidence, interest, motivation, and general learning are among the anecdotal reports from students, teachers, parents, and principals.

Timothy Rasinski, who led the early development stages, comments on the project:

> "Assessing fluency is a bit problematic for many teachers and schools. Generally we ask kids to read and we tape record their readings to keep a record of them. Just the housekeeping with tape recordings is difficult; the technology involved in this particular project where the readings are archived electronically and retrieved easily, not only by teachers, but students themselves can go back and review their own readings and develop their own sense of what fluent meaningful reading is like; . . . that is a particularly positive aspect of this project."

Just as it is not possible to capture every moment of one's life in a photograph album, it is also unlikely that all of the most important classroom moments will be captured in an assessment. Classroom teachers express this sentiment in many ways: "There isn't time to do everything!" "If the standards are the curriculum, what about all of the diversity in my classroom . . . personalities, abilities, interests; they can't all look alike at the end of the year!"

At Educational Service Unit #3 (ESU #3), we believe those sentiments are valid; however, we would add the belief that standards and individual learning are not mutually exclusive. Each child can find his or her own path given enough support and opportunity. Students who are in standards-based classrooms have an opportunity to reach higher, to set goals, all the while becoming more competent and self-sufficient. Rick Stiggins, founder of the Assessment Training Institute in Portland, Oregon, and author of numerous books and articles on quality assessment, says it best:

> "We can use assessment to enhance or destroy a student's motivation and confidence. It depends on how we use it and whether or not we let students in on the process."

The central belief, that quality assessment puts students in the driver's seat while pushing them toward important goals, was the ground from which the Fluency Assessment System© grew. For 2 years, discussions had been developing at ESU #3 about how best to help our member school districts with the assessment and the teaching of reading. One of our local districts, Gretna Public Schools, had experienced some early success with assessing oral reading using electronic portfolios. Their initial efforts were intriguing and led the consultants at ESU #3 to read more about oral reading fluency and its overall relationship to comprehension (Rasinski, 1990, 2003; Rasinski & Hoffman, 2003; Rasinski & Opitz, 1998; Rasinski, Padak, Linek, & Sturtevant, 1994). This became the catalyst that brought a simmering idea to a full boil. The project took 4 years to develop. It began with a conversation in the fall of 1999.

THE BEGINNING

In Nebraska, the hot days of summer suddenly give way to cool, crisp air. It was on one of those days that I walked into Doug Zauha's office with a question. Doug, a technology and curriculum expert, has a natural understanding of how learning and technology fit together. That's one of the reasons I believed he would be enticed by the notion I was about to describe.

"Morning, Doug."

"Morning." Doug doesn't look up from his task, but I can tell he is listening.

"You know how we do the writing assessment here twice a year? Students write to a prompt, send their papers here, and we train raters to do the scoring?" He nods. His face tells me that he is afraid to ask where this is going.

"Do you think it would be possible to collect samples of students' oral reading, organize them here at ESU #3, and assess them using some kind of a rubric?" We had been assessing student writing this way for years, and it seemed as if reading could be done much the same way. Doug looked up.

"Do you mean on audiotape?" He had that "Are you nuts?" tone in his voice. I could see the wheels turning: his mind's eye envisioning 3,000 audiotape reels, with student's recordings; raters attempting to find the appropriate spots on the tape; a nightmare in the making.

"Well, I'm not sure. That's why I'm in your office. Because I know if anyone can figure out a better way, it would be you."

"Okay," he said, against his better judgment. "Tell me more about it."

I described the project that Gretna Public Schools had been doing for a couple of years, using archived fluency samples for student portfolios and for individual assessment purposes. Under the leadership of their Assistant Superintendent, Jef Johnston, they had taken some innovative steps on a district level. I told him about the volumes of research on the importance of reading fluency and the potential to connect assessment and instruction together in a way that could have a huge impact on overall student reading achievement. I explained that the research on fluency and its connection to comprehension were undeniable. In addition, no one else was doing anything like this on a large scale, at least not to my knowledge.

"If no one is doing it, what does that tell you?" He laughed.

"Good point," I conceded. "Just tell me this; would you be willing to work on it if there is interest from our districts in pursuing such an idea?"

He agreed to do it. Neither of us had any idea just how much time we were committing that day, but neither of us would change the course of things, if we did it again.

The next steps were taken. Yes, there was interest. Yes, it made sense to assess reading in this way. We were asked to put together a rationale, get more research support, and put together a proposal. The proposal would include summoning a group of teachers who would create the assessment protocol and pilot the system. The only thing missing was the leadership that a national expert could bring to the project, and Timothy Rasinski was our choice. I wrote to him, asking whether he would work on such a project with us, and to our delight he said "yes"!

Not many days after, Doug came forward with a piece of software that sounded very promising. Family Time Computing (FTC) Publishing Company made a product called Sound Companion that not only had the potential to record student's voices clearly but also sported a visual feature.

Doug explained. "Look," he said, opening up the sound file. "The students will not only hear themselves but also *see* their voiceprint. I'm thinking of the students that were in my special education classroom and how helpful the visual would be." (see Figure 7.1.)

"And since the files can be saved for any platform, it would be easy for students to transfer files from home to school, or even move them to a website. That makes it possible to share with parents and family members. I can envision a parent listening to a sample early in the year and comparing it to samples later on. Could be pretty powerful for parent–teacher conferences."

He told me the base price and explained that FTC would work with us depending on the number of licenses.

We decided to purchase a sufficient number of Sound Companion licenses for the teachers who would participate in the pilot project. They would select texts and make student recordings in their classrooms. The

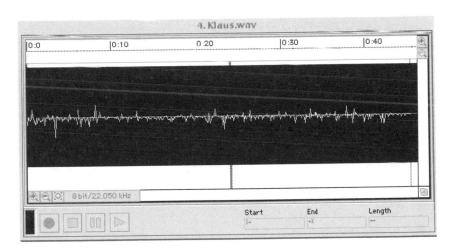

FIGURE 7.1. The Sound Companion file.

collections would be used for scoring practice, to establish anchors, and to design the processes for uploading and storing files.

In the end, what seemed too good to be true turned out to be a long-term relationship with FTC, from whom we have purchased hundreds of copies of Sound Companion. The software has worked flawlessly for hundreds of teachers and thousands of students during the course of the project.

THE PILOT

Timothy Rasinksi came to ESU #3 in 1999 to work with a group of 35 teachers who were willing to develop and pilot the Fluency Assessment System$^©$. They received training in the research base and also learned important classroom strategies for teaching fluency. Michelle Rezek, a fifth-grade teacher and currently one of our lead teachers for the project, remembers it this way:

> "I got involved in the fluency project about 4 years ago. I attended a training at ESU #3 and had an opportunity to hear Tim Rasinksi speak. In listening to him talk about the project and the importance of fluency, I thought, 'Okay, I can kind of buy this,' but I didn't quite have the big picture then. What helped was to bring back the project to school, collect some fluency samples from my students, and then report to ESU #3 how it worked. The power of that was that once I saw how motivated kids were when they were reading into the computer and had a chance to give some feedback with the rubric, I began to see how powerful this could be.
>
> "I had a student that first year that started out reading about 60 words per minute. For fifth graders, we need them to be reading somewhere at about 130, so you know he was behind. Well, we did some of the interventions that Tim suggested, continued to collect some fluency samples, and by the end of the year he was reading at 130 words per minute. Plus when our MAT [Metropolitan Reading Test] scores came back, he was reading for the first time ever at grade level."

The major task of the pilot group was to use the Sound Companion software and to pilot texts that captured students' fluency skills. Tim shared the Multidimensional Fluency Scale (MFS) that he and Jerry Zutell (1991) had developed (see the Appendix at the end of this book). It was adopted for the pilot program. Michelle and her students dubbed the rubric components of the MFS (Expression, Smoothness, and Pace) as ESP. The acronym stuck and is used widely today by students and teachers throughout the area.

Thirty-five teachers at various grade levels collected more than 900 total samples. From those samples, the group selected the most effective texts and, from that pool, began to establish anchor samples that could be used for scoring. An "anchor" is a sample that is representative of one of the levels on the rubric. For example, an anchor representative of a "1" in ESP would fit the descriptors for that level. Each sample was scored by a group of 20–30 "raters." Only when there was 90% agreement between the raters were samples considered good candidates for the anchor pool. In this manner, anchors were established first at grade 4, later at grades 8 and 11.

The group also needed to decide how readability would be determined for the texts. Since this was a large-scale assessment, a standard text would be used for each grade level, in order to collect cohort data for the school district. The team selected the Lexile *Framework*® *for Reading* (2005) as the basis for selecting grade appropriate texts. An explanation of Lexiles and how they work for text selection and grade-level equivalencies can be found at www.lexile.com. The Lexile Framework has been an effective tool in selecting texts because of the large number of trade books that have been assigned Lexile levels. The criteria for selecting texts suggested by Rasinski (Table 7.1) guided us toward books meant for reading

---

TABLE 7.1. Key Indicators of Linguistic Quality

Complete text. Is the text the students read left whole, *or* does it end at a clearly inappropriate place (midconversation, etc.)?

Nature of vocabulary. Watch for too many hard-to-decode words (e.g., Massachusetts); the meaning of words should be appropriate for the grade level.

Syntax. The syntax should be most reflective of natural reading in the classroom.

Narrative. Natural syntax; should include some dialogue to elicit expressive reading.

Readability. Use readability formulas to check for grade appropriateness.

Title. A title assists the reader with building background.

Pictures. Pictures improve the authenticity for young children and also assist with understanding.

TABLE 7.2. Grade-Level Equivalents and Lexile Ranges

Grade	Reader measures (interquartile range, midyear)	Text measures (from Lexile Framework Map)
1	Up to 300L	200L to 400L
2	140L to 500L	300L to 500L
3	330L to 700L	500L to 700L
4	445L to 810L	650L to 850L
5	565L to 910L	750L to 950L
6	665L to 1000L	850L to 1050L
7	735L to 1065L	950L to 1075L
8	805L to 1100L	1000L to 1100L
9	855L to 1165L	1050v to 1150L
10	905L to1195L	1100L to 1200L
11 and 12	940L to 1210L	1100L to 1300L

Note. Data retrieved from www.lexile.com.

aloud. Most of the great authors that teachers and students enjoy together were already assigned a Lexile level, making it easy to find excerpts from quality literature on grade level. The grade level equivalents and Lexile ranges are shown in Table 7.2.

At the end of the first year, we had a bank of oral reading fluency samples, anchors at three grade levels, and a group of teachers who were ready to expand the project. It was time to get serious about the technology needed to carry out the assessment on a larger scale.

THE ASSESSMENT SYSTEM

The Fluency Assessment System© relies on technology, but at the same time, the technology is not the center of the project. It simply allows the students to be in control. When students make recordings in their classrooms, a couple of things happen. First, they are motivated by the use of the computer. Any child loves to hear his or her own voice! Second, he or she gets immediate feedback and can try again without consequence or sanctions. No letter grade, no audience, no evaluation—simply his or her own ears listening for ESP. When students are taught to listen for meaningful, fluent reading, they develop their own sense of where they want to go. This is truly exciting! Jeremy, grade 5, had this to say about his improvement:

"When I read and I use expression, it makes me see what's happening, like it's moving inside my head so I can picture it, so I
understand the book better than just reading. When I first heard
myself read, it told me I needed to do better in ESP 'cause mostly
I used to read choppy and I could hardly hear myself; my expression wasn't that good at first and my pace was pretty fast. But as I
got on to it, I started getting better; my expression, I could hear,
was real good; my pace was just right and not too slow; my
smoothness wasn't choppy or anything.

"It improved me in math because, at the beginning of the
year, I wasn't doing very well in math. But because I started
reading real well, I could read the word problems to know what
happens and know about the problem, and I could figure it out
easier."

The technology allows many things to happen that would otherwise
be impossible. Students can make recordings whenever they want, save
samples over time, listen and practice repeatedly, hear other students
reading, and share samples with parents. Shelly Kramer, third-grade
teacher, shared her thoughts:

"The value of technology, for the kids, is that they can actually
see and hear how they are reading. Before the technology, they
couldn't see or hear themselves, so how could they know what
to improve? With the technology, they can know how they are
doing right away and rate themselves on how well they are doing—do they need to work on their expression, their smoothness, or their pacing? The immediate feedback tells them what
they are doing well and what to work on. I see it work at our February parent–teacher conferences, too, because we go back and
listen to September, and parents really see how much their kids
have grown and they can't believe it. Seeing it on a day-to-day
basis, it doesn't seem like a big improvement, but if they see the
difference from September to February, they are overwhelmed."

The immediate classroom use has turned out to be the real power of
this project. However, the motivation to use fluency instruction and
assessment often comes from the experience with the once-a-year Fluency
Assessment System© service at ESU #3. Chicken and egg aside, one seems
always to enhance and have value for the other. From the beginning, our

TABLE 7.3. The Relationship between Instructionally Supportive Large-Scale Assessment and Classroom Practice

Features of large-scale assessment	Effects on classroom practice
Models the use of technology to assess oral reading fluency.	Technology is made available every day for practice and feedback.
Provides reports on annual student progress.	Provides several archived samples to demonstrate progress over time.
Provides external feedback on oral reading fluency.	Provides immediate feedback to the student on oral reading fluency.
A rater, unknown to the student makes a judgment.	The student makes a judgment.
Procedures are standardized and score is summative.	Process is adjusted for practice, meant to inform learning and teaching.
Assessment results for accountability and for general trends.	Assessment results are used to communicate with students and parents.

vision was to provide a service that would satisfy assessment accountability at the district level, while encouraging student involvement and quality instruction at the classroom level. Unless assessment informs learning on a daily basis, it is not worth doing. An instructionally supportive, large-scale assessment creates an awareness of daily opportunities to learn the skills and processes being assessed. Table 7.3 characterizes this relationship.

HOW THE LARGE-SCALE ASSESSMENT SYSTEM WORKS

Trained raters come to ESU #3 every April to score thousands of oral reading samples without leaving the computer lab. But before that can happen, a series of steps take place:

First, a student reads into a computer in his or her classroom. A sound file is created and saved on the classroom computer.

Then, still from the classroom, the teacher logs on to the system and associates each of the students' audio samples to a space on the server. The teacher simply clicks on the "Upload Audio Files" button to send the files to the ESU server. The screen used by the teachers is shown in Figure 7.2.

SIMS Classroom

Main Menu

Logout

Fluency Assessment

Hello DARCI HEMPEL To Upload Samples: You have selected to upload the Fluency test for grade level 04 of your Homeroom class. If this is not correct, please click the browser's "Back" button once and make a new selection.

For each student you would like to send a file, click the browse button and navigate to the student file located on your computer. Double click the sample file. Once all file(s) have been associated, click the "Upload Audio File(s)" button to send file(s) to the ESU Server.

To Verify Samples: A "Yes" in the last column indicates a sample exists for that student. A "No" in the last column indicates a sample does not exist for that student and one must be sent if one is needed.

Name	Grade	Students Audio Samples	File already on ESU Server
ANDERSON ,RANDAL D.	09	Browse...	No
ANDRESEN ,JOSHUA F	09	Browse...	No
BAUMAN ,KYLE C.	09	Browse...	No
BERGGREN ,KAYLA J	09	Browse...	No
BRUNSTING LAWRENCE D	09	Browse...	No
CONLEY ,AUSTIN J.	09	Browse...	No
GOBLIRSCH ,ERIC S	09	Browse...	No
HAYDUK ,ALEJANDRINA R.	09	Browse...	No
HENSON ,BRANDON S	09	Browse...	No
TJUTNER ,CHELSTE A	09	Browse...	No

FIGURE 7.2. The classroom log-in screen.

Once the files arrive at ESU #3, they are stored for scoring. The system automatically arranges and labels each file, so that a district can receive a final report when the scoring is finished. On the scoring date, raters who have previously been trained arrive ready to work. Each rater is given a set of headphones, a scoring guide, and copies of the standard texts.

The entire rating process is Web-based. Raters log onto the system using a URL (Figure 7.3), click on a sample, and listen. The 1-minute sample is scored using a pull-down menu for each of the three dimensions—Expression, Smoothness, and Pace—according to the scoring guide. The scores are immediately sent to the server, where they are stored for the reports.

Two raters score each reading sample. Since the scores are recorded electronically, each rater is unaware of the scores given by the other. The system compares the two ratings in each of the three dimensions. If the two raters differ by no more than one place on the scale, the system will add the two scores together for each dimension. For example:

Rater 1: 4, 3, 3 = 10   Rater 2: 4, 4, 3 = 11   Total Score = 21

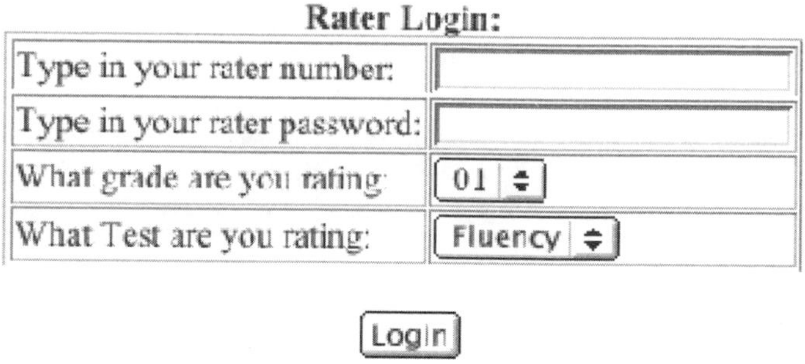

Rater Login:

Type in your rater number:	
Type in your rater password:	
What grade are you rating:	01 ⇕
What Test are you rating:	Fluency ⇕

[Login]

FIGURE 7.3. The log-in screen on scoring day.

When the first and second raters disagree by more than one place on the scale, the system sends the sample to a third rater. The system can retrieve the reliability of the scoring procedure by tallying how well the raters matched. The interrater reliability over 3 years and more than 10,000 samples has been an average 66% exact match between raters, and 92% adjacent match. In other words, 66% of the time raters give the exact same scores, and 92% of the time, they are at least within one point on the scale. That means that 8% of the samples need a third, independent rating.

Finally, the reports are available. Once the scoring session ends, districts are able to access the data, from their own sites, in the form of three reports: by district, by building, and by classroom. These reports are downloaded and printed right in the school, without the waiting for results, as in most large-scale assessment systems. The immediate feedback has been another appealing aspect of the project. If we want to use assessment results *for* learning, then we need to know the results quickly so instruction can be adjusted.

WHY FLUENCY MATTERS: THE RESEARCH

Over the years, attention to fluency has grown. As the body of evidence accumulates, the rationale to dedicate time, money, and energy into the project becomes more compelling. Although, ESU #3 did not produce original research for this project, the rationale was based on the larger body of research on oral reading fluency, including the following highlights:

1983: Richard Allington (1983) calls it the "neglected goal" of the reading program.

1984 to present: Rasinski (1998, 2003), Zutell and Rasinski (1991), Samuels (1979), Carbo (1997), and Rasinski and Hoffman (2003) conduct studies showing positive correlation between oral reading fluency and comprehension.

1995: NAEP (National Assessment of Education Progress) assesses fluency for the first time (Pinnell et al., 1995).

2000: National Reading Panel (2000) affirms fluency instruction as a gateway to comprehension.

2002: No Child Left Behind incorporates fluency as one of five components of a research-based reading program.

Based on the research, the ESU #3 pilot team decided on a definition of fluency that included comprehension:

The ability to read orally or silently with appropriate levels of word recognition, accuracy, phrasing, expression, and good comprehension of the text.

The early work with Rasinski emphasized the notion that fluency must include textual understanding or the reading cannot be considered fluently read. As the project evolved, the attention to prosodic features of reading gained importance. The training for raters, lessons designed for teachers, and general instructional strategies are focused on expressive reading of connected text, paying particular attention to phrasing, volume, the use of pauses, and word emphasis, as well as appropriate speed and accuracy.

Our commitment was further intensified by the NAEP assessment results from 1995, which found 44% of fourth graders to be dysfluent even with grade-level stories that the students had read under supportive conditions. Moreover, that study found a close relationship between fluency and reading comprehension, and overall proficiency scores in reading. The bottom line from the NAEP study was simply this: *Students who are low in fluency have difficulty getting the meaning of what they read.*

The release of the National Reading Panel report in 2000 reinforced this notion, including the theory of automaticity (LaBerge & Samuels, 1974). There are many learning contexts where this theory applies (e.g., driving an automobile, playing a musical instrument, or using a keyboard). When presented with this idea as an intellectual theory, teachers are immediately drawn to it, because it makes intuitive sense based on their experience with students.

In addition to the general body of evidence on oral reading fluency, the research on time with text and on quality assessment supports our schools in their efforts to improve overall reading instruction and assessment.

When students encounter more text, they become better readers. A study by Anderson, Wilson, and Fielding (1998) cements the relationship between time with text and achievement as measured by a standardized norm-referenced achievement test. This study of 500,000 students found that children in the 98th percentile on a standardized achievement test spent 90.7 minutes per day engaged in reading, and read a total of more than 4,000,000 words in books per year. Students at the 60th percentile spent an average of 18.1 minutes per day and read 432,000 words in books per year. Students at the 2nd percentile read .2 minutes per day, computing to 0 words in books per year.

Studies by Stiggins, Arter, Chappuis, and Chappuis (2004), Marzano (2001), and Black and William (1998) reveal that students show achievement gains when

- The criteria are clear.
- The feedback is immediate and specific to the task.
- They have time and opportunity to practice skills.
- They are involved in self-assessment.
- Their parents are involved.
- Their teacher provides multiple opportunities to learn.

The Fluency Assessment System©, when used together with ongoing instruction and assessment at the classroom level, meets all of these conditions. Particularly exciting is the anecdotal evidence in the stories that students, parents, teachers, and principals tell. Their words are recorded in the ESU #3 unpublished video *Testimonies from the Classroom*. The following section contains transcripts from that video.

SUCCESS STORIES:
TESTIMONIES FROM THE CLASSROOM

The Papillion LaVista School District comprises 8,500 students in a suburban area with two high schools, two junior high schools, and 12 elementary schools. One of the elementary buildings, G. Stanley Hall, is unique in its demographic, with a higher percentage of Title I students. Michelle Rezek, a fifth-grade teacher at G. Stanley, is also one of the lead teachers for the Fluency Assessment System©. She led the building initiative to implement fluency assessment and instruction in every G. Stanley Hall first- through sixth-grade classroom. The building became a model for the district, outscoring many of its more affluent neighbors on standardized achievement tests in just 1 year's time.

Shelley Kramer, a grade 3 teacher, tells this story about Tara, a girl in her class.

> "Tara is a student who, at the beginning of the year, was in a Title I reading group. She has improved her reading so much through Sound Companion, and just by practicing her oral reading a lot, that she is not in that group any more. It's raised her confidence level and she has become more motivated to read. She wants to sit down and read, because she knows that she can do it and understand what she is reading."

The day of the filming for *Testimonies from the Classroom*, Tara's mother came for an interview. The following conversation about reading fluency occurred among Tara, her mom, and her teacher.

TEACHER: What are the three things that we listen for?

TARA: Expression, smoothness, and pace.

TEACHER: What is expression?

TARA: Whatever you want to say out loud that expresses yourself.

TEACHER: What about smoothness?

TARA: You don't stutter between sentences.

TEACHER: And what about pace?

TARA: You're not reading too fast or too slow. You just want to read right in the middle.

MOM: Using it in parent–teacher conferences helps me to know where she needs to work. At home we work on expression, smoothness, and pace—things like pausing after periods. She's been reading chapter books now and understanding what she's reading. And some of the book reports and projects that Ms. Kramer has had them do in class—she enjoys not only the interaction of that, but she really understands more of what she is reading. She stops to listen to herself and realizes "Hey, that doesn't sound very good." In September, when she heard herself on the computer, she wanted to work hard so that she made sense to herself. The practice has helped her read more smoothly, and when she reads smoother, she understands it better.

TARA: I've been reading a lot of chapter books. I just got new chapter books from my Grandma, which I'm very anxious to read. When you read stories, you can learn how to write words you didn't know how to write.

TEACHER: When you read into the computer, how does that make you better with ESP?

TARA: Because when I listen to the one that I just did, then I know that I have to work on some things for the next time I do it.

The final conversation at G. Stanley Hall was with Bernie Gordon, the principal, who not only understands the qualities of good assessment, but he also has an appreciation for the work of teachers and students in the learning process.

"We allow students to make the recordings whenever they want. If they're working on it and they want that immediate feedback to rate themselves and see how they are doing, they'll do that—that's really important. One of the things we know about learning is that students need feedback; they need it specifically, and they need it frequently. This is another tool that allows for that to happen.

"It's really been nice to be able to play a sample early in the year and then come back again in mid-February, when we do our second conferences, and let the children talk about what they've learned. And for the parent to hear that fluency sample is pretty overwhelming and exciting.

"I see a lot more smiles now from kids and parents when they leave conferences. A lot more feedback from parents that they really enjoy the conferences. But more importantly, they understand what this learning process is all about and what is being done. What amazes them a bit is the amount of interest their children have in their learning process. Once you can make that happen for kids, you really can't stop them.

"Sound Companion and the work we are doing with fluency is really for all students; whether they are good readers, bad readers; it doesn't really matter. The important thing to note is that with just a few strategies that are very simple to do, you'll see growth across the board with all students. And isn't that what we really want to see?"

The Fluency Assessment System© project at ESU #3 is a source of pride. It is research-based, user-friendly, a good match between large-scale and classroom-based assessment, and is proving to have an impact on the motivation and confidence of its most important users—the students. The work continues to evolve as the relationship between fluency and comprehension is better understood.

For more information about the Fluency Assessment System©, contact Educational Service Unit #3 in Omaha, Nebraska. Or visit our website at esu3.ishareinfo.org/fluency/.

REFERENCES

Allington, R. L. (1983). Fluency: The neglected goal of the reading program. *Reading Teacher, 36,* 556–561.

Anderson, R., Wilson, P., & Fielding, L. (1988). Growth in reading and how children spend their time outside of school. *Reading Research Quarterly 23,* 285–303.

Black, P., & William, D. (1998). Inside the black box: Raising standards through classroom assessment. *Phi Delta Kappan, 80*(2), 139–148.

Carbo, M. (1997). Every child a reader. *American School Board Journal, 124*(2), 33.

LaBerge, D., & Samuels, S. J. (1974). Toward a theory of automatic information processing in reading. *Cognitive Psychology, 6,* 293–323.

Lexile® Framework for Reading. (2005). Durham, NC: MetaMetrics.

Marzano, R. (2001). *Classroom instruction that works.* Alexandria, VA: Association for Supervision and Curriculum Development.

National Reading Panel. (2000). *Report of the National Reading Panel: Teaching children to read: Report of the subgroups.* Washington, DC: U.S. Department of Health and Human Services, National Institutes of Health.

Opitz, M., & Rasinski, T. (1998). *Good-bye round robin: 25 Effective oral reading strategies.* Portsmouth, NH: Heinemann.

Pinnell, G. S., Pikulski, J. J., Wixson, K. K., Campbell, J. R., Gough, P. B., & Beatty, A. S. (1995). *Listening to children read aloud: Data from NAEP's Integrated Reading Performance Record (IRPR) at grade 4.* Washington, DC: Office of Educational Research and Improvement, U.S. Department of Education.

Rasinski, T. V. (1990). Investigating measures of reading fluency. *Educational Research Quarterly, 14*(3), 37–44.

Rasinski, T. V. (2003). *The fluent reader: Oral reading strategies for building word recognition, fluency, and comprehension.* New York: Scholastic.

Rasinski, T. V., & Hoffman, J. (2003). Theory and research into practice: Oral reading in the school literacy curriculum. *Reading Research Quarterly, 38*(4), 510–522.

Rasinski, T. V., Padak, N., Linek, W., & Sturtevant, E. (1994). Effects of fluency development on urban second-grade readers. *Journal of Educational Research, 37*(3), 158–165.

Samuels, S. J. (1979). The method of repeated readings. *Reading Teacher, 32,* 403–408.

Sound Companion for Hyperstudio. (1997). Bloomington, IL: FTC Publishing Group.

Stiggins, R. J., Arter, J. A., Chappuis, J., & Chappuis, S. (2004). *Classroom assessment for student learning.* Portland, OR: Assessment Training Institute.

Testimonies from the Classroom. (2003). Unpublished digital video by Educational Service Unit #3, Omaha, Nebraska, featuring G. Stanley Hall Elementary School, Papillion–LaVista Schools in Nebraska.

Zutell, J., & Rasinski, T. V. (1991). Training teachers to attend to their students' oral reading fluency. *Theory Into Practice, 30,* 211–217.

CHAPTER 8

"Everybody Reads"

Fluency as a Focus for Staff Development

CAMILLE L. Z. BLACHOWICZ
MARY KAY MOSKAL
JENNIFER R. MASSARELLI
CONNIE M. OBROCHTA
ELLEN FOGELBERG
PETER FISHER

Evanston Skokie District 65 is a leafy lakefront suburb north of Chicago, with a richly diverse population reflected both in the teachers and students in its schools. Education is critical to this town with three universities, and the gap between achieving and nonachieving students receives a lot of attention. Looking at the district benchmark assessments, it appeared that fluency of reading was one factor that differentiated achieving students from those who were lagging behind. The district reading coordinator contacted the Reading Center at National–Louis University, where fluency instruction was a regular emphasis in its reading improvement programs and in the training of reading specialists. Together, the district and the college embarked on a collaborative investigation to see whether instruction for fluency could improve student performance. Along the way, the process of developing this program resulted in a staff development program and volunteer program that is continuing beyond the scope of the initial project.

The project, called Everybody Reads, was funded by the Illinois State Board of Education. It had three goals:

1. To develop classroom-tested models for building reading fluency in grades K–3.
2. To design a tutoring model for fluency to be delivered by volunteer tutors.
3. To increase the impact of the process by not only training teachers and tutors but also developing a cadre of teacher leaders who could direct the project after the grant period ends.

In this chapter, we describe the ways in which fluency instruction had a threefold outcome for the district. It improved the fluency of the elementary students in the project, provided an excellent focus for the development of an effective volunteer tutoring program, and provided a point of departure for teacher staff development that led teacher inquiry far beyond this single instructional issue.

WHY WAS *FLUENCY* THE TARGET FOR STUDENTS?

The ability to read fluently (at a good rate, with good accuracy and proper intonation and phrasing) is highly correlated with many measures of reading competence (Kuhn & Stahl, 2000; Strecker, Roser, & Martinez, 1998). For the reader, fluency requires good decoding skills, the strategies to orchestrate these in reading real text, and comprehension to monitor what is being read to make sure it sounds like language.

For the teacher, listening to students read and charting their development in fluency is also a way to measure the effect of instruction and to provide input for further instructional planning. Unlike most standardized measures, which only show large changes in behavior, fluency measurement is sensitive to small increments of improvement (Shinn, 1989). And unlike standardized measures, the practice involved in the reading of a fluency measurement passage can also help students' reading. Fluency is not only a good *measure* of reading performance, but working toward fluency is also a good *treatment* for reading difficulties. Having students do a lot of reading at an appropriate level, with a teacher, tutor, or peer supporting them and helping them self-monitor, is a good way for students to practice their way to competence (Rasinski, Padak, Linek, & Sturtevant, 1994).

WHY IS FLUENCY A GOOD FOCUS FOR STAFF DEVELOPMENT?

With respect to staff development, fluency work also embeds several issues that are critical to classroom instruction and deal with the real empirical questions of teachers. Teachers who are concerned with their students' fluency need to ask and answer several questions that have ramifications far beyond the realm of fluency instruction:

> How do I know what my class can handle?
> What materials do I need so that everybody can read?
> How do I build activities into the day so that every student reads every day at an appropriate level?
> How do I measure and show growth?

These rich questions grow out of investigations of fluency but have much further reaching effects on classroom instruction.

WHAT WAS THE WORKING MODEL FOR THE STAFF DEVELOPMENT COMPONENT?

Two primary teachers from each of Evanston's 12 public schools and one participating private school worked for 2 years, after school and during the summer, to design the project, which was supported administratively by the district Director of Reading. University faculty led monthly meetings and worked with three master teacher–facilitators. Over 300 students were involved in the project, with four targeted students from each classroom also receiving extra individual help.

Teachers came together to ask questions about fluency and to receive resources, articles and books, videos, and ideas from the facilitators. After each meeting, teachers tried strategies, read articles, and brought back ideas to the group. Each teacher who volunteered received either a stipend or district credit for pay scale advancement. Participants needed to commit to trying out strategies and reporting back to the group and their principals. They decided on the goal of developing a set of classroom activities that would not add another layer of curriculum to the day but would "put a fluency spin" on all the instruction typically done (Rasinski & Zutell, 1990). This "fluency spin" would increase the incidence of the following instructional activities:

- More modeling of fluent reading.
- More support during reading in the roles of teacher, tutor, or partner.
- More repeated reading practice in various forms.
- More emphasis of good phrasing and expression in reading.
- More careful matching of students and texts.

As an example, teachers using poetry would be sure to read aloud the poem under study several times, or have students hear a recorded version of the poem, so they would have good first models. The class would do choral reading or support reading, with the teacher's voice fading in and out as the students became confident readers. After the readings of the poem, teachers might conduct a mini-lesson on punctuation and phrasing, often having students draw pause marks or stop signs as reminders to stop, and underline phrases where the words went together. Then they read to each other, in partner sets or with take-home poems, for further practice. The materials were now easy for the students to read independently, and this provided an easy way to share their new skills with family members.

Teachers worked during the year to develop a handbook of teacher resources (a favorite was Opitz, Rasinski, & Bird, 1998; also Stahl & Kuhn, 2002) and sample videos. The teachers, along with district and university staff, created transparencies, handouts, and PowerPoint presentations to match the issues that teachers decided were important and could be shared with other teachers in school mini-workshops (these are available for downloading at www.illinoisreads.com). The handbooks were organized around these topics, which reflected the inquiry questions pursued over the course of the year:

1. What is fluency, and why is it important?
2. How do I assess and observe my students and make a fluency snapshot of my whole class?
3. How do I match students with materials?
4. What are some methods for increasing fluency in the classroom?
5. What is an individual tutorial model for increasing fluency?

A teacher can't do fluency work without knowing students' reading levels and what materials match their needs. For assessment, teachers decided to use the Classroom Fluency Snapshot (Blachowicz, Sullivan, & Cieply, 2001) to provide a quick overview of each classroom in the fall, winter, and spring as a "thermometer" of progress (see Figure 8.1). Once it was clear that there was a range of reading levels in each class, the teachers asked for sessions on material leveling, then organized their own work sessions on leveling. They developed and shared ways to store and share materials in schools and created a video for others on organizing materials. So the seemingly simple concept of fluency led to a significant amount of teacher inquiry and sharing.

WHY IS FLUENCY A GOOD "HOOK" FOR A VOLUNTEER PROGRAM?

Not only the district staff development initiatives but also the school volunteer program benefited from the stimulus of investigating fluency. Schools and classrooms are often encouraged to make use of reading volunteers, but the suggestion is often more complicated than it seems (Blachowicz, 1999). Tutors must be trained so that what they teach is appropriate to the students with whom they are working. They need to understand the task and to be able to see progress. Furthermore, many tutors have a limited amount of time to donate to their tutoring, sometimes only one time a week, so continuity for the students must be built into programs. Finally, the tutoring must not take too much attention away from the teacher, or the value becomes questionable. Given all these concerns, fluency work is a "natural" for tutoring, because fluency is a simple concept to explain, and one that is salient to most nonprofessionals. They know when a student "sounds good." Also, methods for building fluency can be routinized, so that a simple model can be developed and used by several tutors who may work on different days with the same child.

The first step in the Everybody Reads tutoring component, which began in year 2 of the project, was adapting the teachers' model for individual instruction in order to make a Tutor Handbook (available for free download at www.illinoisreads.com). The model used was a modified repeated reading format (see Figure 8.2). The teacher would select an appropriate book, one that was familiar or on an appropriate level for the

Reading in September 2001	Words Correct Per Minute	Reading in January 2002
Katie (158)	160	Jeb (172)
	155	
	150	
	145	Mary (146) Katie (143)
	140	
Mary (136)	135	
Andy (127)	130	
	125	Haley (123)
	120	Andy (121)
	115	
	110	
	105	
Haley (96)	100	Louis (99) Neal (99)
	95	
Chuck (90)	90	Chuck (91) Barbara (89)
	85	Kathy(86) Catherine (84)
Emily (80) Kathy (76)	80	
Jeb (73) Barbara (73)	75	Emily (72)
Louis (67)	70	Jenny (68) Nancy (67)
	65	Richard (63) Pablo (63)
Catherine (59) Neal (59)	60	Alison (60)
Nancy (54) Jenny (52)	55	
	50	
Alison (45)	45	
Chris (41)	40	
Pablo (31)	35	
	30	
Richard (26)	25	
	20	
	15	

FIGURE 8.1. Classroom Fluency Snapshot—second grade. In January, these second graders read the first few pages of the grade 2 text *Commander Toad and the Planet of the Grapes* by Jane Yolen. Shading indicates typical oral reading rates for second graders as indicated in Barr, Blachowicz, Katz, and Kaufman (2001, p. 25).

1. Select a book or passage of approximately 100–150 words at instructional level. Count the number of words, write on a Post-It, and place it at the end of the passage.

2. Ask the student read the passage orally. Time how many seconds it takes from start to finish, noting the error(s) as the child reads.

3. Have a calculator available to calculate the reading rate:
   (use the record sheet if you have one)
   # of words in the passage − # of miscues = # of words read correctly
   # of words read correctly × 60 divided by # of seconds = number of words read correctly in 1 minute (WCPM)!

If the number of errors is more than 15 (or 85%), an easier text should be chosen.

4. Review the errors with the student and ask him or her to read again. Time the reading. Calculate the errors and rate. Praise any improvement and discuss goals.

5. One more time, review the errors with the student and ask for one last reading. Time the reading. Calculate the errors and rate. Praise improvement and discuss goals. Remember that increased rate is not the goal for everyone. Some students need more attention to phrasing and intonation. You may wish to not calculate rate for some students.

6. Chart the rate and errors from all three readings. Display the impressive results.

7. You may want to continue this process for several days until a predetermined rate has been achieved. Be sure to chart each improvement.

Typical oral reading rates

First grade	30–70 words per minute
Second grade	60–90
Third grade	80–110
Fourth grade	95–120
Fifth grade	110–140
Sixth grade	110–150

FIGURE 8.2. Time repeated reading procedure.

student to be tutored, and put it in the Tutor Handbook. After an introduction and any modeling necessary, the tutor would have the student
read the book two or three times and record rate and accuracy. After each
reading, the pair also evaluated the reading and filled in a record sheet
(see Figure 8.3). At the end of the session, the tutor and child made a
graph showing reading rate and miscue rate over several readings for the
student to take home (see Figure 8.4).

Child's Name _____   Date _____

Book Title _____

Start Page _____   End Page _____   Number of Words ___

Recorder _____

···

First Reading

Number of Seconds _____   Number of Miscues _____

___ words − ___ miscues = ___ correct words − ___ seconds × 60 = ___ wcpm

(e.g., 100 words − 5 miscues = 95 correct words − 120 seconds x 60 = 48
words correct per minute)

	Always				Rarely
Correct use of punctuation	5	4	3	2	1
Read with expression	5	4	3	2	1

···

Second Reading

Number of Seconds _____   Number of Miscues _____

___ words − ___ miscues = ___ correct words − ___ seconds × 60 = ___ wcpm

	Always				Rarely
Correct use of punctuation	5	4	3	2	1
Read with expression	5	4	3	2	1

···

Third Reading

Number of Seconds _____   Number of Miscues _____

___ words − ___ miscues = ___ correct words − ___ seconds × 60 = ___ wcpm

	Always				Rarely
Correct use of punctuation	5	4	3	2	1
Read with expression	5	4	3	2	1

···

FIGURE 8.3. Fluency Record Sheet.

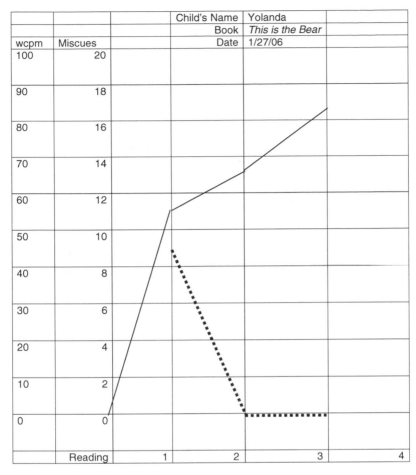

wcpm	Miscues		Child's Name	Yolanda	
			Book	*This is the Bear*	
			Date	1/27/06	
100	20				
90	18				
80	16				
70	14				
60	12				
50	10				
40	8				
30	6				
20	4				
10	2				
0	0				
	Reading		1	2	3	4

wcpm ——————————

Miscues ▪▪▪▪▪▪▪▪▪▪▪▪▪▪▪▪

FIGURE 8.4. Sample fluency graph.

Each classroom had a Volunteer Notebook in place, with pockets and sections for the following:

- The current book for the child
- Blank record sheets
- A pocket pouch with colored pencils, ruler, and stopwatch or digital watch
- A book list with the books listed by level, with the number of

words indicated for a quick calculation of words correct per minute (wcpm)
- A record section for each child
- A communication section for written notes between the tutors and teachers

Using this notebook, if one volunteer worked with a student on Monday, the next volunteer could pick up at the appropriate point on Wednesday, and each could see the other's notes and comments, and responses from the teacher. Each student had at least two individual volunteer sessions per week, and each usually averaged 15–20 minutes.

The volunteers had a first training session using the visuals and handouts prepared by the team. They were mentored during the year by the teacher and the volunteer supervisor, and were also invited to two to three more meetings for learning and debriefing. The volunteer supervisor was a parent/volunteer who was also enrolled in a graduate program in reading. Over the course of the year, lead volunteers emerged. These community members who had special interest in the project added to and refined the Volunteer Handbook and strategies, a process which is continuing.

WHAT WERE THE RESULTS?

Student Growth in Fluency in the Classroom

The primary goal had, of course, been the improvement of student fluency. Second grade was the target grade for this project, because that is when students must move beyond the initial stages of decoding to develop some fluency to make the next leap in reading improvement. Three second-grade classrooms participating in the project were compared to contrasting classrooms from the same grade and school that did not participate; an analysis of covariance that controlled for pretest level was used to examine the fluency gains in words correct per minute. The gains in the project classrooms were statistically superior to those of their matched grade-level and school contrast classrooms ($F = 2.472$; $p < .038$) (see Figure 8.5).

Individual Improvement

There was also a statistically significant effect for those students receiving the volunteer fluency training. Figure 8.6 shows gains in fluency when the

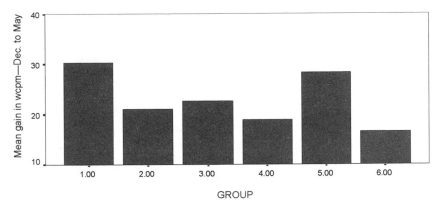

FIGURE 8.5. Second-grade fluency gains by class. Experimental: 1, 3, 5; contrast: 2, 4, 6.

students who received the individual volunteer tutoring were compared in matched pairs to students with the same pretest benchmark scores. T-tests showed that tutored students experienced significantly greater gains in fluency over the course of the 6-month trial than students in the control group ($t = -2.86$, $p < .010$). It is interesting to note that the effect seemed to be greatest for the most dysfluent students. In all but two pairs, all students were also "gap" students who represented ethnic minorities of

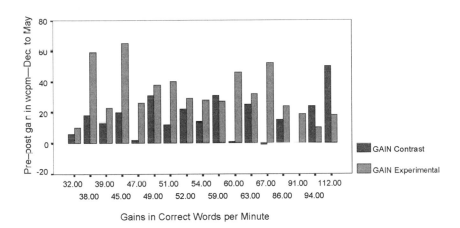

FIGURE 8.6. Second-grade fluency gains—comparison of matched pairs. Students in the Fluency Project are the right-hand bar of each pair.

the district. This provided lots of impetus for teachers to help gap students catch up in their reading through extra reading practice and instruction.

Teacher Growth

All 25 participating teachers filled out a postprogram evaluation on their learning, using a 5-point Likert scale and anecdotal comments. The mean response scores were the following:

Increased my knowledge and expertise	5.0
Provided new techniques and strategies	4.9
I intend to continue using these strategies after the project	4.8
Encouraged me to undertake further professional development	4.8

With respect to whether the program could be extended further, in the anecdotal comments section, 17 of the 25 teachers said they had used the new assessment strategies to share information with parents during conferences. All of the teachers reported sharing materials and strategies with others in their school.

As a further test of the commitment of teachers to supporting and spreading the project, participating teachers volunteered to offer an in-district course on fluency using the created materials. Seventy-three new district teachers signed up for the course, which was then offered at four different school sites in the district. This continued in year 4 of the project, 2 years after university and state support ended. The local press and media have shared the project with the community in print and video, and the Illinois State Board of Education now makes a complete set of project materials available on its website. Teachers have also presented the project at local and state reading councils, and have gone to other schools and districts to disseminate the model.

Volunteers

Volunteers surveyed were uniformly positive about the program and had many fine ideas for extension and refinement. Seventy percent of the volunteers committed to another year. The second year, the number of volunteers grew from 42 to 57, with more coming forward every day. Four volunteers have begun programs to become certified teachers or reading specialists. The district has hired the volunteer coordinator from the project, and one of last year's volunteers has volunteered to assist her. The volunteer coordinator has received many calls from other districts about sharing the model.

A FINAL WORD

Like Topsy, Everybody Reads is a project that "just growed." It demonstrates how a simple concept such as fluency development can inspire deep and meaningful inquiry by classroom teachers and volunteers, who then take charge of the direction and development of further investigation. Project teachers are deciding how to continue and refine the project. Several have been stimulated to undertake graduate study because of the incentive provided by the project. Some first-grade teachers, dissatisfied with lack of fluency study in beginning reading improvement, have started a project called Rethinking First-Grade Instruction that looks at the precursors to fluency instruction. In addition, committed volunteers are modifying the Volunteer Handbook with their own ideas. As one volunteer who is also a district parent said:

> "This has gotten a lot of us really excited about what *we* can do to help our children, and it helped me understand one thing the teachers are doing to make our children better readers. With the charting process we can *see* the growth in the children, and so can they and their teachers. We all get excited. It's motivating for all of us and makes us feel successful and want to do more. We're the 'Everybody Reads' Team!"

REFERENCES

All materials for Everybody Reads can be found on the Illinois State Board of Education site for professional development, www.illinoisreads.com. Click on the links to "educators" and then on "professional development."

Barr, R., Blachowicz, C. L. Z., Katz, C., & Kaufman, B. (2001). *Reading diagnosis for teachers: An instructional approach*. White Plains, NY: Longman.

Blachowicz, C. L. Z. (1999, May 4). *Preparing reading specialists for their roles*. Paper presented at the 44th Annual Convention of the International Reading Association, San Diego, CA.

Blachowicz, C. L. Z., Sullivan, D., & Cieply, C. (2001). Fluency snapshots: A quick screening tool for your classroom. *Reading Psychology, 22*(2), 83–94.

Kuhn, M. R., & Stahl, S. (2000). *Fluency: A review of developmental and remedial strategies.* Ann Arbor, MI: Center for the Improvement of Early Reading Achievement.

Opitz, M., Rasinski, T., & Bird, L. (1998). *Good-bye round robin: Twenty-five effective oral reading strategies.* Portsmouth, NH: Heinemann.

Rasinski, T. V., Padak, N., Linek, W., & Sturtevant, E. (1994). Effects of fluency development in urban second-grade readers. *Journal of Educational Research, 87,* 158–165.

Rasinski, T. V., & Zutell, J. B. (1990). Making a place for fluency instruction in the regular reading curriculum. *Reading Research and Instruction, 29,* 85–91.

Shinn, M. R. (1989). *Curriculum-based measurement: Assessing special children.* New York: Guilford Press.

Stahl, S. A., & Kuhn, M. R. (2002). Making it sound like language: Developing fluency. *Reading Teacher, 55*(6), 582–584.

Strecker, S. K., Roser, N. L., & Martinez, M. G. (1998). Toward understanding oral reading fluency. *National Reading Conference Yearbook, 47,* 295–310.

CHAPTER 9

Meaningful Oral and Silent Reading in the Elementary and Middle School Classroom

Breaking the Round Robin Reading Addiction

Gwynne Ellen Ash
Melanie R. Kuhn

Many teacher educators and educational researchers find the persistence of round robin reading in public schools in the United States disconcerting. Given the common understanding that round robin reading is not only an ineffective strategy but also one that actively damages learners' comprehension of text (Allington, 1980; Opitz & Rasinski, 1998; Stanovich, 1980), teacher educators and educational researchers are puzzled as to why it remains common practice. However, to teachers it is no puzzle. They have purposes, *real purposes*, for using round robin reading. In most cases, teachers' use of round robin reading is focused on meaningful goals, such as improving student learning, supporting struggling readers, or maintaining classroom management. For them, round robin reading is a means to an end. Although there may be downsides, many teachers believe that their goals for instruction are purposeful and therefore supersede the negative aspects of round robin reading. They are addicted to round robin reading.

This addiction has led to the founding of Round Robin Reading Anonymous (RRRA), modeled on other "Anonymous" programs. We at RRRA believe that all teachers want to be the best teacher possible, but addiction may be getting in the way of good instruction. RRRA invites you to take our quiz (Figure 9.1) to see if you are addicted to round robin reading.

How did you do? Are you a teacher who may have a problem with round robin reading? If so, this chapter is written especially for you. If you do not yet have a problem with round robin reading, you still may find this chapter, and the alternatives it offers, to be compelling.

You might ask, "Why does using round robin reading matter so much?" To researchers, teachers' use of round robin reading seems problematic because it runs counter to research on good literacy instruction. To teachers, the research seems to be getting in the way of their goals. Because of this, teachers may be ignoring research (or they may not, as we see later), but they are doing so in an "ends justify the means" choice. Perhaps, it is a choice that researchers have not taken the time to understand. In the words of Elizabeth Moje, "It may be that inconsistencies lie not between what teachers believe and what they practice, but between what researchers believe and what teachers practice" (1996, p. 191).

As members of RRRA, we suggest that teachers examine their purposes for using round robin reading; when they do so, they will probably find that there are more effective reading strategies that will meet their purposes *and* help to improve their students' literacy learning. Choosing round robin reading may be the most straightforward or simplistic choice, but there may be other choices—choices that are more beneficial for learners. Or, in the words of RRRA, once we admit we have a problem, we can begin to solve the problem. Once teachers admit to themselves that the compromises involved in using round robin reading are not likely to compensate for its benefits, they might feel ready to change. In this chapter, we examine the purposes that teachers give for using round robin reading, then suggest alternative practices that will help teachers meet their purposes and improve their literacy instruction at the same time. We also discuss some teachers' observations regarding why they use round robin reading, and why it may not be the best possible solution to their problems, even if it seems to be at times.

Please complete the following questionnaire; answer yes or no to each question.

___ Do you believe that hearing their peers read aloud helps students understand the text and the content they are covering better than if they read it themselves?

___ Do you have students read aloud in class, without preparation, even though they dislike reading aloud in front of their peers?

___ Do you think that your students will not read text that they are assigned to read independently, so reading it aloud in class is the only way to make sure the content is covered?

___ Do you believe that round robin reading, where students read short, unprepared pieces of text on demand, helps improve students' fluency and comprehension?

___ Do you believe that round robin reading is an efficient use of your instructional time?

___ Do you regularly (at least once a week) have your students read aloud, in front of their peers, without preparation?

___ Do you believe that your students will like you better if you use round robin reading?

___ Do you ever have behavior problems in your class while you are using round robin reading?

___ Do you understand the research on fluency, yet you wouldn't know how to run your class if you didn't use round robin reading?

___ Have you tried to stop using round robin reading, only to go back to it again and again?

___ Do you hide your use of round robin reading from your coworkers and superiors?

___ Have you ever felt that your instruction would be better if you didn't use round robin reading?

Did you answer YES four or more times? If so, you are probably already in trouble with round robin reading. Why do we say this? Because teachers who have admitted their addiction to round robin reading have said so in research. They found out the truth about themselves—the hard way.

But again, only *you* can decide whether you think Round Robin Reading Anonymous is for you. Try to keep an open mind on the subject. If the answer is yes, we'd be glad to tell you how we stopped using round robin reading ourselves, and how we've helped hundreds of teachers to stop as well.

RRRA does not promise to solve all of your teaching problems. But we can show you how we are learning to teach without round robin reading. And our teaching is better. When we got rid of round robin reading, we found that teaching became much more meaningful.

FIGURE 9.1. Round Robin Reading Anonymous questionnaire. We use the framework of the Alcoholics Anonymous questionnaire with great admiration for the work the organization does with people who have difficulties with alcohol. Although this is a parody, no disrespect is meant to the organization, or to the work that it does.

WHAT SPECIFICALLY IS ROUND ROBIN READING, AND WHY IS IT SO PROBLEMATIC?

Round robin reading, or "the outmoded practice of calling on students to read orally one after the other," may not be so outmoded in the classroom (Harris & Hodges, 1995, p. 222). Although it is a practice that "no authority recommends, including those who write and promote basal readers" (Cox & Zarrillo, 1993, p. 170), round robin reading is actively used by even some of the more "savvy" teachers of today (Cunningham & Allington, 1999; Ivey, 1999; Opitz & Rasinski, 1998), not only in elementary schools but also in the middle and secondary grades. As such, even a teacher who "knows and uses 'best practice' teaching strategies . . . resorts to round robin reading and low-level questions during social studies and science" (Cunningham & Allington, 1999, p. 174).

Because of its negative connotations, round robin reading has persisted as a group of related practices. The round robin reading family includes practices teachers have alternatively referred to as

- *Popcorn reading* (the students read aloud in "random" order, without prior practice with the text).
- *Combat reading* (the students call on each other to read, without prior practice with the text, attempting to catch each other "off task").
- *Popsicle reading* (the students have their names written on popsicle sticks; the teacher draws the popsicle sticks, and students read—unprepared—in the order their names are drawn).
- *Round robin reading* (the students are called in a predetermined order, usually following their current seating arrangement, to read an unpracticed text orally).

In fact, in two studies (Ash & Kuhn, 2001; Ash, Kuhn, & Walpole, 2003), teachers differentiated between and among these practices, often claiming to be avoiding round robin reading by using popcorn, combat, or popsicle reading.

One of the interesting things about round robin reading is that most teachers are reluctant to admit to their use of the practice. Acknowledging round robin reading as "something we know we're not supposed to do," teachers still do it, calling it "popcorn" or "combat" reading, and suggesting that it is less damaging when the students, rather than the teacher, call on their peers, or when the selection of readers is "random" (Ash & Kuhn, 2001). Furthermore, some teachers indicate that they are embarrassed to admit to using round robin reading, because its use seems to go against their scholarly knowledge of reading instruction.

The fact that some teachers admit guilt when using round robin reading reflects its broad condemnation as a strategy in reading research and theory. For instance, in his studies of dysfluent readers in the primary grades, Allington (1977, 1980) found that the turn-taking aspect of round robin reading means that these students got very little practice in actual reading. Stanovich (1986) also argued that one result of limited access to connected text is increased difficulties in the literacy development of struggling readers which, in turn, increases the gaps in achievement between fluent and dysfluent readers. Furthermore, Allington (1980) found that the interruptive nature of turn taking provides poor models of skilled reading for students by presenting dysfluent oral reading examples. Such interruptions further prevent students from developing their proficiency in word decoding, since peers or teachers often provide struggling readers with the words before they can decode them independently. Developing such independence in decoding is considered crucial to reading development, since it is intricately linked to the automaticity that is a key component of fluent reading (LaBerge & Samuels, 1974; Stanovich, 1980).

Additionally, round robin reading has been demonstrated to be damaging to students' social and emotional growth (Opitz & Rasinski, 1998). In her case study of middle school readers, Ivey (1999) found that the practice of round robin reading caused great stress for the students who were not reading on grade level (as well as boredom for those who were). One student felt embarrassed to read aloud without practice. Another student who appeared to enjoy round robin reading, often volunteering to read, later confessed, "I raise my hand [to read] 'cause I want to read and get it done with 'cause the slow people read, and it takes them forever to get it done, what we have to read" (p. 186). And while emotional and social damage is problematic enough, students' embarrassment and anxiety, when connected to reading, seems to work against their development of positive identities as readers.

DO TEACHERS STILL USE ROUND ROBIN READING, AND IF SO, WHY?

Although teachers may express guilt about the practice of round robin reading, they are still using it. Few researchers (Santa, Isaacson, & Manning, 1987; Wolf, 1998) have conducted intervention research that actually attempts to end teachers' use of round robin reading. Although these isolated cases resulted in teachers changing their oral reading practice, the widespread use of round robin reading continues, even in the face of research that discourages its use and teachers' awareness of that research.

In two surveys of elementary and middle school teachers in several sites in the United States, we found that almost 60% of the teachers surveyed used some form of round robin reading regularly in their teaching (Ash & Kuhn, 2001; Ash et al., 2003). The teachers who used round robin reading had a different understanding of the research on fluency, and its implication for the use of round robin reading, than did their peers who did not use it. Of teachers who did not use round robin reading, more than 80% were able to describe the research on fluency accurately; only 30% of teachers who used round robin reading regularly were able to do so. Seventeen percent of teachers who used round robin reading incorrectly interpreted fluency research to support its use, claiming that research sanctioned Round Robin Reading as a means of improving students' fluency and comprehension (many teachers also indicated this was especially the case for readers who struggle). Only 3% of teachers who did not use round robin reading regularly misstated the findings of fluency research.

What might be more significant is that 70% of teachers who used round robin reading regularly could not accurately describe fluency research (17% were inaccurate, giving responses such as "I know we should use it because those who struggle can improve their comprehension"; 21% indicated they had little or knowledge of the research; 17% gave information unrelated to fluency; and 15% left the item blank). In contrast, only 18% of teachers who did not use round robin reading regularly had this difficulty (3% misstated the research, and 15% left the item blank).

It would be simplistic to suggest that once teachers learn about the fluency research, they will abandon their use of round robin reading. More than 30% of the teachers who used round robin reading regularly could articulate the research on fluency, yet many actively contradicted this knowledge ("I believe that it's not a preferred approach, but it's still used"). Others suggested that the research was wrong because the practice was popular in their classrooms. While it is important for teachers to understand the research on fluency (as shared elsewhere is this book), it is not enough. Teachers need practices that meet their goals; in order to change practice, there needs to be an alternative available.

COMMON GOALS/PURPOSES
FOR USING ROUND ROBIN READING

We asked teachers who use round robin reading regularly to explain their goals when using the practice. The teachers' most commonly stated goals were the evaluation/assessment of students' reading and the improvement of students' fluency. Other common responses included:

1. Providing a common level of knowledge/content for the class as a whole.
2. Providing oral reading practice.
3. Improving the students' comprehension of the text being read.
4. Pleasing the students (i.e., the students like it).
5. Engaging the students in the reading.
6. Improving the students' self-confidence in oral reading.
7. Improving the students' listening skills.
8. Covering content/material speedily and accurately.
9. Improving the students' word identification accuracy.
10. Improving the students' vocabulary knowledge.

In addition to the goal of evaluating/assessing students' reading, all remaining goals fit in the following three categories: improving students' fluency (items 2, 6, and 9 in the preceding list), improving students' comprehension of content (items 1, 3, 7, 8, and 10), and improving students' motivation/engagement with the text (items 4 and 5).

Taking these four primary goals into account, we would like to recommend alternative practices that not only help teachers meet those goals but also are recognized best practices for reading instruction. We remind teachers that these strategies are effective not only in reading classes per se but also for content area reading and instruction. In our opinion, these practices, once established, are easy to manage, easy to implement, make difficult materials accessible, and provide an opportunity for teachers to assess students' growth. So although a practice may be listed in a particular goal category, we have tried to select practices that offer support across multiple categories.

PRACTICES FOR IMPROVING STUDENTS' FLUENCY

Although many practices in this book focus on improving students' fluency, we have included two here: fluency-oriented reading instruction

(FORI) and radio reading. FORI is an entire classroom organization, and radio reading is a read aloud practice that on the surface may seem similar to round robin reading, but differs through its inclusion of practice before performance and a focus on comprehension.

Fluency-Oriented Reading Instruction

FORI (Stahl et al., 2003) was designed for reading and content area instruction in the primary grades. It involves students in repeatedly reading a selected text, usually a story from the classroom's literature anthology or basal reader, several times over the course of a week. The text is first read aloud by the teacher, with the students following along in their own copy. A discussion is held in order to direct attention to the importance of comprehension early on in the lessons. Over the next few days, the students echo-, choral-, and partner-read the text, and also take it home for additional practice as needed. These readings are followed by the extension activities that usually occur as part of the literacy curriculum.

Radio Reading

In radio reading (Greene, 1979; Opitz & Rasinksi, 1998; Searfoss, 1975), students are assigned segments of the text, which they are to practice reading. After they have practiced reading their section, they are to develop questions to ask their peers regarding that section. The following day, the students read their section aloud, as if they are radio announcers. Once their section is finished, they may ask their peers the questions they developed. If necessary, they may reread sections of their selection in order to help their classmates answer the questions. Although this may seem similar to round robin reading, it differs in one very specific way: Students are given time to practice their reading *before* they are asked to read in front of their peers.

PRACTICES FOR IMPROVING STUDENTS' COMPREHENSION OF CONTENT

In the cooperative groups implemented in jigsaw (Aronson, Blaney, Sikes, Stephan, & Snapp, 1978; Aronson, Blaney, Stephan, Rosenfield, & Sikes, 1977) and the other practices discussed in this section, students are responsible for their own learning; however, they also have the opportunity to construct meaning socially with their peers. As with teacher-led guided reading, instructional organizations for structuring small-group work with text allow students the opportunity to "mimic" what good readers do. These practices frame reading with activities that mirror what good readers do while they read and allow students to practice strategy use in a supportive environment.

Peer-Assisted Learning Strategies

Peer-assisted learning strategies (PALS; e.g., Fuchs, Fuchs, & Burish, 2000) is a form of partner reading. Teachers assign partners to match higher and lower needs students (see Table 9.1). The partners engage in a series of turns reading, rereading, and retelling. Beyond first grade, PALS focuses on three activities to support fluency and comprehension: (1) partner reading, (2) paragraph shrinking, and (3) prediction relay. Working together in pairs, each partner takes the lead as Coach, alternating with the role of Reader. As in peer repeated reading (discussed later in

---

TABLE 9.1. Choosing Partners for Peer-Supported Activities

When pairing up students for partner activities, the conventional wisdom has been to match the most gifted reader with the one who needs the most help, the next-most-gifted reader, with the student who needs the next-to-most help, and on and on, until the two middle readers are matched with each other. Unfortunately, this method is not the most useful one for matching students who can support each other's reading. Often the more proficient reader takes over, doing all of the reading and depriving the reader who needs support the practice he or she might need to become a better reader. Likewise, in the next-to-most pair, the needs-support reader cannot support the gifted reader in his or her needs.

To pair students, list them in descending order from the most proficient reader to the reader who needs most support. In a class of 24, that would mean that the most proficient reader was #1 and the one who needs the most support is #24. Divide the class list in half, so that you have numbers 1–12 on one list, and numbers 13–24 on another. Align the two lists, so that #1 is lined up with #13, #2 with #14, #3 with #15, and so on, until #12 is matched with #24.

With students matched in this way, in each pair, there will be a student who is capable of supporting the student with greater needs, but there will not be such a great difference between their proficiencies. The student with greater needs will still be able to be an active partner, and he or she will also be able to support the more proficient reader.

---

the chapter), the reader reads aloud, and the coach listens and provides positive feedback on his or her reading. Together, the students work to ask questions as they read, shrink paragraphs (a form of structured summarization), and relay their predictions (following the steps of predict, read, check, and summarize).

Jigsaw

Jigsaw (e.g., Aronson et al., 1977, 1978; Gunter, Estes, & Schwab, 1995) is an adaptation of a basic strategy to increase student interdependence. First, students are assigned to one of several heterogeneously grouped study teams with a text or text segment to read and a set of questions or goals to discuss. All the students in this group become "experts" on that particular text. These "experts" are responsible for teaching the content of their area to other students, who read and become "experts" on other sections of text. Once the study groups have answered their questions or met their goals, each member of the study team "jigsaws" or joins representatives from each other's team to form a "jigsaw" group. Each member of the new group teaches the piece with which he or she has developed "expertise" from his or her study team. The teacher then evaluates the students' knowledge of all of the information either individually or according to "jigsaw" groups.

Reciprocal Teaching Plus

Reciprocal teaching plus (Ash, 2002) was recently developed based on the reciprocal teaching activity (Palincsar & Brown, 1984). Reciprocal teaching is a strategy that focuses students on four aspects of their reading: making and revising predictions, asking questions, clarifying difficult points and vocabulary, and summarizing the material. In the beginning, the teacher models reciprocal teaching with the students, demonstrating how to use the four parts of the strategy, and eventually moving students toward using the strategy in peer-led small groups or pairs. In these small groups or pairs, students read predesignated sections of text silently, stopping at designated stopping points and taking turns, leading a discussion that includes questioning, summarizing, clarifying, and predicting.

The adaptation takes this very effective strategy and incorporates critical literacy perspectives. In addition to the four elements, reciprocal teaching plus asks students to address a fifth element, the critical evaluation of a text, identifying the author's perspective and analyzing what points of view are left out of the current text. Prompts that teachers can use to help students with the fifth element—analyzing the perspective of the author and text—include:

- Whose story is being told? What is the author's point of view or perspective?
- Is the author taking one side or another? Does the author tell the reader that he or she is doing this?
- Whose story is not being told? Why might that be?
- What might another point of view or perspective be?

Reciprocal teaching plus models how students can read literally, inferentially, and critically, with guidance and feedback from their peers and their teacher.

PRACTICES FOR IMPROVING STUDENTS' MOTIVATION/ENGAGEMENT

Research suggests that students are more motivated to complete their reading if they are given a specific purpose or task to complete through their reading. The two activities presented here, problematic perspectives and SPAWN, ask students to gather, evaluate, and apply knowledge from their reading to creative discussion and writing tasks.

Problematic Perspectives

In problematic perspectives (Vacca & Vacca, 2005), a teacher designs a hypothetical scenario related to the content in the reading assignment. For example, a teacher getting ready to have students read a text on the Revolutionary War in the United States might ask the students to consider the following scenario:

> You are a 14-year-old son of a prosperous Tory farming family, living in a rural part of the Massachusetts Bay Colony in 1774. You know that in Boston, and in other parts of the Colonies, there have been men who have protested recent taxing acts of the English government. Your family, as Tories, is loyal to King George III, and your family (mostly your father) finds these protests to be traitorous. Yet you have friends in families who believe that England has violated their rights, taxing them in this way, and prevent-

ing them from having power to decide on tax laws that affect them, their products, and their profits. You also believe that it is unfair for England to prevent people from making a living, due to the high taxes they have levied ("levied" means to impose) to pay for the French and Indian War. At dinner, your father tells you that you must not spend time with friends who are not Tories. To spend time with your friends, you must defend their beliefs, even though you are unsure of your own beliefs yourself, and even though you know that your father greatly disapproves of your friends' beliefs. What would you say to your father? Why? Can you imagine a similar situation happening in the United States today? What might it be based on?

Before asking the students to read, the teacher presents the scenario, allows the students to discuss the problem, asks the students questions that might help them think about the scenario in different ways, and seeks possible solutions from the students. Then the teacher asks the students to read the text, thinking about the scenario and how their possible solutions might be affected by the information they read. Following their reading, students are asked to reconsider the scenario and again share possible solutions.

SPAWN

SPAWN (Special Powers, Problem Solving, Alternative Viewpoints, What If, Next; Martin, Martin, & O'Brien, 1984) is a series of writing assignments that ask students to consider the content that they are about to read from multiple perspectives, and to creatively apply their knowledge to their writing or discussion tasks. Before reading a section of *Holes* (Sachar, 1998), the teacher shares the following assignments:

- S *(Special Powers)*—You have been granted special powers. You are able to read minds, and you discover the purpose for having the boys dig the holes. Who would you tell? Why? How would telling someone affect the story and its outcome?
- P *(Problem Solving)*—When Stanley had the sunflower seeds, he chose to take responsibility for their theft and, even though he did not steal them, to hold his place in the pecking order of the boys of Tent D. How could you have handled the problem differently?
- A *(Alternative Viewpoints)*—Pretend you are Mr. Pendanski (Mom). How do you view the boys of Tent D in particular, and the boys of Camp Green Lake in general? How do you view Mr. Sir and the War-

den? What do you think the purpose of your job is? What do you think the Warden thinks that the purpose of your job is?

- *W (What If)*—What if the Warden had punished Stanley, instead of punishing Mr. Sir, for the theft of the sunflower seeds? How might the story have been different?
- *N (Next)*—You are a "camper" at Camp Green Lake. You see Zero walk away; then later, Stanley also runs away. What might you do next?

After using these prompts to set students' purpose for reading, the teacher has them read the selected section silently. After reading the section, students are placed in heterogeneous small groups and are asked to discuss some of the assignments in their group, and to write individual responses to others.

PRACTICES FOR ASSESSING/EVALUATING AND DEVELOPING STUDENTS' READING

Although many teachers indicate that they use round robin reading for assessment, further questioning reveals that they are rarely able to use the practice to monitor their students' fluency and growth. This is partially because it violates our assumption that assessment is an individual act. In order to assess students' fluency (and their use of comprehension strategies), we need to take the time to listen to students read individually. On the other hand, we can monitor students' development through instructionally based practices—practices that can be supported effectively in peer-based activities.

Timed Repeated Readings

A long-standing instructional practice for monitoring students' fluency development is timed repeated readings (Samuels, 1979). In timed repeated readings, students are placed in pairs and asked to read text of an instructional, or just above instructional, level. Students usually read passages of 50–100 words; a copy of each text being read is needed for each student. They should each have a copy of a repeated readings chart and a pencil; each pair should share a stopwatch.

First, students read the texts silently. Then, taking turns, one student reads the passage aloud, while the other student times the reading and marks errors. The student should read as quickly as he or she can, while maintaining appropriate expression. After a student reaches rate–accuracy goals for the passage or after a set number of readings (usually six), the student records the information on a chart, and the other student reads. These charts can be gathered weekly to monitor students' growth. Teachers can meet with each student to review the charts and have the student read a brief text to confirm the measurements.

Peer Repeated Readings

Peer repeated readings (Koskinen & Blum, 1986) is a practice very similar to timed repeated readings, but without the need for stopwatches. Students read a text that has been read in class previously. Again, using a short passage (50–100 words), the student pairs first read the text silently. Then, taking turns, the students read the text orally. After the first reading, the student who is reading assesses his or her own reading. After the second reading, the student again self-assesses, and the student who is listening comments on how the reading is improving (see Figure 9.2). Then the student reads a final time, self-assessing, and listening to his or her partner's positive comments. Then the partners switch roles, with the new reader self-assessing his or her own first reading, and proceeding through the three readings of the text.

Reading 2

How did your partner's reading get better?

He or she read more smoothly.   _____

He or she knew more words.   _____

He or she read with more expression.   _____

Tell your partner one thing that was better about his or her reading.

Reading 3

How did your partner's reading get better?

He or she read more smoothly.   _____

He or she knew more words.   _____

He or she read with more expression.   _____

Tell your partner one thing that was better about his or her reading.

FIGURE 9.2. Paired repeated readings peer evaluation.

WHY SHOULD I CONSIDER JOINING RRRA AND TRYING THESE PRACTICES?

When surveyed, teachers identified what they believed to be the positives of using round robin reading in their classrooms. Among these were student engagement resulting from listening to others read; ease of gathering information for assessing reading development; improving struggling readers' literacy development; the fact that all the students are able to hear all the reading material; good readers serving as role models; the provision of student support and interaction; and round robin reading's ability to help students read and understand challenging text.

However, these identified benefits seemed to conflict with the disadvantages that also emerged in the survey. For example, teachers identified disadvantages, such as students being off task or failing to attend when others (particularly poor readers) are reading; the time-consuming nature of round robin reading; the difficulty and discomfort experienced by those students who are not reading on grade level; the pressure exerted on students who struggle; the recognition that struggling readers provide poor models of fluency; and a lack of sufficient time to assess individual readers properly.

Similarly, when teachers who used round robin reading practices were asked to identify how students responded to the practices, they suggested overwhelmingly that their students enjoyed round robin reading. (Although one teacher gave the very telling response, "I can't say that any student of mine really loves oral reading, but they do it anyway") However, when asked to consider if all of their students responded in the same way, teachers often backed away from this assertion.

Teachers suggested that struggling readers, proficient readers, English language learners, students with learning disabilities, students with behavioral/emotional disabilities, students with attention-deficit/hyperactivity disorder, and students with other identified special education needs did not enjoy round robin reading. These students responded (according to the teachers' own observations) with avoidance of reading, emotional distress, off-task behavior, and preference for other methods of reading.

Students who avoided reading did things such as refusing to read aloud, avoiding eye contact, asking to go the bathroom, giving up and asking other students to read for them, asking to be skipped, "trying to disappear," and coming to the teacher ahead of time and asking to read shorter pieces of text aloud. In addition to avoiding reading, students who struggled indicated their emotional distress through reluctance, embarrassment, stress, shyness, and fear. Other students also felt frustrated by slower readers.

Teachers also suggested that although they said students liked round robin reading, they experienced many off-task behaviors, including students losing attention/focus/place and students openly refusing to attend to the lesson (e.g., putting their heads down, not making eye contact). In the category of preference for other methods, it was suggested that students prefer to read alone rather than have to complete a "cold" read in front of others.

If you are ready to take the step away from round robin reading, welcome. We believe that a number of strategies here, and throughout the book, can help you break your addiction. However, if you think that round robin reading is working in your classroom, we would like for you to take a week when you closely observe all of your readers while you are engaging in round robin reading. Ask your students how they feel about it and why. Assess their comprehension, and compare it to their comprehension when using a practice such as jigsaw. Ask yourself if the benefits that you perceive in round robin reading really exist, and if they really outweigh having the students avoid reading, feel humiliated or frustrated, or act out. Then, if you feel you are ready, come back to this chapter and its practices. And in the words of RRRA, "Keep coming back!"

REFERENCES

Allington, R. L. (1977). If they don't read much, how are they ever going to get good? *Journal of Reading, 21,* 57–61.

Allington, R. L. (1980). Teacher interruption behaviors during primary grade oral reading. *Journal of Educational Psychology, 72,* 371–377.

Aronson, E., Blaney, N., Sikes, J., Stephan, G., & Snapp, M. (1978). *The jigsaw classroom.* Beverly Hills, CA: Sage.

Aronson, E., Blaney, N. T., Stephan, C., Rosenfield, R., & Sikes, J. (1977). Interdependence in the classroom: A field study. *Journal of Educational Psychology, 69,* 121–128.

Ash, G. E. (2002, March). Teaching readers who struggle: A pragmatic middle school framework. *Reading online: The Online Journal of the International Reading Association, 5*(7). Available at www.readingonline.org/articles/art_index.asp?href=ash/index.html

Ash, G. E., & Kuhn, M. R. (2001, December). *Round Robin Reading Anonymous (RRRA): Investigating inservice and preservice teachers' continued pursuit of round robin reading*. Paper presented at the National Reading Conference, San Antonio, TX.

Ash, G. E., Kuhn, M. R., & Walpole, S. (2003, December). *Flying in the face of research: Inservice teachers and their use of round robin reading (research in progress)*. Paper presented at the National Reading Conference, Scottsdale, AZ.

Cox, C., & Zarrillo, J. (1993). *Teaching reading with children's literature*. New York: Macmillan.

Cunningham, P. M., & Allington, R. L. (1999). *Classrooms that work: They can all read and write* (2nd ed.). New York: Longman.

Fuchs, D., Fuchs, L. S., & Burish, P. (2000). Peer-assisted learning strategies: An evidence-based practice to promote reading achievement. *Learning Disabilities Research and Practice, 15*, 85–91.

Greene, F. (1979). Radio reading. In C. Pennock (Ed.), *Reading comprehension at four linguistic levels* (pp. 104–107). Newark, DE: International Reading Association.

Gunter, M., Estes, T., & Schwab, J. (1995). *Instruction: A models approach*. Needham Heights, MA: Allyn & Bacon.

Harris, T. L., & Hodges, R. R. (Eds.). (1995). *The literacy dictionary: The vocabulary of reading and writing*. Newark, DE: International Reading Association.

Ivey, G. (1999). A multicase study in the middle school: Complexities among young adolescent readers. *Reading Research Quarterly, 34*, 172–192.

Koskinen, P. S., & Blum, I. H. (1986). Paired repeated reading: A classroom strategy for developing fluent reading. *Reading Teacher, 40*, 70–75.

LaBerge, D., & Samuels, S. J. (1974). Toward a theory of automatic information processing in reading. *Cognitive Psychology, 6*, 293–323.

Martin, C. E., Martin, M. A., & O'Brien, D. G. (1984). Spawning ideas for writing in the content areas. *Reading World, 11*, 11–15.

Moje, E. B. (1996). "I teach students, not subjects": Teacher–student relationships as contexts for secondary literacy. *Reading Research Quarterly, 31*, 172–195.

Opitz, M. F., & Rasinski, T. V. (1998). *Good-bye round robin*. Portsmouth, NH: Heinemann.

Palincsar, A. S., & Brown, A. L. (1984). Reciprocal teaching of comprehension-fostering and comprehension-monitoring activities. *Cognition and Instruction, 2*, 117–175.

Sachar, L. (1998). *Holes*. New York: Farrar, Straus and Giroux.

Samuels, S. J. (1979). The method of repeated reading. *Reading Teacher, 32*, 403–408.

Santa, C. M., Isaacson, L., & Manning, G. (1987). Changing content instruction through action research. *Reading Teacher, 40*(4), 434–438.

Searfoss, L. (1975). Radio reading. *Reading Teacher, 29*, 295–296.

Stahl, S. A., Bradley, B. A., Smith, C. H., Kuhn, M. R., Schwanenflugel, P.,

Meisinger, B., et al. (2003, April). *Fluency-oriented reading instruction: Instructional effects*. Paper presented at the annual meeting of the American Educational Research Association, Chicago.

Stanovich, K. E. (1980). Toward an interactive compensatory model of individual differences in the development of reading fluency. *Reading Research Quarterly, 16,* 32–71.

Stanovich, K. E. (1986). Matthew effects in reading: Some consequences of individual differences in the acquisition of literacy. *Reading Research Quarterly, 21,* 360–407.

Vacca, R., & Vacca, J. (2005). *Content area reading* (8th ed.). Boston: Allyn & Bacon.

Wolf, S. A. (1998). The flight of reading: Shifts in instruction, orchestration, and attitudes through classroom theatre. *Reading Research Quarterly, 33,* 382–415.

CHAPTER 10

Paired Reading

Impact of a Tutoring Method on Reading Accuracy, Comprehension, and Fluency

KEITH J. TOPPING

WHAT IS FLUENCY?

Fluency is not an entity, benchmarkable competence, or static condition. Fluency is an adaptive, context-dependent process. Even expert readers will show dysfluency when confronted with a text on an unfamiliar topic that provides challenge greatly beyond their independent reading level, however high that level might be. Fluency is of little value in itself; its value lies in what it enables.

For silent reading, I define fluency as "the extraction of maximum meaning at maximum speed in a relatively continuous flow, leaving spare simultaneous processing capacity for other higher-order processes." This definition assumes the text is at an appropriate level of difficulty for the reader.

For reading out loud, the task (and therefore the definition) is more demanding, since among the higher-order processes, the reader must have an awareness of audience needs and the capability to manage the prosodic demands for expressiveness (varying phrasing, stress, intonation, pitch, rhythm, loudness, pauses, etc.).

Already two definitions of fluency have been implied, and it becomes more complex. Simple assumptions can prove misleading. For example, just reading faster might result in reduced accuracy. Fast reading, even if still accurately decoded, might not automatically result in good comprehension. A number of factors interact with each other in the area of fluency. An attempt is made to map these factors in the model of fluency presented here. All of this has implications for how we might effectively intervene to enhance fluency, and how we might usefully measure it.

This chapter thus asserts a fluid definition of fluency, conceptualized within an information-processing or "resource allocation" model, while mapping the many varieties of fluency and the consequently varied implications for intervention and measurement. Socioemotional factors are given equal prominence with cognitive aspects.

THE DEEP PROCESSING FLUENCY MODEL

The deep processing fluency (DPF) model presented here (Figure 10.1) groups relevant factors into four sectors, arranged sequentially:

- Predisposing factors
- Surface fluency factors
- Strategic fluency factors
- Deep fluency factors

This suggests further definitional complexity—three different kinds of fluency! These progress toward fluency as both input and output in the "deep processing" of reading. Additionally, even the apparent linearity of the model is beguiling, since there are feedback loops, including from "end" to "beginning." Actually the model is recursive. However, its components are explored here in a stepwise manner.

Predisposing factors facilitating the development of fluency ("entry skills," if you prefer) include:

- Management of text difficulty. (Since fluency is not likely to be developed on material that is much too hard or easy, have teachers leveled books and taught students readability self-checking strategies?)
- Time exposed; time on task; time engaged. (Simply allocating silent reading time is not enough. Have teachers ensured that time is allo-

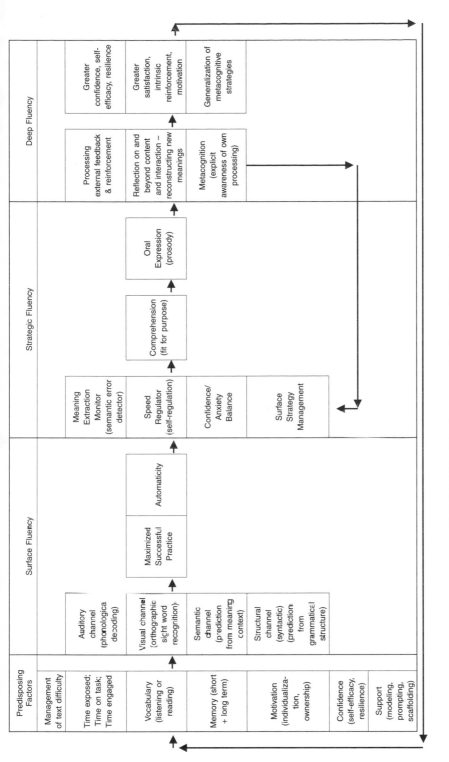

FIGURE 10.1. The deep processing fluency (DPF) model.

175

cated for reading to ensure exposure to text, and that that time is spent on task, and that that time is spent actually engaged with the task?)

- Vocabulary (listening or reading). (Have teachers, parents, and peers engaged students in increasingly complex dialogue and had them listen to stories to develop their receptive vocabulary and facilitate decoding when these words are encountered in print?)

- Memory (short and long term). (Both visual and verbal, short- and long-term memory are needed. Teachers can help develop memory but should avoid abstract games that might have no effects generalized to reading.)

- Motivation (individualization, ownership). (Have teachers considered individual student reading preferences, offered balanced access to fiction and nonfiction to tap existing motivation, respected multiple and gendered literacies and home cultures, and sought to bridge discontinuity between home, community, and school interests and competences, rather than promote only "schooled" literacy experiences?)

- Confidence (self-efficacy, resilience). (Have teachers created a classroom ethos free of a fear of failure, shame at error, and obsession with "the right answer," where strategic risk-taking is seen as normal? But beware abstract self-esteem-building exercises that might not generalize to reading. And remember that too much confidence is almost as unhelpful as too little; students benefit from high but realistic expectations.)

- Support (modeling, prompting, scaffolding). (Have teachers made available a variety of supports for those attacking texts above their current independent readability level—involving assistants, volunteers, or peers with modeling of fluent reading, prompting while reading, and other forms of scaffolding, such as audiotapes?)

Even if a highly energetic teacher were able to provide all these, different students always have different profiles of strengths and weaknesses across these factors. With luck and good management, they make the best of what they have available as they seek to develop fluency.

In developing "surface fluency," different students also have different profiles of strengths and weaknesses in the four major channels for extracting meaning:

- Auditory channel (phonological decoding)
- Visual channel (orthographic sight word recognition)
- Semantic channel (prediction from meaning context)
- Structural (syntactic) channel (prediction from grammatical structure)

Stanovich (1984) described this as an "interactive–compensatory" model. Of course, some written languages and some specific texts, or parts of texts, are intrinsically more accessible through particular channels (e.g., Finnish through the auditory channel, Mandarin through the visual channel). Unfortunately for our students, English is a complex mongrel language, requiring some capability in all channels.

Nonetheless, given reasonable availability of predisposing factors and reasonable competence in most, if not all, of the channels, students who have substantial practice at reading will over time develop automaticity in extracting meaning—it will become less effortful, require less concentration, use up fewer mental resources—until, of course, the difficulty of the book increases and the student has to start trying hard all over again. Some students prefer to avoid this never-ending struggle for self-improvement and might at the age of 7 decide that they can read ("fluently"), and coast along reading at that level for the rest of their lives. In fact, it is not "practice that makes perfect," but *successful* practice *at an appropriate level of difficulty* that yields wider automaticity. Consequently, teachers need to monitor not only volume of student practice in and out of school, but also its quality, its challenge level in relation to student proficiency, and the successfulness of that practice in leading to high-quality comprehension.

Some revealing quotes from students about their real reading strategies during sustained silent reading were recorded by Griffith and Rasinski (2004, p. 134):

> "I only read the third paragraph of each page. My teacher was always at her desk grading papers, so it didn't really matter."

> "I started at the top, skipped a hunk, and then read the bottom."

> "I lifted up the book in front of my face and looked for the 'fancy' words."

> "I looked at the pictures and then told the story by the pictures."

> "I wanted to read as fast as my friend, so I watched her as she read. I only read the bottom line of each page and turned the page when she did. But she made 100% on her Accelerated Reader quiz and I only made 20%."

Notwithstanding these difficulties and evasions, many students do achieve a reasonable degree of surface fluency, albeit in some cases almost accidentally; that is, given a book at their independent readability level, they can read it reasonably accurately, at a reasonable speed, and with reasonable continuity (this can be construed as a definition of surface fluency).

Some unfortunately see this as the end of the road. In fact, this automaticity gives them spare processing capacity that can be deployed to move on to the next stage of fluency development—strategic fluency.

However, moving on requires more focused strategy on the part of the reader. Some readers try to apply their strongest surface fluency channel to all words, on a "one size fits all" basis. Given the nature of the English language, this is only likely to be effective and efficient a quarter of the time. Other readers apply their strongest surface fluency channel to all words first, then quickly revert to their second strongest if that proves ineffective, and so on. Still other readers apply any channel that comes to mind, hoping for the best from random chance. However, the most capable readers tend to analyze the nature of the problem word and choose a channel they judge most likely to maximize success for that word. Such surface strategy management does not necessarily operate at an explicit level; it might have developed inductively or intuitively and been automatized without ever having been made explicit, much as how to ride a bicycle is rarely made explicit. It is typically done at considerable speed.

Furthermore, moving on also requires awareness that greater speed might result in reduced accuracy, and greater accuracy might result in reduced speed. It requires a balancing act between a notional meaning extraction monitor (semantic error detector) and a speed regulator in the child's brain, the balance suited to the purpose of the reading task in hand. The spare processing capacity available has to be able to handle two competing processes at the same time—and to do so at some speed. (Perhaps boys tend to be weaker readers because they can't multitask?). The well-known U-shaped relationship between anxiety and performance is also relevant here. If the student regards the book as easy, anxiety will be low and confidence high, and the speed regulator will be dominant: The student will read fast but possibly not accurately, even though the book is easy. If the student regards the book as hard, anxiety will be high and confidence low, and the meaning monitor will be dominant: The student will read accurately but very slowly. Of course, if speed becomes very slow, the interaction with memory becomes important; by the time the last word in the sentence has been decoded, the student has forgotten the beginning, let alone why on earth he or she wanted to read it in the first place.

If the student manages this balancing act with reasonable success, good comprehension will result. Remember (from Figure 10.1) that there are no guarantees that *surface* fluency will lead to good comprehension—only that it will lead to rapid and accurate decoding, which might be little

more than "barking at print." In strategic fluency, however, good comprehension is almost inevitable. Of course, there are interesting questions
about what exactly "good comprehension" is. Does it mean extracting
every last drop of meaning the author put in there? Was the author aware
of all the meaning that might be in there? And can any text mean exactly
the same to all readers? How "good" comprehension has to be might vary
according to the purposes and intentions of the reader—which might
change as they are reading the text.

Leaving such complexities aside for the moment, we now behold a
generally strategically fluent silent reader who is a "good comprehender."
The final step within strategic fluency requires even more spare processing capacity—moving to fluent oral reading with expression (prosody).
As noted earlier, this requires all of the foregoing; in addition, the reader
must have an awareness of audience needs and the capability to manage
the prosodic demands for expressiveness in response to audience needs
and text complexities (varying phrasing, stress, intonation, pitch, rhythm,
loudness, speed, pauses, etc.).

Having mastered all of this to a greater or lesser extent, our strategic
reader has good reason to feel pleased, but the next stage of deep fluency
beckons, which requires even more spare processing capacity—the ultimate goal in the DPF model. At this stage, readers not only have excellent comprehension of text content but also have spare capacity to go
beyond it in personal reflection on content—reconstructing new meanings. They are also able to process and reflect upon external feedback and
reinforcement, such as audience responses to a read-aloud. Perhaps most
importantly, they have spare capacity to begin to develop metacognition
(explicit awareness of the nature of their own processing, most and least
effective strategies in specific contexts, and their relative strengths and
weakness). This has connections to the Reutzel concept of "metafluency"
(see Chapter 4, this volume). Such explicit awareness is a prerequisite for
more effective self-regulation of deeply fluent reading, and the DPF model
(Figure 10.1) shows a feedback loop back into surface strategy management.

From these developments stem powerful socioemotional effects, not
the least of which are greater confidence, self-efficacy, and resilience as a
reader (and perhaps as a learner in general). The reader feels greater satisfaction, the intrinsic reinforcement and motivation that is associated
with learner autonomy. Additionally, the metacognitive awareness gained
in the area of reading might generalize spontaneously or deliberately to
other subjects or other aspects of the student's life.

Given that this definition of fluency is complex, there are many difficulties with measuring fluency in a reliable and valid way. This is all very well, the practitioner might think, but what am I supposed to *do* about it?

PAIRED READING (DUOLOG READING)

A method specifically designed for peer-assisted learning (also widely used by parents, classroom assistants, and volunteer tutors) is "paired reading" (PR). It features many of the desirable components in the model of fluency (Figure 10.1). Unfortunately, over the years, this name for this structured and well-evaluated method has sometimes been applied by other workers to vaguely similar or quite dissimilar practices that have not been evaluated. Consequently, the structured and evaluated method was renamed "duolog reading" in an attempt to establish a name that was more distinctive (this name was chosen by 100 teachers in Texas). In this chapter, however, I continue to refer to it by its original name.

The PR method for peer or parent tutoring is a form of supported oral reading that enables students to access and comprehend texts somewhat above their independent readability level, within a framework of predictable and nonintrusive error correction. This structured support used with high-motivation texts offers dysfluent readers a flow experience, which is likely to impact on their reading style and socioemotional aspects of the reading process.

What Is Paired Reading?

PR is a straightforward and generally enjoyable way for more able readers to help less able readers develop better reading skills (i.e., a form of cross-ability tutoring). Pairs should not be too distant in reading ability, or there is little chance of reading ability gains for the helpers. The method is adaptable to any reading material, and tutees select texts that are of intrinsic interest to them but a little above their independent readability level (otherwise, the support of PR is pointless). This might include newspapers, magazines, community literature, or texts in electronic environments. Of course, the texts must be within the independent readability level of the tutor, but a relatively modest differential in reading ability is recommended if the hope is to improve the reading of the tutor as well as the tutee. The pair might use the "five-finger test" of readability:

1. Open a page at random.
2. Spread five fingers on one hand.
3. Place fingertips on the page at random.
4. Tutor attempts to read the five words.
5. Repeat on another four pages.
6. If the tutor has struggled on more than one or two words, the book is too hard.

This is not perfectly scientific, but it gives the pair a ritual to remind them to think about readability. Additionally, if the tutee has a fanatical interest in one topic that is not shared by the tutor, a little negotiation about book choice is needed.

Encouragement to read "little but often" is usual. Pairs commit themselves to read at least three times per week for at least 10 minutes per session for at least 6 weeks. This frequency is needed in order to develop automaticity (fluency, even) with the technique, and to give it a fair test. At the end of 6 weeks, pairs consider whether they wish to continue with greater or lesser frequency, or at all, and perhaps vary partners or some aspect of the method.

The technique has two main aspects. Initially, tutor and tutee read out loud simultaneously in close synchrony. This is termed "reading together." The tutor adjusts their reading speed to the tutee's pace as necessary. The tutee must read all the words out loud correctly. Errors are corrected merely by the tutor again giving a perfect example of how to read the error word, and ensuring that the tutee repeats it correctly. Then the pair continues reading.

The second aspect is termed "reading alone." When the tutee feels confident enough to read a section of text unsupported, the tutee signals by a knock, nudge, or other nonverbal signal for the tutor to be silent. The tutor praises the tutee for taking this initiative, and subsequently praises the tutee very regularly, especially for mastering very difficult words or spontaneously self-correcting.

When the tutee makes an error when reading alone, the tutor corrects this as before (by modeling and ensuring perfect repetition), and then joins back in reading simultaneously. Any word not read correctly within a pause of 4 seconds in treated as an error—the tutee is not left to struggle. (However, tutors often have difficulty learning to give tutees this time to self-correct—without which they will never learn to self-correct). Throughout, there is a great deal of emphasis on praising the tutee for correct reading and pausing from time to time to discuss the meaning of the text. A flowchart describes the flow of the aspects of the technique (Figure 10.2).

Initially, much reading is usually done simultaneously, but as the tutee improves and makes more appropriate choices of reading materials, more and more independent reading occurs (until the tutee becomes more ambitious and chooses harder books, of course). Any tendency to rush on the part of the tutee is usually resolved by consistent use of the correction procedure (although sometimes a shorter pause is needed initially) and/or visually "pacing" the reading by the reader pointing to each word as it is to be pronounced (usually only on harder texts with smaller print and closer spacing).

Young readers sometimes assume that they are expected to read more and more alone as they get better at reading. In fact, this is only true if they stick to books of just the same difficulty. It is probably more advanta-

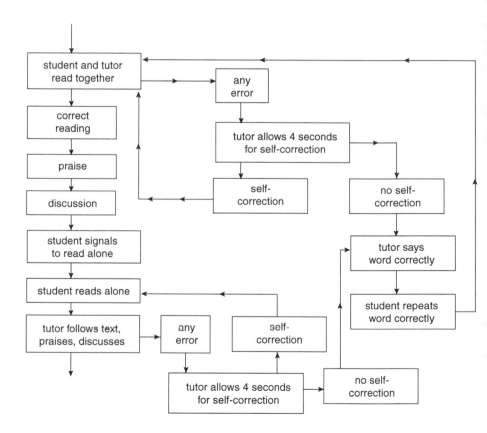

FIGURE 10.2. Paired reading.

geous if, as they get better, they tackle harder and harder books and there-fore still need a good deal of support from reading together. Some readers regard silent reading as the "grown-up" way of reading and might be resis-tant to reading together, especially if the point of it is not made clear to them and they do not use it to attack texts beyond their independent readability level.

PR can do a lot of good, but equally important is that it seems to do lit-tle harm and is widely ideologically acceptable. PR at home works in paral-lel with a school reading curriculum based on look-and-say, phonics, lan-guage experience, pictograms, precision teaching, direct instruction, or any other kind of approach. Those who wish to read more about the theoretical underpinnings of PR and its connections with the wider literature on how children learn to read should consult Topping and Lindsay (1992c).

It will now be clear that "paired reading" is a specific name for a spe-cific technique. It is *not* any old thing that two people feel like doing together with a book. Unfortunately, the name has become widely mis-used. You will often meet people who say, "Oh, yes, we do that paired reading." When you actually *look* at what they are doing, you often find that it is nothing like the specific method described earlier.

Further details of the method can be found in the sources listed in the Resources section at the end of the chapter, including specimen leaf-lets for peer and parent tutors, checklists for monitoring implementation integrity, and so on. Topping (2001) gives detailed organizational advice for planning and operating a good-quality implementation.

What Are the Advantages of Paired Reading?

1. Children are encouraged to pursue their own interests in reading material. They have more enthusiasm for reading about their own favorite things, and so try harder. PR gives them as much support as they need to read whatever book they choose.

2. Children are more in control of what's going on. Instead of having reading crammed into them, they make decisions themselves in the light of their own purposes (e.g., about choice of books, going on to reading alone, going on longer in the session).

3. There is no failure. It is impossible not to get a word right within 4 seconds or so.

4. PR is very flexible. The child decides how much support is neces-sary according to the current level of interest, mood, degree of tiredness, amount of confidence, difficulty of the books, and so on.

5. The child gets lots of praise. It's much nicer to be told when you're doing well, instead of just being moaned at when you go wrong.

6. There's lots of emphasis on understanding, getting the meaning out of the words, and that's what reading is all about. It's no use being able to read the words out loud mechanically without following the meaning.

7. PR gives continuity. It eliminates stopping and starting to "break up" hard words. Doing that often leaves children having forgotten the beginning of the sentence by the time they get to the end. With PR, it is easier for children to make sensible guesses at new words, based on the meaning of the surrounding words.

8. During reading together, a child can learn (by example) to read with expression and the right pacing (e.g., by copying how the tutor pauses at punctuation or gives emphasis to certain words).

9. Children are given a perfect example of how to pronounce difficult words, instead of being left to work it out themselves, and then perhaps thinking their own half-right efforts are actually 100% correct.

10. When doing PR, children get a bit of their own peaceful, private attention from their helper, which they might not otherwise have had. There is some evidence that just giving children more attention can actually improve their reading.

11. PR increases the amount of sheer reading practice children get. Because children are supported through books, they get through them faster. The number of books read in a week goes up, the number of words children look at in a week goes up, and more words stick in the child's memory.

12. PR gives tutors a clear, straightforward, and enjoyable way of helping their children—so no one gets confused, worried, or bad-tempered about reading.

In short, PR addresses many components of the process model of fluency (Figure 10.1). Additionally, an extended version of the technique (paired reading and thinking) provides a specific methodology to bridge students into strategic fluency and deep fluency (see Resources at the end of the chapter).

Does Paired Reading Work?

PR is a well-evaluated method and has been the focus of a great many studies over the years. The English government included it in their review of what works in literacy interventions (Brooks, 2002), and now recommends it as part of the national literacy strategy. Importantly, it has been shown to work both in carefully controlled research studies and in naturalistic large-scale field trials. It has been used as an intervention for students with reading delay, and also as a broad-spectrum mainstream method deployed inclusively for all students (although it tends to show larger effects with students with reading delay, it shows good effects for students with no delay). Gains in reading comprehension, as well as reading accuracy, are very commonly reported. The PR research literature has been reviewed by Topping and Lindsay (1992a) and Topping (1995, 2001).

Studies reported in the literature include 19 control or comparison group studies. Control group studies are generally considered by researchers to yield better quality data capable of supporting firmer conclusions. However, the quality of studies varies even within this category. Weaker studies might have flaws such as small size of experimental or control group, doubtful comparability of control and experimental groups irrespective of method of allocation to groups, impurity of PR technique as trained, and other atypical factors in project organization, such as poor monitoring, infrequent tutoring, overcontrol of reading materials, and unusually short or long project periods. Compensating research design strengths include blind testing and equivalent extra reading practice for control groups. Overall, in the 19 control group studies, the mean experimental accuracy gain was 2.5 times larger than the control group gain. For comprehension, experimental gain was 2.1 times larger than control gain. Where effect sizes were calculable for parent-tutored projects, the mean effect size was 1.6 for accuracy and 1.4 for comprehension. Where effect sizes were calculable for peer-tutored projects, the overall effect size for reading accuracy was 2.2, and that for reading comprehension 1.6 (but with great variability), including results from peer tutors and tutees. These effect sizes are large when compared to those cited in other meta-analytic reports. Fifteen studies compared PR to some other intervention technique. Overall, PR gains averaged 1.5 times alternative intervention gains.

Topping (1995) reported large-scale field study data from one school district, with a substantial majority of district schools participating (i.e., no selection of "cooperative" or "enthusiastic" schools). In 37 comparison or control group projects (n = 580 participant and 446 comparison children), scores in both accuracy and comprehension for participant children were statistically significantly greater than for controls. Overall effect sizes were 0.9 for reading accuracy and 0.8 for comprehension, less than reported on average in the literature (as might have been expected), but nevertheless substantial (although reduced by high control group variance). Twenty-three projects featured baseline measures (total n = 374), using each student as his or her own control over time. Overall, gains in the intervention phase in reading accuracy were twice as large as gains in the baseline period. However, in reading comprehension, both baseline and pre–post gains were high, and the difference not statistically significant. Follow-up data were gathered in 17 projects over short periods (typically 4 months) and longer periods (typically 12 months). PR students continued to show accelerated rates of gain over the follow-up period, although not as sharply as during the intensive phase of the intervention (some of these students would have continued with PR, some would not). There was no evidence of "washout" of experimental gains over time. It is considered unrealistic to expect acceleration at above-normal rates to continue indefinitely.

Children from all social classes were involved in projects, 60% of participants being of below-average socioeconomic status for this disadvantaged school district. There was a tendency for participants of lower socioeconomic status to make larger gains in reading accuracy. Gains in reading accuracy were similar for parent-tutored, same-age peer-tutored, and cross-age peer-tutored participants. Pre–post gains of peer tutors were greater than those of peer tutees in reading accuracy, but the difference was not statistically significant.

Data from 10 peer-tutor projects were reported in Topping (1987), the follow-up data in Topping (1992b), the socioeconomic data in Topping and Lindsay (1992b), data on the effectiveness of paired reading in ethnic minority homes in Topping (1992a), subjective feedback from a great many participants in Topping and Whiteley (1990), and the effect of gender differences in PR peer pairings in Topping and Whiteley (1993). Research on the use of PR with adults of restricted literacy was reported in Scoble, Topping and Wigglesworth (1988).

Subsequently, PR studies have emanated from a number of other countries, including Brazil (Cupolillo, Silva, Socorro, & Topping, 1997; Murad & Topping, 2000).

The most recent wave of research in the United Kingdom has been associated with the national Read On project (see Resources section at the end of the chapter for website link including evaluation), which focused mainly on classwide cross-age peer tutoring in elementary schools, developing PR into paired reading and thinking (PRT), and moving even further into strategic and deep fluency territory. Teachers participating in the Read On pilot project evaluation ($n = 34$) observed widespread gains in student motivation, confidence, and social relationships within the PR sessions, with substantial socioemotional effects generalized beyond the sessions, including impact on self-esteem. McKinstery and Topping (2003) found PRT very effective in high school settings, and Topping and Bryce (2004) found that PRT added value in thinking skills for tutees in elementary school when compared with standard PR.

What about Paired Reading and Fluency?

Given the difficulties of finding a measure of fluency that is more than superficial (mentioned earlier), directly researching the impact of PR on fluency in a way in keeping with the model of fluency (Figure 10.1) is a tough assignment. However, there have been some studies (often small-scale) that explored aspects of the model in relation to PR. These include studies of the impact of PR on fluency, reading style, self-correction rates, and reader confidence with both elementary and high school students. More detail of these studies may be found in Topping (1995); just the main findings are summarized here.

If children "learn to read by reading," one factor in the effectiveness of PR (or any supplemental tutoring intervention) might be expected to be the influence of extra reading practice alone. Thus, other things being equal, more time spent doing PR should be associated with greater gains in reading skill. Some workers have explored this relationship. However, only small correlation coefficients between reading accuracy/comprehension gains and time spent reading during a PR project have been found, so PR does not work merely by increasing time spent on reading, although it does that as well.

A number of studies have measured changes in rate of reading on fixed test passages on a pre- and post-PR basis. This has yielded somewhat various results (since for some children, to read more slowly is to read more effectively in terms of accuracy and comprehension, while for others the converse is true). Other researchers measured rate of reading on samples of text specifically selected for the purpose from a variety of sources. Several studies of changes in "reading style" have applied some form of miscue or error analysis on a pre–post basis, using parallel but different texts of similar readability on the two occasions. Four studies report data for reading style change from parent-tutored projects.

Considering parent- and peer-tutored studies together, in eight studies, error rates have been found to reduce in paired readers, and in no cases have error rates increased. In seven studies, paired readers showed decreases in rates of refusal to attempt to read a word, and in two cases an increase. In seven studies, use of context showed an increase; in one case no difference was found, and in no case was there a decrease. In four studies, the rate or speed of reading showed an increase, and in no case was there a decrease. In four studies, self-correction rate showed an increase, and in no case a decrease. In three studies, the use of phonics showed an increase, and in no case was there a decrease. Although not all these differences reached statistical significance (unsurprising in small-scale studies) and only a few studies used either nonparticipant control or alternative treatment comparison groups, strong consistent trends emerge from all these studies considered together.

The general pattern is of PR resulting in fewer refusals (greater confidence), greater fluency, greater use of the context, and a greater likelihood of self-correction, as well as fewer errors (greater accuracy) and better phonic skills. There are implications here for all stages of the DPF model (Figure 10.1).

SUMMARY AND CONCLUSION

Fluency is an adaptive, context-dependent process. On a text of an appropriate level of difficulty for the reader, it involves the extraction of maximum meaning at maximum speed in a relatively continuous flow, leaving spare simultaneous processing capacity for other higher-order processes. An information-processing or resource allocation model of fluency is proposed that groups relevant factors into four sectors: predisposing factors, surface fluency, strategic fluency, and deep fluency.

The specific structured method for peer, parent, or volunteer tutoring, known as paired reading (PR) or duolog reading, was described and its advantages outlined. PR is a well-evaluated method, has been the focus of a great many studies over the years, and is included in governmental evidence-based recommendations. Research has included many positive control and follow-up studies. Effect sizes from studies in the literature are very large, and those from unselected schools in districtwide field trials still substantial. Pre–post reading gains of peer tutors were greater than those of peer tutees. Weaker readers and those of lower socioeconomic status tended to gain more. PR does not work just by increasing time engaged with reading. PR has been found to result in fewer refusals (greater confidence), greater fluency, greater use of the context, and a greater likelihood of self-correction, as well as fewer errors (greater accuracy) and better phonic skills. There are implications here for all stages of the fluency model. PR has also now been broadened into PRT, extending higher-order reading skills (Topping, 2001).

REFERENCES

Brooks, G. (2002). *What works for children with literacy difficulties?: The effectiveness of intervention schemes*. London: Department for Education and Skills. Available at www.dfes.gov.uk/research/dara/uploadfiles/rr380.pdf

Cupolillo, M., Silva, R. S., Socorro, S., & Topping, K. J. (1997). Paired reading with Brazilian first-year school failures. *Educational Psychology in Practice, 13*(2), 96–100.

Griffith, L. W., & Rasinski, T. V. (2004). A focus on fluency: How one teacher incorporated fluency with her reading curriculum. *Reading Teacher, 58*(2), 126–137.

McKinstery, J., & Topping, K. J. (2003). Cross-age peer tutoring of thinking skills in the high school. *Educational Psychology in Practice, 19*, 199–217.

Murad, C. R., & Topping, K. J. (2000). Parents as reading tutors for first graders in Brazil. *School Psychology International, 21*(2), 152–171.

Scoble, J., Topping, K. J., & Wigglesworth, C. (1988). Training family and friends as adult literacy tutors. *Journal of Reading, 31*, 410–417.

Stanovich, K. E. (1984). The interactive–compensatory model of reading: A confluence of developmental, experimental, and education psychology. *Remedial and Special Education, 5*(3), 11–19.

Topping, K. J. (1987). Peer tutored paired reading: Outcome data from ten projects. *Educational Psychology, 7*, 133–145.

Topping, K. J. (1992a). The effectiveness of paired reading in ethnic minority homes. *Multicultural Teaching, 10*(2), 19–23.

Topping, K. J. (1992b). Short- and long-term follow-up of parental involvement in reading projects. *British Educational Research Journal, 18*, 369–379.

Topping, K. J. (1995). *Paired reading, spelling and writing: The handbook for teachers and parents*. London: Cassell.

Topping, K. J. (2001). *Thinking reading writing: A practical guide to paired learning with peers, parents and volunteers*. New York: Continuum.

Topping, K. J., & Bryce, A. (2004). Cross-age peer tutoring of reading and thinking: Influence on thinking skills. *Educational Psychology, 24*, 595–621.

Topping, K. J., & Hogan, J. (1999). *Read On: Paired reading and thinking video resource pack*. London: British Petroleum.

Topping, K. J., & Lindsay, G. A. (1992a). Paired reading: A review of the literature. *Research Papers in Education, 7*, 199–246.

Topping, K. J., & Lindsay, G. A. (1992b). Parental involvement in reading: The influence of socio-economic status and supportive home visiting. *Children and Society, 5,* 306–316.

Topping, K. J., & Lindsay, G. A. (1992c). The structure and development of the paired reading technique. *Journal of Research in Reading, 15,* 120–136.

Topping, K. J., & Whiteley, M. (1990). Participant evaluation of parent-tutored and peer-tutored projects in reading. *Educational Research, 32*(1), 14–32.

Topping, K. J., & Whiteley, M. (1993). Sex differences in the effectiveness of peer tutoring. *School Psychology International, 14*(1), 57–67.

RESOURCES

The Thinking, Reading, Writing website (www.dundee.ac.uk/fedsoc/research/projects/trw) has many free resources for PR and other methods associated with the book *Thinking Reading Writing* (Topping, 2001). The Web resources include the Topping (1995) review of outcome research on PR.

The Read On project website (www.dundee.ac.uk/fedsoc/research/projects/readon) includes many free practical resources, an online teacher's manual, data on evaluation, and links to online text for paired reading and thinking (www.dundee.ac.uk/fedsoc/research/projects/readon/onlinetext) and a video pack (below).

A video resource pack for peer tutoring in paired reading and paired thinking (Topping & Hogan, 1999) is also available (www.dundee.ac.uk/fedsoc/research/projects/readon/resourcesforteachers/downloads/BT-LT.pdf). Note that this video is VHS PAL, not VHS NTSC, which is common in North America. Modern multisystem video machines should handle both. The International Reading Association distributes a paired reading video pack made by the North Alberta Reading Specialist Council in consultation with the author (www.reading.org), which includes work with adults with reading difficulty. Renaissance Learning distributes a video pack in the United States, which focuses on peer tutoring in schools (www.renlearn.com), but look for the "new" name "duolog reading."

Topping, K. J. (1989). Lectura conjunta: Una poderosa técnica al servicio de los padres. *Comunicación, Lenguaje y Educación, 3–4,* 143-151. (Spanish translation of Topping, K. J. [1987]. Paired reading: A powerful technique for parent use. *Reading Teacher, 40,* 608–614.)

Topping, K. J. (2001). *Peer- and parent-assisted learning in reading, writing, spelling and thinking skills* (Spotlight No. 82). Edinburgh: Scottish Council for Research in Education. Available at www.scre.ac.uk/spotlight/spotlight82.html

Topping, K. J. (2001). *Peer assisted learning: A practical guide for teachers*. Cambridge, MA: Brookline Books.

Topping, K. J. (2001). *Tutoring by peers, family and volunteers*. Geneva, Switzerland: International Bureau of Education, United Nations Educational, Scientific and Cultural Organisation. (Also in translation in Catalan, Chinese, and Spanish.) Available at www.ibe.unesco.org/International/publications/educationalpractices/prachome.htm

Topping, K. J., & Ehly, S. (Eds.). (1998). *Peer-assisted learning*. Mahwah, NJ: Erlbaum.

CHAPTER 11

"Jonathon Is 11 but Reads Like a Struggling 7-Year-Old"

Providing Assistance for Struggling Readers with a Tape-Assisted Reading Program

MERYL-LYNN PLUCK

"Jonathon is 11 but reads like a struggling 7-year-old."

"Ben can't read even the simplest of books, and he'll be turning 9 next month."

"Jonathon decodes at a very slow pace, with no fluency at all."

"Katie can decode at a reasonable level, but her comprehension is very poor."

"Danielle is a very reluctant reader—she cannot read well and won't practice."

"Jason is 10 and refuses to read the books at his instructional reading level of 6 years."

Comments like these, substantiated by objective data, were typical of those written on the 85 referrals for reading assistance that flooded my desk when I was Resource Teacher of Reading (RTR) in Nelson, New Zealand. These 85 referrals were from 19 schools serviced by one RTR, and there were probably hundreds of other, equally needy students whose teachers hadn't bothered filling in referrals that they knew would get no further than my desk. What was I to do? Realistically, I could provide assistance to 10–12 students a year at most, if I ran myself ragged visiting students in their schools, tutoring them individually for half an hour, four times a week. Half of these students would be discontinued after a year; then they needed ongoing monitoring to ensure that they continued to make gains in their reading.

I was no mathematician, but it was obvious to me that I would never clear the backlog of current and future referrals in my lifetime. Also, decisions about who should be included on the roll when a space became available were extremely difficult to make. Would the best choice be a younger student who didn't have a lot of ground to cover to catch up, or an older student for whom this might be his or her last chance to receive specialized assistance? Also, with so many students awaiting assistance, how long could individual assistance be justified for those on the roll? Should I risk discontinuing students early if they had almost caught up with their peers but could so easily drop back without support?

When I sat down to consider what needed to be done, I knew I needed a program that would meet the needs of not only students waiting for assistance but also the many struggling readers who hadn't been referred for help. The program should also help the RTR to prioritize students who needed intensive individual instruction, and support those students who had recently been discontinued from the RTR roll but still needed support and practice. This program would need to reach readers at a "rainbow" of levels and their teachers as well.

Because I believed these students could be helped if I had the time and resources, it became a major concern to me that I wasn't doing anything. I started to lie awake at night worrying about what I wasn't doing for the struggling readers of Nelson! When I did sleep, I dreamed of illiterate, delinquent, suicidal teenagers!

A plan of action was clearly needed.

PROGRAM DESIGN

Looking at the economic and staffing realities, I wanted to set up an intervention that could be implemented easily, effectively, and economically by teachers and paraprofessionals in the schools. Being Reading Recovery–trained and further educated as a postgraduate at Auckland

University in the theory and practice of teaching older struggling readers, I had firm ideas about what would characterize an effective intervention. An effective intervention would need to

- Be capable of lifting, maintaining, and continuing to improve students' reading skills, including comprehension.
- Be supportive and nonthreatening for students who were afraid of failing.
- Be enjoyable for students who were turned off to reading.
- Result in improved attitudes toward reading.
- Provide a good model for students to aspire to and emulate.
- Engage students in lots of reading (Stanovich, 1992).
- Feature texts that were not only leveled so that students could experience success with them at their instructional reading levels but also of high interest for students whose interest levels exceeded their reading levels.
- Incorporate repeated reading (Samuels, 1979).
- Require students to demonstrate their reading to a tutor conversant with the techniques of praising, pausing, and prompting (McNaughton, Glynn, & Robinson, 1985).
- Encourage independence and allow students to make decisions and take control.

I had read about the success Chomsky (1976) and Carbo (1978) experienced with struggling readers using tape-assisted reading programs, and it became apparent to me that a form of tape-assisted reading could be tailored to incorporate the features I believed would make an effective intervention for the struggling readers in my district. Furthermore, I believed schools could implement such a program easily, that it would be cost-effective, because paraprofessionals could work with small groups of students, and that students would enjoy it.

Getting this program off the ground took many hours of seeking permission from publishers and authors to tape-record their stories, fundraising for equipment, book leveling, tape-recording and tape-copying, writing initial guidelines, and sorting and organizing equipment, staff, work spaces, and students. Fifteen schools in my district took up the challenge to make a difference for their struggling readers, and 43 of the 85 students referred for assistance and over 100 of their peers joined the program (Pluck, 1995) and became Rainbow Readers. The first pilot study would be used both to measure and to refine the process; it would be an example of formative research.

RAINBOW READING PILOT STUDY (PLUCK, 1995b)

Participants

Eighty-five students had been referred to the RTR for assistance with their reading and writing. These students, between 6.5 and 13.0 years of age, were from Nelson and Richmond primary and intermediate schools. Their instructional reading levels ranged from 5 years to over 13 years. Some students had been on Reading Recovery programs for 6-year-olds, and all were students for whom teachers had the most concern and difficulty in providing programs, because they had the most significant difficulties in reading in their schools.

Of the 85 referrals, 15 were found to be reading at levels considered at the time too low for Rainbow Reading (below 6.5 to 7-year reading levels), so they were initially tutored individually. They typically joined Rainbow Reading groups later, when their skills levels improved, but their data are not included in this study. Thirteen students were found to have reached reading levels at least equivalent to their chronological ages while they were awaiting assistance, so they were removed from the referral list. A further eight students had either moved away from the district or on to college (secondary school), where students cannot be assisted by the RTR.

The remaining 49 students were considered to have needs that could be met by the Rainbow Reading program. Their reading levels were below their chronological ages, yet they could read at or above the 6.5- to 7-year level. This group was reduced in number to 43, because six students moved away from the district during the year, and follow-up data were unavailable. The 43 Rainbow Reading students ranged in age from 7.8 to 12.8 years (average 10.1 years) at initial testing in February 1993. Their reading levels at this time range was 6.5–7 years to 10–11 years, with an average level of 8–8.5 years.

Measures

In February 1993, the 85 students who had been referred to the RTR for assistance with their reading were assessed using unseen graded text or

Informal Prose Inventory passages (New Zealand Department of Education Reading Advisory Service, 1984) to establish their current instructional reading levels. An "instructional reading level" was defined as the highest level a student could read after a minimal, standard orientation, with 90% accuracy or more. Comprehension was also checked, but for the purposes of this study was not used as a criterion for establishing reading level. For the 43 Rainbow Reading program students, this assessment was repeated in August, again in December by independent testers in schools, and yet again the following February. Students' instructional reading levels at initial assessment in February were their starting levels on the Rainbow Reading program, which for most began in March. If students were initially assessed as having an instructional reading level of 6.5–7 years, they started at the 7- to 7.5-year level, which was at the time the easiest level in the Rainbow Reading program.

Materials

With the help of generous donations, the following equipment was purchased by the RTR service and loaned to students: personal cassette players with headphones, battery chargers, rechargeable batteries, taped stories, book bags, and handbooks.

Stories used were chosen from *New Zealand School Journals* (these are published each year, so no date is given), which are distributed free of charge to all schools. Those chosen consisted of 130 short (200–600 words), high-interest stories and articles. Permission to record stories was obtained from the publisher and from authors. Stories were graded at six different levels of difficulty (7–12 years) according to the publishers' recommendations based on the Elley Noun Frequency Method (Elley & Croft, 1989). Stories were identified in the order of the colors in a rainbow, which resulted in the Rainbow Reading program name. Stories were recorded on tape by trained readers who read fluently but slowly enough for students to follow along. For ease of use, just one story was recorded on each tape.

The Instructional Setting and Tutors

Groups of between four and six students were withdrawn from their classrooms to work with teachers or paraprofessionals employed by the schools. Handbooks and minimal training were provided for tutors. Initial training of teachers and teacher aides took place in a large group of 40 interested people and lasted 45 minutes. Rainbow Reading practice can take place in students' classrooms, but all the tutors in this study preferred to withdraw students to practice. The places to which groups were withdrawn varied markedly, from libraries, staff rooms, spare classrooms, or offices to book storage rooms. In all cases, it was emphasized that Rainbow Reading practice was in addition to the regular classroom reading program.

Liaison and Monitoring

To ensure fidelity of treatment, liaison visits by the author, the RTR, initially took place fortnightly and were later reduced to just once every 3 weeks. During liaison visits, tapes were exchanged, students' and teachers' records in the students' handbooks were checked, and progress, promotion, and any concerns were discussed.

Instructional Process

The instructional process was also standardized, so that the treatment could be examined. Each school and tutor followed the same process and agreed that

- Schools would operate the program for an hour, five times a week, until students' instructional reading levels matched their chronological ages.
- Students would work with a teacher or paraprofessional in a small group of four to six students.
- Teachers could pull students out of their classroom for practice or work in the classes.
- Rainbow Reading practice should be in addition to the regular classroom reading program.
- Students would be assessed to determine their instructional reading level, the optimal starting level of the program.
- Students would read instructional-level material and receive an orientation to the book.
- Students would practice reading the book while listening to the audiotape until they believed they could read the book well without the tape.
- Students would read the book aloud independently to confirm whether they needed more practice with or without the book, or whether they were ready to conference with their teacher.

- During the conference, the teacher would listen to the student read and check for accuracy, comprehension, and fluency (expression). If the student reads easily with 95%+ accuracy, good understanding, and fluency, the process would begin again with a new book.
- A record of practice would be kept in the student's handbook, where the student noted the book titles and how many practices were needed before he or she could read the books easily. After each conference, the teacher would write a brief positive note about what he or she observed and recommendations for future practice.
- Students would be assessed for readiness to move on to a new level when they could read an unseen book at their current level easily, with good understanding and fluency. Alternatively, they could demonstrate readiness to practice with books at the next level if they could read unseen books at that next level with instructional accuracy.

Results

Forty-three students spent between 9 and 32 weeks (average 27.5 weeks) on the Rainbow Reading program. Time spent on the program varied due to factors such as the school or class timetable, availability of tutor time and space, student interest, or discontinuation because skills level had reached the point where continued practice on the program was no longer considered necessary.

Students made, on average, gains of 2.2 years and up to 4 years in their reading level. At retesting, in February 1994, 23 of the 43 students could read at levels equivalent to or higher than their chronological ages. These particular students averaged 28.2 weeks on the program.

Before students began practicing on the Rainbow Reading program, they were, on average, reading 1.7 years below their chronological ages; ranging between 0.5 and 3.5 years behind what is considered to be average for their ages. Twelve months later, after an average of 27.5 weeks on the program, and after a 6-week holiday break, students had improved their reading to the extent that they were reading on average just 0.5 years below their chronological ages.

The four students initially assessed as having instructional reading levels of 6.5–7 years all made significant progress, ranging from 1.75 to 2.75 years in reading level. The majority of students made the most progress in the first 18 weeks of their programs between March and August, only improving on average by 0.17 of a year between August and December. Most students continued to improve their reading level over the holiday break, making average gains of 0.4 year between December and February.

CONFIRMATORY STUDIES

Since the initiation of the program in Nelson, over two-thirds of New Zealand's schools have begun to use Rainbow Reading, and a number of action research and other studies have been carried out. Two that are reported here are of special interest, because the subjects were older students, typically with more delay, a longer history of struggle, and corresponding poor attitudes about learning to read.

Tape-Assisted Repeated Reading for a Group of Low-Progress Readers in a Secondary School

Langford (2001) chose Rainbow Reading as the intervention for her class of 15 low-progress readers (many of whom spoke English as a second language) from years 8–10 (12- to 14-year-olds) in an Auckland Secondary school. A paraprofessional facilitated the program, providing students with half an hour daily reading practice for 8 weeks. Analyses of test results revealed that students made on average 1.2 years progress in reading level and comprehension, along with an average gain of 9.7 months in word recognition skills. Five of the students made 2 years' progress in reading. The overwhelming response of the students to the program was positive. All 15 selected students agreed to participate, felt that they had made good progress, and enjoyed the sessions. The researcher concluded, "It is a very worthwhile intervention to recommend for secondary schools who need assistance in meeting the needs of their low-progress readers" (p. 21).

Is Tape-Assisted Reading an Effective Support Program?

Harlow (2001) introduced Rainbow Reading to year 8 (12- and 13-year-old) students in her Dunedin intermediate school, following the instructional protocol. Twenty-four students made average gains of 1.9 years in reading level (range: 1–3 years) in just 15 weeks on the program, as tested using the PROBE reading test (Prose Reading Observation, Behavior, and

Evaluation; 1999). The average number of Rainbow Reading levels (a level is equivalent to 12 months' progress in reading) moved was 3.6. The lowest number of levels moved was three, which was achieved by three students. The highest number of levels moved was five, which was achieved by two students. Harlow reported that

> children on the program made significant gains in their reading ability [and that] the program itself has proven to be an effective one. . . . It provides a good model by a good reader, it focuses on what reading is all about (understanding the author's intent), it reinforces and extends the child's existing language patterns, it allows for the much needed extra practice without pressure from others, it shifts the focus away from getting all the words right and the child has control over their learning environment. (p. 10)

Furthermore, students enjoyed the program, rarely had to be reminded to practice, asked to take the books home to read to their parents, and were generally very positive.

Using Audiotaped Read-Along Stories with Low-Progress Readers

In 2001, an action research study was commissioned to determine the effect of the program on students' reading, writing, and related skills (Nalder & Elley, 2004). In this study, 30 students in eight New Zealand elementary schools, who were, on average, 2 years behind in reading, were tutored with the Rainbow Reading tape-assisted program for 18 weeks. The research was designed to investigate whether, and how much, the Rainbow Reading program would assist slow-progress students of several age groups, across a range of schools. The students came from eight schools in suburban Auckland, the largest city in New Zealand.

The schools represented a wide range of socioeconomic levels, from below average to high, and included many different ethnic and language groups. At the outset of the study, the mean age of the subjects was 9 years, 6 months, with a range from 7 years, 2 months to 12 years, 2 months. The students for whom English was a second language (L2) came from a variety of countries, including Samoa (4), South Korea (3), Tonga (2), and several East European countries. Most had lived in New Zealand between 1 and 3 years, and most spoke their first language at home. Particular research questions were addressed:

1. How much progress in reading ability does a selected group of 30 low-progress readers make when students follow the tape-assisted Rainbow Reading program for a period of 4 months?
2. Do the benefits of such a program spread to writing, spelling, and oral language skills?
3. Do second language (L2) learners benefit as much as first language (L1) users?

The selected students were required to participate in the Rainbow Reading program at least four times each week, over a period of two school terms (18 weeks). Three students ended their treatment prior to the end of the two school terms (after 8, 11, and 12 weeks, respectively), because they had made enough progress to manage without further assistance, and four students continued for another 4–6 weeks, because they needed more time to be able to work at their current class level.

Even when a maturation factor was allowed for, results showed significant gains in reading age levels, in word recognition, reading accuracy, comprehension, writing fluency, spelling, and oral language, with L2 students showing strong gains. Because the intervention took place over a period of 4 months, it was judged important to allow for this time lapse in evaluating the results. Such an adjustment has not been common in earlier studies, because most delayed readers make little progress at all in an intervention of only 2 or 3 months. Hence, for each test with age norms, the actual pretest scores were increased by 2 months, which represents half the duration of the project. The assumption is made that these students, who had made less than half the normal rate of progress since starting school, might have been expected to make no more than 2 months' progress in the 4 months of the intervention. No such adjustment was made for the writing and oral language tests, because they had no age norms.

Reading Age Levels

All but two of the students made good progress up the Rainbow Reading Level (RRL) scale during the intervention. A sign test shows a significant difference ($z = 4.65$, $n = 29$, $p < .01$). Fourteen students were able to read text at a level over 2 years higher than that at which they started, and 12 more moved up by 1.8 years. With the aid of the audiotapes and guided practice, these 26 students, who had made so little progress before, had

202 BEST PROGRAMS, BEST PRACTICES

caught up over two grade levels on average, and were thus able to read books at their expected grade level.

Word Recognition

On the Burt Word Reading Test (1981), 24 out of 29 students (83%) showed greater progress than expected, and seven of them gained more than 12 months in the 4-month intervention. The researchers used a rank test of paired observations to test for significance and found a z score of 4.20 ($n = 28$), $p < .01$. On the skill of recognizing words in isolation, students have shown a significant improvement during the intervention. Six of the L2 students demonstrated noticeable gains of more than 12 months on this skill, while only one of the L1 students did so.

Reading Accuracy

On the Neale Accuracy Test (1999), 21 out of the 28 students (75%) showed greater progress than expected ($z = 3.66$, $n = 28$, $p < .01$), and three of them gained by 12 months or more. Their ability to read text aloud without error clearly improved during the intervention. Once again, the L2 students showed greater gains. In fact, the student profiles for word recognition and accuracy in reading text aloud were very similar. The gain scores rose and fell together.

Reading Comprehension

On the Neale Comprehension Test (1999), 17 students (out of 28) exceeded expectation, which was only just enough to show a marginally significant gain on a one-tailed test ($z = 2.05$, $n = 28$, $p < .05$). It seems that the ability to comprehend unfamiliar text while reading aloud is given a boost by a 4-month tape-assisted reading intervention, but the gain is less impressive than that for the other skills.

Spelling

On the Peters Spelling Test (1970), 18 out of 25 students (72%) exceeded expectation, indicating that there were positive effects on the students' spelling ability during the intervention ($z = 3.11$, $n = 25$, $p < .01$). Six students gained by more than a year. (The number of participants was reduced to 25 on this test due to absences.)

Writing

Although there were no norms in the writing test to allow for a matura-tion factor during the 4-month intervention, as there were for the previ-ously mentioned assessments, it was clear that most students made large gains in the volume of their writing. Overall, 25 out of 29 students showed gains in volume (86%), and 21 students increased their score by more than the standard deviation (16.0). The rank test for paired obser-vations produced a significant z value of 4.44 ($n = 29$, $p < .01$).

Oral Language

On the Van Hees Oral Language Pretest (1999), three students had a per-fect score, so with three absentees, the sample was reduced to 23. Of these students, 18 showed improvement (78%), and 13 improved by more than the pretest standard deviation of the whole group. The sign test was used to check significance, because there were many tied ranks, and the result-ing z value was 3.84 ($n = 23$, $p < .01$).

English Language Learners

The third research question asked whether L2 students had also benefited from a tape-assisted reading program. The researchers conclude that on this matter there is little room for doubt. The L2 students actually showed more consistent gains than the L1 students. Thus, the L1 students showed clear improvements in 71% of the comparisons made between their respective pre- and posttest scores, while the L2 students showed gains on 85%. The main difference was found in the Neale Comprehension Test, where L1 students showed gains on 47% of the comparisons, while L2 stu-dents showed gains on 85%. On all tests, L2 students improved as much or more than L1 students. Looked at another way, the rate of improve-ment for L2 students was more than twice the L1 rate in the case of read-ing comprehension and spelling, and almost as great (1.90 and 1.86 times the L1 gains) in the case of word recognition and reading accuracy, respectively.

The Highest and Lowest Achievers

When scores were compared across the measures, it was discovered that five students stood out because they showed very few gains. These students failed to show improvement on 51% of the test comparisons made, and these same students made minimal progress on the Rainbow Program also. Three of them moved up by less than a year, whereas the typical gain was over 2 years. Analysis of the research records showed that two of these students had fewer sessions than most, and another student was described as "low ability."

By contrast, 10 students stood out because they made impressive gains on most tests. For instance, an L2 (South Korean) student improved over 4 years on the Rainbow levels, over 2 years in spelling, and over 12 months in both word recognition and accuracy, in a period of only 4 months. The Rainbow Reading program was clearly of great benefit to him. The nine other "rapid recoverers" showed consistent gains in nearly every case, with several jumps of more than 2 years. Again, the improvement of the L2 students is apparent.

Teachers and students spoke positively about the program, and most students claimed to enjoy reading after the intervention. Further analysis showed that the students who read the most books during the intervention improved the most. The researchers noted that, in many cases, the program was not always administered as intended. For example, teachers had committed to implementing the program for half an hour, four times a week, but there were many distractions in that period. Thus, students had an average of 50.45 sessions, which is 22 fewer than the number prescribed. Under ideal conditions, the researchers reported, the level of impact might well have been greater. Nevertheless, the results were very pleasing. For students making regular progress, which these students were not, if we expect 1 month of gain for 1 month of instruction, we would expect these students to make 4 months' progress in their reading. These students, however, made, on average, gains of 26 months, or more than six times the expectation. The researchers concluded that there is a definite place for a tape-assisted reading program in helping low-progress students to improve their reading and language abilities.

GLOBAL INTEREST

With the introduction of a website, we started to get requests for information from all around the world. For example, there are many users in both Australia and Sweden, where the program is used to support students learning English as a second language. As an educator first and foremost, I was comfortable with sending our product to Australia and the United

Kingdom, where it was well-received by teachers and students. I was also comfortable with sending it to Sweden, where it was used very successfully to assist students learning to speak and read in English. We were actually highly amused, on a visit there, to be surrounded with New Zealand–sounding voices!

I was, however, far less comfortable about having our materials used in the United States in its current format with standard English spelling, New Zealand voices on the audiotapes, and topics and illustrations to which a lot of American students would not easily relate. However, materials adapted, rerecorded, and tailored to American students have been well received and widely used.

FUTURE DEVELOPMENTS

Innovation, it is clear, is never a finite business. The world changes, and ongoing research contributes to our knowledge and understanding, which influence how we, as educators, choose to teach, and what we, as publishers, choose to publish to support teachers. The latest research that has me buzzing with enthusiasm, and yes, has turned me back into an insomniac, centers around the hot topic of fluency. After my first perusal of Tim Rasinski's book *The Fluent Reader* (2003), I congratulated myself, because it seemed that our tape-assisted reading programs incorporated the key features of good fluency-building programs emerging around the world:

- Text at an appropriate level of difficulty.
- Repeated readings when students practice, with and without the audiotape.
- Modeled reading by the voice on the audiotape.
- Supported reading with the audiotape.
- Opportunities for students to respond to what they've read, with optional text-related activities.
- Performance demonstration when students read to their teacher.

Indeed, Rasinski (2003) refers to our program as being "synergistic" (p. 123) because it incorporates so many successful features and strategies of his own work. However, niggling at the back of my mind is the question most frequently asked of me by educators: "How do you get students, particularly the older ones, to engage in the repeated readings we know they need?" My answer usually involves factors relating to the nature of the books, such as having the books be of high interest and written in such a manner (often with a surprise ending) that students want to read them again and again.

Other suggestions are dependent on convincing the students that such practice is worthwhile or necessary:

- Explaining to students that repeated readings are a requirement of the program that will help them to become better readers.
- Comparing repeated reading to the practice students do in other areas of their life in which they want to achieve well, such as sports or music practice.
- Ensuring that when students demonstrate their reading to their teacher, it needs to be easy, fluent, and well understood before they are given permission to move on to another book. In other words, "If you're bored with the book you're reading, read it well, and you won't have to read it any more!"

When I attended the Fluency Institute at the International Reading Association in Orlando, Florida, in 2003, and learned more about Readers Theatre, I believed I'd been presented with the best means yet to get students to engage happily and willingly in repeated readings: They need to be fluent if they are going to perform for an audience of their peers. No student I've ever encountered wants to be perceived publicly as a stumbling reader. Repeated readings would definitely be needed to achieve the level of fluency required for performing to an audience or making a recording. And how much more powerful the scripts would be if they were accompanied by a specially prepared audiotape for modeling and support.

It has, hence, been my mission since attending the Institute to trial test Readers Theatre scripts in schools, and write the guidelines for teachers and students. Early indicators are that the teachers and students love them. There are no problems with getting students to engage in repeated reading practice. The biggest problem now is keeping the sessions to 30 minutes, because students and teachers simply don't want to stop practicing when they're having so much fun! As well as enjoying the practice, it is clear that students' fluency is also much improved, and both the presenters and the audience really look forward to performance days.

From the schools involved in field-testing the Readers Theatre and from those simply using the original texts, the comments I'm now more likely to receive from teachers are as follows:

"Ben is 11. He has no trouble with his reading since making over 4 years' progress in 2 years on the Rainbow Reading program."

"Jonathon loves books since he's been practicing on the New Heights Reading Program. He now reads with good pace and excellent expression."

"Katie's been working on New Heights, and her comprehension is much improved."

"Danielle is a no longer a reluctant reader. New Heights has helped her to become a much better reader, and she's now a bit of a bookworm."

"Jason is now 12. He has made fantastic progress in his reading, happily practicing with the Rainbow Reading books at his instructional reading level."

And last, one of my favorites:

"Jonathon is now 12 and, thanks, to Rainbow Reading, reads fluently at an age-appropriate level."

REFERENCES

Carbo, M. (1978). Teaching reading with talking books. *Reading Teacher, 32*(3), 267–273.

Chomsky, C. (1976). After decoding, what? *Language Arts, 53*(3), 288–296.

Elley, W. B., & Croft, A. C. (1989). *Assessing the difficulty of reading materials: The noun frequency method.* Wellington: New Zealand Council for Educational Research.

Harlow, S. (2001). *Is tape assisted reading an effective support program?* Unpublished manuscript.

Langford, J. (2001, July). Tape assisted reading for a group of low progress readers in a secondary school. *Reading Today for Tomorrow, Auckland Reading Association Newsletter,* pp. 14–21.

McNaughton, S., Glynn, T., & Robinson, V. (1985). *Pause, prompt and praise: Effective tutoring for remedial reading.* Birmingham, UK: Positive Products.

Nalder, S., & Elley, W. (2004). Interesting results from Rainbow Reading research, 2001–2003. *Reading Forum, 19*(1).

Neale, M. (1999). *Neale analysis of reading ability.* Melbourne: Australian Council for Educational Research.

New Zealand Council for Educational Research. (1981). *Burt Word Reading Test.* Wellington, NZ: Author.

New Zealand Department of Education Reading Advisory Service. (1984). *Informal Prose Inventory*. Wellington, NZ: Author.

New Zealand School Journals. Wellington, NZ: Learning Media, Ltd.

Peters, M. L. (1970). *Success in spelling*. Cambridge, UK: Cambridge Institute of Education.

Pluck, M. J. (1995). Rainbow Reading program: Using taped stories: The Nelson Project [*Reading Forum*, Term 1]. Auckland: New Zealand Reading Association.

PROBE (Prose Reading Observation, Behaviour and Evaluation of Comprehension). (1999). *Informal Reading Inventory*. Whangarei, New Zealand: Triune.

Rasinski, T. V. (2003). *The fluent reader: Oral reading strategies for building word recognition, fluency, and comprehension*. New York: Scholastic.

Samuels, S. J. (1979). The method of repeated readings. *Reading Teacher, 32*, 403–408.

Stanovich, K. (1992). Differences in reading acquisition: Causes and consequences [*Reading Forum*, Term 3]. Auckland: New Zealand Reading Association.

Van Hees, J. (1999). *Diagnostic and literacy assessment in English*. Auckland, New Zealand: Kohia Teachers' Center.

CONTACT INFORMATION
ABOUT COMMERCIALLY PRODUCED MATERIALS

New Heights. Learning Media Limited, Box 3293 Wellington 6001, New Zealand. Distributed in the United States by Pacific Learning, P.O. Box 2723, Huntington Beach, CA 92647-0723.

New Zealand School Journals. Learning Media Limited, Box 3293, Wellington 6001, New Zealand.

P.R.O.B.E (Prose Reading Observation, Behaviour and Evaluation of Comprehension). (1999). Informal Reading Inventory. Triune Publications, Box 10023 Te Mai, Whangarei, New Zealand.

Rainbow Reading Program. Rainbow Reading Program, Ltd., P.O. Box 561, Nelson, New Zealand.

CHAPTER 12

Readers Theatre across the Curriculum

LILA UBERT CARRICK

Readers Theatre is a highly motivational reading strategy that provides a context for purposeful reading. It is an interactive process in which students are actively involved in responding to and interpreting literature. It reinforces the social nature of reading, provides an occasion for students to work together in a cooperative learning environment, and enhances students' ability to understand and transform text (Stayter & Allington, 1991). According to Harris and Sipay (1990), script reading is one of the most interesting oral reading activities and encourages children to read using natural expression. In addition, Readers Theatre provides an opportunity for students to study literature, develop better speech habits, and participate in self-expressive activities before an audience (Coger & White, 1967).

WHAT IS READERS THEATRE?

Readers Theatre integrates oral reading, literature, and the performing arts. Unlike traditional theatre, Readers Theatre does not require makeup, sets, costumes, props, or memorization of lines; only a script is needed. Reading aloud from the script, the readers use their voices, facial expressions, and bodies to interpret the emotions, beliefs, attitudes, and motives of the character. The narrator "paints a picture" by communicating the story's setting and action and provides the commentary necessary for transition between scenes (Carrick, 2001).

Today, in an effort to improve the student's reading and writing ability and better standardized test scores, large blocks of time may be allotted to teach literacy in a teacher's daily schedule; therefore, little time remains to teach subjects of equal importance, including mathematics, science, and social studies. Moreover, teachers are encouraged or required to provide instruction in technology, the visual and performing arts, and world languages as set forth in the state's and/or district's curriculum content standards. As a result, classroom teachers are faced with the challenge of "finding time" in the daily schedule to teach all subjects.

One of the best solutions to this dilemma is to integrate language arts and a content area subject matter into one activity or experience. The multifaceted nature of Readers Theatre makes it a logical choice for integrating the content of several subjects across the curriculum, while at the same time addressing or meeting the standards. No extensive training or expensive materials and supplies are required; only a script is needed to implement this highly motivating reading strategy.

THEORETICAL AND RESEARCH FOUNDATIONS OF READERS THEATRE

Theories and Paradigms Supporting Readers Theatre

To understand and appreciate the educational value of using Readers Theatre as a reading strategy to promote fluency and comprehension, it is important to recognize the theoretical applications and research supporting the various aspects of Readers Theatre. Several of the theories of reading and educational paradigms embedded in the many facets of Readers Theatre are described in Table 12.1.

Research Supporting Readers Theatre

Support for Readers Theatre to promote fluency and comprehension can be found in repeated reading of the text and dramatically interacting with

TABLE 12.1. Theories and Paradigms Supporting Readers Theatre

Theory or paradigm	Description and effects
Automaticity (Samuels, 1979)	Through repeated reading of the text, the reader decodes words quickly and accurately and focuses attention on bringing meaning to the text.
Prosodic cuing (Schreiber, 1980)	Through repeated readings of the text, as well as hearing "fluent reading," the reader produces the appropriate phrasing of the sentences in a passage, which enables the reader to read with greater ease, reproduce the appropriate phrasing, and have a greater understanding of the reading task.
Transactional theory (Rosenblatt, 1978)	The reader and the text are partners in the interpretive process. The text acts as a stimulus for eliciting various past experiences, thoughts, and ideas from the reader. The reader takes an efferent or aesthetic stance when reading and participates in a transaction with the text to produce meaning.
Multiple intelligences (Gardner, 1985)	Verbal–linguistic, interpersonal, visual–spatial, or bodily kinesthetic intelligences allow for multiple ways of understanding.
Cooperative learning (Johnson & Johnson, 1985; Slavin, 1987)	Heterogeneous group of students work together on an activity or project, or to accomplish a task, which enhances both cognitive and social learning.

the text. Furthermore, studies demonstrate positive effects of Readers Theatre on fluency, comprehension, attitude toward reading, and appreciation of literature when used in whole-class and/or small-group instruction (Carrick, 2000; Maberry, 1975, Millin, 1996).

Several studies demonstrated that the practice of repeated reading of the text increases students' reading rate and word recognition (Dowhower, 1987; Rasinski, 1990b; Samuels, 1979). Furthermore, other studies revealed that students achieve significant gains in comprehension when using a repeated reading procedure (Chomsky, 1976; LaBerge & Samuels, 1974; O'Shea, Sindelar, & O'Shea, 1985). In addition, students with varying learning abilities became more fluent readers through the repeated reading of the text. These include students with learning disabilities (Rashotte & Torgesen, 1985), students with a mental handicap

(Samuels, 1979), and students who read below grade level (Carver & Hoffman, 1981; Herman, 1986), as well as those who function at grade level (Dowhower, 1987; O'Shea et al., 1985; Rasinski, 1990a).

Using drama as a whole-class teaching tool encourages participation of all children, regardless of academic ability. According to Wilhelm and Edmiston (1998, p. 30), "Drama is one of the most powerful discoveries and techniques at a teacher's disposal for helping students become more masterful readers and learners." Dramatic reading of the text provides the reader an opportunity to experience literature and identify with the story characters; therefore, the reader can become a character, interpret how and what the character feels, and understand what the character experiences (Stayter & Allington, 1991). The use of appropriate speech patterns and language, including voice quality, intonation, pitch, inflection, and volume to convey the physical and emotional state of a character promotes fluency. The ability to create and maintain a dramatic context requires the reader to think critically, ask questions, and evoke higher-order thinking and problem-solving skills (Booth, 1985); therefore, as thinking skills are sharpened, comprehension increases (Yaffee, 1989).

Even though Readers Theatre, as a reading strategy, has been used in the classroom for over 30 years, experimental studies investigating its effectiveness are limited. Maberry (1975) compared silent reading to listening to two oral interpretation methods, one a solo performance, and the other a Readers Theatre performance. Maberry's study revealed that high school students who listened to a Readers Theatre performance had higher comprehension scores, retained the material for a longer period of time, and had a greater appreciation of the literature when compared to the other two groups. Millin (1996) investigated the effectiveness of using Readers Theatre in small-group instruction in a pullout program with second graders who qualified for Title I services. This study demonstrated that students who participated in Readers Theatre read faster and more fluently, received higher comprehension scores, and had a more positive attitude toward reading compared to students who received traditional instruction that included worksheets, review of reading skills, and playing games. Carrick (2000) examined the effectiveness of using Readers Theatre on fluency and comprehension as whole-class instruction with fifth-grade students in regular education classrooms. When compared to groups using the traditional method of instruction, a basal reader, and groups using a paired reading method, the Readers Theatre groups revealed higher gains in fluency, including reading rate and word accuracy.

THE SCRIPT

Choosing a good script is the essential element to having successful Readers Theatre experiences. The script should be age- and grade-level appropriate, written at the readability level of the students engaged in reading the script, and interesting. Scripts should offer a rich vocabulary, be grammatically correct, and contain content area material (e.g., the water cycle, measurement, or Native American culture), and/or language arts topics (e.g., similes, fairytales, or cause and effect).

Readers Theatre scripts can be purchased through publishing companies, book vendors, or script services. In addition, many scripts suitable for a variety of grade and reading levels, and representing a range of genres and content matter, are available on the Internet. These scripts can be easily downloaded or printed and are generally available free of charge. Publishers' resources for Readers Theatre scripts are listed in Appendix 12.1; books that are written to be read by two or more readers and are easily adapted to Readers Theatre are listed in Appendix 12.2; and websites offering free Readers Theatre scripts are listed in Appendix 12.3. Educators and administrators should make themselves aware of all applicable copyright laws that allow for use of these scripts in the classroom. In addition, students can write and perform their own Readers Theatre scripts.

Creating a Script from Text

Creating a script from quality children's literature offers another option. Literature that contains lively, spirited dialogue and/or is written from the third-person point of view offers greater flexibility for developing a worthy script (Adams, 1999). A narrator's role should be evident, since the narrator describes the action of the characters, establishes the setting, and "paints the picture" for the listener.

Literature with a lively, spirited dialogue, such as *How Big Is a Foot* (Myller, 1991), *Moira's Birthday* (Munsch, 1987), and *I Wish I Were a Butterfly* (Howe, 1987), are excellent choices. Poems that can be scripted include "Casey at the Bat" by Earnest Thayer (1989) and "Crocodile's Toothache" by Shel Silverstein (1974). In addition, nonfiction or informational texts, such as *The Magic School Bus Inside a Hurricane* (Cole, 1996), *Heartland* (Siebert, 1995), and *Mojave* (Siebert, 1992), also lend themselves to being used as Readers Theatre material.

Procedures for converting the text of a book or poem into a script vary. Some teachers prefer to photocopy the pages of a book and then mark the speaking parts of each character and narrator, using different colors of high-lighter pens. Others prefer to convert the text into the script format. Some tips to consider when converting the text to a script (Adams, 1999) follow.

A character can read what he or she says, thinks, or does, including any actions. More than one narrator can be created for a script; however, it is important that the narrator remain the same for a specific character throughout the script. A narrator may be the narrator for more than one character as long as the narrator maintains these roles throughout the entire script. In keeping with the quality of good literature, if the text is too lengthy, it is considered acceptable to delete words or sections of the text. Repetitious phrases such as "he said" or "asked the girl" can be eliminated once the character has been solidly identified. It is considered unacceptable to add words or change the wording of the text, because then it is no longer the original work of the author.

The procedure (Adams, 1999) to convert text into a script is as follows: To mark the text and distinguish the speaking parts of the characters and narrators, place a solid line or bracket at the beginning and ending of what a character or narrator says. Above this bracketed text place a symbol, initial, or word to indicate who speaks that amount of text. An example of how to mark the text (*described in italics*) follows:

$$N_1$$

[One hot, sultry day Brett and Greg were walking home from soccer practice when they noticed a huge object on Brett's lawn].
- *Place a mark [in front of "One" and behind "lawn"].*
- *Above this sentence write* N_1 (Narrator 1).

$$B \qquad\qquad N_1$$

["What is that?"] [shrieked Brett.]
- *Place a mark [in front of "What" and behind "that"].*
- *Above this sentence write* B (Brett).
- *Place a mark [in front of "shrieked" and behind "Brett"].*
- *Above this sentence write* N_1 (Narrator 1).

$$G \qquad\qquad N_2$$

["It looks like a spaceship,"] [replied Greg.]
- *Place a mark [in front of "It" and behind "spaceship"]. Above this sentence write* G (Greg).
- *Place a mark [in front of "replied" and behind "Greg"].*
- *Above this sentence write* N_2 (Narrator 2).

N_3

[The door on the object began to open and an odd-looking creature began to emerge.]

- *Place a mark [in front of "The" and behind "emerge"].*
- *Above this sentence write* **N_3** (Narrator 3).

G **N_2**

["Let's get out of here!"] [shouted Greg.]

- *Place a mark [in front of "Let's" and behind "here"].*
- *Above this sentence write* **G** (Greg).
- *Place a mark [in front of "shouted" and behind "Greg"].*
- *Above this sentence write* **N_2** (Narrator 2).

N_1 and N_2 **N_3**

[Before the boys could run,] [a creature with eyes like a frog and legs like an octopus stepped out.]

- *Place a mark [in front of "Before" and behind "run"].*
- *Above this sentence write* **N_1** and **N_2** (Narrators 1 and 2 speaking together indicating both boys).
- *Place a mark [in front of " a" and behind "out"].*
- *Above this sentence write* **N_3** (Narrator 3).

C **N_3** **C**

["I am famished,"] [said the creature.] ["A round, dirty, tasty, rubbery soccer ball is just what I need."]

- *Place a mark [in front "I" and behind "famished"].*
- *Above this sentence write* **C** (Creature).
- *Place a mark [in front of "said" and behind "creature"].*
- *Above this sentence write* **N_3** (Narrator 3).
- *Place a mark [in front of "A" and behind "need"].*
- *Above this sentence write* **C** (Creature).

B

["Not my soccer ball."], ~~said Brett.~~

- *Place a mark [in front of "What" and behind "that"].*
- *Above this sentence write* **B** (Brett).
- *Mark through "said Brett." (Brett at this point in the text is identified and recognized in the text/script; therefore, repeated phrases like "said Brett" or "he said" can be deleted from this point on in the script.)*

After the text has been marked, the text can be formatted into a script in which each of the speaking parts is identified.

NARRATOR 1: One hot, sultry day Brett and Greg were walking home from soccer practice when they noticed a huge object on Brett's lawn.

BRETT: What is that?

NARRATOR 1: Shrieked Brett.

GREG: It looks like a spaceship.

NARRATOR 2: Replied Greg.

NARRATOR 3: The door on the object began to open and an odd-looking creature began to emerge.

GREG: Let's get out of here!

NARRATOR 2: Shouted Greg.

NARRATORS 1 AND 2: Before the boys could run,

NARRATOR 3: A creature with eyes like a frog and legs like an octopus stepped out.

CREATURE: I am famished.

NARRATOR 3: Said the creature.

CREATURE: A round, dirty, tasty, rubbery soccer ball is just what I need.

BRETT: Not my soccer ball.

After the text has been arranged into a script and the appropriate number of copies made, individual scripts can be stapled into a manila folder for durability. A teacher's copy (director's copy) can be developed in the same manner. This copy can be used to indicate content to be addressed or taught (e.g., vocabulary words, content material, examples of writing techniques, cause and effect, main idea and detail, and figurative language), questions, or thoughts.

A PROCEDURE FOR IMPLEMENTING READERS THEATRE IN THE CLASSROOM

Using a Readers Theatre script to teach reading or content area subject matter can last several days, varying with the length of the script and the amount of daily class time set apart for reading. The average time spent on one script is generally 5–10 days. Shorter scripts and poetry may take less time. The following is a day-by-day outline of how a 5-day project might progress (Carrick, 2001):

Day 1

- Give a copy of the script to each student.
- Read the title of the script and its author.
- Ask students to make predictions about the story, characters, and so forth.
- Read the script orally to the students as they follow along, looking at their copy of the script.
- Upon completion of reading the script, ask for feedback: What did you like about the story? Is this story similar to another story you read? Were our predictions correct? Did anything in the story surprise you? What questions do you have about the story?
- With student input, create a list of vocabulary words from the script. Write the words on the board or on large sheets of paper. Keep the list posted while the script is being used and refer to the list daily, focusing on the pronunciation, spelling, and meaning of the words.

Day 2

- Divide the class into groups of two. Assign a number of pages to be read, keeping in mind that a longer script can be divided into several parts. Students should take turns reading every other entry in the script; this ensures that they will all have the same amount of material to read. If students finish before the end of the assigned reading time, they can read the selection again and read entries other than the ones they initially read.
- While the students read the script, the teacher circulates around the room and offers assistance in pronouncing the words correctly, reading with feeling and emotion, and reading at an appropriate rate and volume.
- Close the session by doing a group read-around of the script or by assigning roles and having students perform a segment of the script.

Days 3 and 4

- Continue the paired repeated reading and circulating and modeling, until all students read the entire script.

- Once the students become familiar with the script, they can begin working in groups of three or more students, with each group member reading an assigned role or roles.

Day 5

- *Option 1*: Assign parts and let the students perform informally for their class or for other classes. To avoid having students with smaller parts see themselves as poorer readers or lose interest or enthusiasm in reading, every student should be given the opportunity to read as equal a portion of the script as possible. To accomplish equality among the readers in the amount of material read, assign readers more than one part or role.
- *Option 2*: On certain occasions, the students can engage in giving a performance on a grander scale. Assigning roles, transforming the class-room into a theatre, and issuing an invitation to other classes or parents is generally well received by the performers and audience alike. Such a pro-duction may feature two or three groups of readers, with each group read-ing a different script. These productions may have a theme (e.g., insects, mathematics, holidays, or deserts). See Figure 12.1 for an example of an invitation to a Readers Theatre performance.

Readers Theatre is a suitable activity for thematic teaching, teaching content area material, or teaching a specific unit. For example, a unit on Native Americans can include scripting both *Knots on a Counting Rope* (Archambault & Martin, 1997) and *Jumping Mouse* (Steptoe, 1984), and downloading "The Hidden One" (1995d) from Aaron Shepard's website (www.aaronshep.com/rt/rte.html).

Scripts for a unit on fables are available from Lisa Blau's website (www.lisablau.com/freescripts.html) and include "The City Mouse and the Country Mouse" (1998b), "The Lion and the Mouse" (1998c), and "Belling the Cat" (1998a). In addition fables are available in *A Readers Theatre Treasury of Stories* (Braun & Braun, 1996) including "The Ant and the Grasshopper," "The Goose That Laid the Golden Egg," and "The Miller, The Boy, and the Donkey."

A unit on multicultural folktales can be obtained by downloading scripts from Aaron Shepard's website (www.aaronshep.com/rt/rte.html), and include "The Calabash Kids: A Tale of Tanzania" (1995b), "A Frog Who Went to Heaven: A Tale of Angola" (1995c), and "The Sea King's Daughter: A Russian Legend" (1995e).

A unit on measurement could include scripting the following books:

Mrs. Henderson's Third-Grade Class Presents a Holiday Readers Theatre Performance:

The Baker's Dozen (Shepard, 1995)

Even Steven Odd Todd (Cristaldi, 1996)

The Seven Days of Kwanzaa (Pieffinger, 1994)

The Night Before Christmas (Moore, in Braun & Braun, 1996)

You are invited to a

Winter Readers Theatre Performance.

It will be held at Pioneer School,

Friday morning, December 23, 2006,

in Room 207, at 11:30 AM.

FIGURE 12.1. Invitation to a Readers Theatre performance.

How Big is a Foot (Myller, 1991) can be scripted to teach nonstandard measurement, and linear measurement such as feet and inches, and *50 below Zero* (Munsch, 1989) can be scripted to teach temperature.

CLASSROOM APPLICATIONS

Readers Theatre scripts, whether taken from the Internet, from books of scripts, or created by the teacher or students from literature, can be used to teach a variety of concepts and skills. For example, a script at the

Aaron Shepard site, "The Baker's Dozen: A Saint Nicholas Tale" (1995a), supplies content that can be used to teach concepts or reading skills, as well as mathematics or social studies concepts. In this story, the origin of the term "baker's dozen" is told through the eyes of a baker, Van Amsterdam, who owns and operates a very successful bakery in Colonial New York. Van Amsterdam prides himself on his baked goods and gives his customers exactly what they ask for, nothing more, nothing less. However, this practice eventually ruins his business. Then, on St. Nicholas Day, December 6, an old woman visits his bakery and he learns the true meaning of generosity. Reading activities to accompany this script include the following:

- Compare and contrast the script version of the story to another version of the story, such as *The Baker's Dozen: A Colonial American Tale* (Forest, 1993).
- Choose a character in the story. Determine the character traits, and justify these traits using examples from the script, using a character traits chart (see Figure 12.2).
- Sequence the important events of the story.
- Find examples of cause and effect in the story. This could include a singular cause and effect or several causes leading to one effect.

Social studies activities could include researching the following:

- From where did the Dutch settlers come?
- Why did they come to America?

Character: The Baker	
Trait	Prove it
Honest	He balanced and checked his scales; he took care of his customers and gave them exactly what they paid for.
Sad	His customers left; his bakery goods did not turn out right, and he went sadly to bed.
Wanted customers in his shop	After his dream, he began baking, and when the old lady visited his shop, he gave her 13 cookies.
Successful	"He had more customers than ever." "He grew wealthy."

FIGURE 12.2. Character traits and prove-it chart.

- Where was New Amsterdam, and how did the Dutch Colonists acquire it?
- Compare and contrast winter holiday events or celebrations around the world.

Mathematics activities to accompany this script include the following:

- Using a recipe, make gingerbread cookies, or use a recipe and make a frosting and have the students decorate cookies as described in the script.
- According to the script, St. Nicholas Day is December 6. With the students, generate a list of things, terms, and so forth, that can be associated with the word or number *six* (see Figure 12.3).
- Having completed the chart about the number six, have the students, working independently or in small groups, make a list about the number 12 and compare their lists.

Things about the Number 6	
Soda comes in a six-pack.	There are six colors of M&M's.
I live a 66 Elm Street.	June is the sixth month.
My birthday is February 6.	An insect has six legs.
I have #6 on my soccer jersey.	Saturn is the sixth planet.
Six-Flags Amusement Park	It can be written three ways: 6, six, VI.
There are six grades in our school.	I have six brothers and sisters.
My brother is in the sixth grade.	There are six people in my family.
Six is a half-dozen.	My sister is six years old.
John Quincy Adams was the sixth president of the United States.	Massachusetts was the sixth state admitted to the Union (ratify the Constitution).
F is the sixth letter of the alphabet.	Six is an even number.
A fact family of 6 is: $4 + 2 = 6$; $2 + 4 = 6$; $6 - 4 = 2$; $6 - 2 = 4$	There are six habitable continents—excluding Antarctica.
There are six players on a hockey team.	6 on a clock can be 6 A.M. or 6 P.M.
A cube has six faces.	A hexagon has six sides.

FIGURE 12.3. Number 6 activity (grades 2 and up).

ASSESSMENT

"Readers Theatre is enhanced by evaluation that supports student learning" (Dixon, Davies, & Politano, 1996, p. 97). Several aspects of fluency, including volume, rate, tempo, pitch, and intonation, can be measured when students are familiar with a script (see Figure 12.4). Elements of making an oral presentation, such as stance, posture, and mannerisms, can also be measured. Evaluation may focus on how students work together as a group. Furthermore, it can measure comprehension, including skills such as cause and effect, sequencing, or main idea and details; concepts that were features of the script, such as characterization (see Figure 12.5) and story elements; and vocabulary. Using a self-evaluation tool,

Student									Date
Script									
	Low							High	
Volume	Weak, too soft, voice does not project	1	2	3	4	5	6	7	Strong, loud
Clarity	Unclear	1	2	3	4	5	6	7	Clear
Intonation	Reads at one tone without any inflections or emotions	1	2	3	4	5	6	7	Uses pitch, stress, emotions, inflections
Tempo	Too fast or too slow	1	2	3	4	5	6	7	Appropriate rate
Punctuation	Ignores punctuation markers	1	2	3	4	5	6	7	Uses punctuation markers
Comments									

FIGURE 12.4. Fluency Evaluation Form (Carrick, 2000; Dixon, Davies, & Politano, 1996).

Name	Date
Script	
Role or character	
I learned several things about my character. These include . . .	
In the beginning of the script my character feels, seems, thinks, does, acts . . .	
At the end of the script my character feels, seems, thinks, does, acts . . .	
I think this change happens because . . .	
If I could talk to my character, I would ask or tell my character . . .	

FIGURE 12.5. Character Assessment Form (Carrick, 2000; Dixon, Davies, & Politano, 1996). The narrator can choose a character from the scripts and complete the form.

students can reflect on how they feel about Readers Theatre, what they need to improve, and how they worked as a group or with other group members (see Figure 12.6). An audio- or videotape of the Readers Theatre activities or the final performance can also be used as an evaluation tool and can be placed in students' portfolios.

CONCLUSION

Readers Theatre is an interactive activity in which students are energized and actively involved in responding to, interacting with, and interpreting a text. The nature of Readers Theatre demonstrates the social aspect of

Name   Date
Today, during Readers Theatre I . . .
In reading the script, I am really good at . . .
In reading the script, I need to improve at . . .
I plan to improve by doing the following . . .
Things I like about Readers Theatre are . . .
If I could change anything about Readers Theatre, I would . . .
I would like my teacher to know the following about my experience with this script, with my group, or with Readers Theatre . . .

FIGURE 12.6. Student Self-Evaluation Form (Carrick, 2000; Dixon, Davies, & Politano, 1996).

reading and provides a cooperative learning environment, where students of varying abilities can work together as a team. Readers Theatre brings energy and excitement to the classroom and acquaints students with the element of drama, while integrating literacy and content area learning. It magically transforms any classroom into a stage (Carrick, 2001).

Even the most reluctant readers become enthusiastic about reading and experience confidence in reading and speaking before a group. Students of a wide range of reading abilities indicate that they read more fluently, recognize and pronounce more words, and read using the punctuation markers; furthermore, they look forward to Readers Theatre time and wish "it would last forever" (Carrick, 2000, p. 136).

By utilizing the techniques and information described in this chapter, the teacher can raise the curtain in the classroom, encourage every reader to take center stage, and provide every reader the opportunity to be a star.

APPENDIX 12.1. PUBLISHED RESOURCES
FOR READERS THEATRE SCRIPTS

Braun, W., & Braun, C. (1995a). *Readers Theatre: More scripted rhymes and rhythms*. Calgary, AL, Canada: Braun and Braun Educational Enterprises.

Braun, W., & Braun, C. (1995b). *Readers Theatre: Scripted rhymes and rhythms*. Calgary, AL, Canada: Braun and Braun Educational Enterprises.

Braun, W., & Braun, C. (1996). *A Readers Theatre treasury of stories*. Calgary, AL, Canada: Braun and Braun Educational Enterprises.

Braun, W., & Braun, C. (1998). *Readers Theatre for young children*. Calgary, AL, Canada: Braun and Braun Educational Enterprises.

Crawford, S. A., & Sanders, N. I. (1999). *15 irresistible mini-plays for teaching math*. New York: Scholastic.

Crawford, S. A., & Sanders, N. I. (2000). *25 science plays for emergent readers*. New York: Scholastic.

Crisco, B. L., & Lanasa, P. J. (1995). *Fairy tales for two readers*. Englewood, CO: Teacher Ideas Press.

Glassock, S. (1995). *10 American history plays for the classroom*. New York: Scholastic.

Glassock, S. (2001). *10 easy-to-read American history plays that reach all readers*. New York: Scholastic.

Haven, K. (1996). *Great moments in science*. Englewood, CO: Teacher Ideas Press.

McCann, A. (1994a). *Fable plays for oral reading*. North Billirica, MA: Curriculum Associates.

McCann, A. (1994b). *Fairy tale plays for oral reading*. North Billirica, MA: Curriculum Associates.

Pugliano-Martin, C. (1998). *25 just-right plays for emergent readers*. New York: Scholastic.

Pugliano-Martin, C. (1999). *25 emergent reader plays around the year*. New York: Scholastic.

Tripp, V. (1995). *Five plays for girls and boys to perform: The American Girl collection*. Middleton, WI: Pleasant Co. Publishing.

APPENDIX 12.2. BOOKS WRITTEN
FOR TWO OR MORE READERS

Archambault, J., & Martin, B., Jr. (1984). *Knots on a counting rope*. New York: Lothrop Lee & Shepard.

Baylor, B. (1978). *Everybody needs a rock*. New York: Atheneum.

Baylor, B. (1981). *When Clay sings*. New York: Holiday House Publishing.

Baylor, B. (1987). *The desert is theirs*. New York: Scott Foresman.

Baylor, B. (1993). *Desert voices*. New York: Aladdin Library.

Fleischman, P. (1988). *Joyful noise: Poems for two voices*. New York: Harper.

Fleischman, P. (1989). *I am Phoenix: Poems for two voices*. New York: Harper Trophy.

Fleischman, P. (2000). *Big talk: Poems for four voices*. Cambridge, MA: Candlewick Press.

Hoberman, M. A. (2001) *You read to me, I'll read to you: Very short stories to read together*. New York: Little, Brown.

Pappas, T. (1991). *Math talk: Mathematical ideas in poems for two voices*. San Carlos, CA: Wide World/Tetra.

APPENDIX 12.3. WEBSITE RESOURCES FOR READERS THEATRE SCRIPTS

Blau, L. *Monthly scripts reader's theatre language arts ideas*. Retrieved March 3, 2005, from www.lisablau.com/freescripts.html

Gallagher, C. *Teaching is a work of heart*. Retrieved March 3, 2005, from www.teachingheart.net/readerstheater.htm

Lansky, B. *Classroom theatre*. Retrieved March 3, 2005, from www.fictionteachers.com/classroomtheater/theater.html

Readinglady. *Teacher resource for elementary school comprehension, reading, writing, and books*. Retrieved March 3, 2005, from www.readinglady.com

Shepard, A. *Reader's Theatre (Readers Theatre, free scripts)* Retrieved March 4, 2005, from www.aaronshep.com/rt/rte.html

Swallow, R. *Readers Theatre and language arts for teachers*. Retrieved March 4, 2005, from www.surfcitydelux.com/readerstheater/index.html

Telus Learning Connection Project Centre. *Readers Theatre K–3*. Retrieved March 4, 2005, from www.readerstheatre.ecsd.net/

REFERENCES

Adams, W. (1999, July). *Script making for Readers Theatre*. Paper presented at the Readers Theatre Workshop, London, UK.

Blau, L. (1998a). Belling the cat. In *Monthly Script Reader's Theatre Language Arts Ideas*. Retrieved March 4, 2005, from www.lisablau.com/freescripts.html

Blau, L. (1998b). The city mouse and the country mouse. In *Monthly Script Reader's Theatre Language Arts Ideas*. Retrieved March 4, 2005, from www.lisablau.com/freescripts.html

Blau, L. (1998c). The lion and the mouse. In *Monthly Script Reader's Theatre Language Arts Ideas*. Retrieved March 4, 2005, from www.lisablau.com/freescripts.html

Booth, D. (1985). "Imaginary gardens with real toads": Reading and drama in education. *Theory Into Practice, 24,* 193–198.

Braun, W., & Braun, C. (1996). *A Readers Theatre treasury of stories*. Calgary, AL, Canada: Braun and Braun Educational Enterprises.

Carrick, L. U. (2000). *The effects of Readers Theatre on fluency and comprehension in fifth grade students in regular classrooms*. Unpublished doctoral dissertation, Lehigh University, Bethlehem, PA.

Carrick, L. U. (2001, July/August). Internet resources for conducting Readers Theatre. *Reading Online, 5*(1). Retrieved March 2, 2002, from www.reading-online.org/electronic/elec_index.asp?href=carrick/index.html

Carver, R. P., & Hoffman, J. V. (1981). The effect of practice through repeated reading on gain in reading ability using a computer-based instructional system. *Reading Research Quarterly, 16*, 374–390.

Chomsky, C. (1976). After decoding: What? *Language Arts, 53*, 288–314.

Coger, L., & White, M. (1967). *Readers Theatre handbook*. Glenview, IL: Scott, Foresman.

Cole, J. (1996). *The magic school bus inside a hurricane*. New York: Scholastic.

Cristaldi, K. (1996). *Even Steven odd Todd*. New York: Scholastic.

Dixon, N., Davies, A., & Politano, C. (1996). *Learning with Readers Theatre*. Winnipeg, MB, Canada: Peguis.

Dowhower, S. L. (1987). Effects of repeated reading on second-grade transitional readers' fluency and comprehension. *Reading Research Quarterly, 22*, 389–406.

Forest, H. (1993). *The baker's dozen: A colonial American tale*. New York: Voyager.

Gardner, H. (1985). *Frames of mind: The theory of multiple intelligences*. New York: Basic Books/HarperCollins

Harris, A. J., & Sipay, E. R. (1990). *How to increase reading ability: A guide to developmental and remedial methods* (9th ed.). White Plains, NY: Longman.

Herman, P. A. (1986). The effect of repeated reading on rate, speech pauses, and word recognition accuracy. *Reading Research Quarterly, 20*, 553–564.

Howe, J. (1987). *I wish I were a butterfly*. New York: Gulliver Books.

Johnson, D., & Johnson, R. (1985). The internal dynamics of cooperative learning groups. In R. Slavin, S. Sharon, S. Kagan, R. Hertz-Lazarowitz, C. Webb, & R. Schmuck (Eds.), *Learning to cooperate, cooperating to learn* (pp. 103–124). New York: Plenum Press.

LaBerge, D., & Samuels, S. J. (1974). Toward a theory of automatic information processing in reading. *Cognitive Psychology, 6*, 293–323.

Maberry, D. R. (1975). *A comparison of three techniques of teaching literature: Silent reading, solo performance, and Readers Theatre*. Unpublished doctoral dissertation, North Texas State University, Denton.

Millin, S. K. (1996). *Effect of Readers Theatre on oral reading ability and reading attitudes of second grade Title I students*. Unpublished doctoral dissertation, West Virginia University, Morgantown.

Moore, H. C. (1996). Twas the night before Christmas. In W. Braun & C. Braun, *A Readers Theatre treasury of stories* (pp. 23–26). Calgary, AL, Canada: Braun and Braun Educational Enterprises.

Munsch, R. (1987). *Moira's birthday*. Toronto, ON, Canada: Annick Press.

Munsch, R. (1989). *50 below zero*. Toronto, ON, Canada: Annick Press.

Myller, R. (1991). *How big is a foot?* New York: Random House.

O'Shea, L. J., Sindelar, P. T., & O'Shea, D. J. (1985). The effects of repeated readings and attention cues on reading fluency and comprehension. *Journal of Reading Behavior, 17*, 129–142.

Pieffinger. C. R. (1994). *Holiday Readers Theatre*. Englewood, CO: Teacher Ideas Press.

Rashotte, C. A., & Torgesen, J. K. (1985). Repeated reading and reading fluency in learning disabled children. *Reading Research Quarterly, 20*, 180–188.

Rasinski, T. V. (1990a). Effects of repeated reading and listening-while-reading on reading fluency. *Journal of Educational Research, 83*, 147–150.

Rasinski, T. V. (1990b). Investigating measures of reading fluency. *Educational Research Quarterly, 14*(3), 38–44.

Rosenblatt, L. (1978). *The reader, the text, the poem: The transactional theory of the literary work*. Carbondale: Southern Illinois University Press.

Samuels, S. J. (1979). The method of repeated reading. *The Reading Teacher, 32*, 403–408.

Schreiber, P. A. (1980). On the acquisition of reading fluency. *Journal of Reading, 12*, 177–186.

Shepard, A. (1995a). The baker's dozen: A Saint Nicholas tale. In *Reader's Theatre editions*. Retrieved March 4, 2005, from www.aaronshep.com

Shepard, A. (1995b). The calabash kids: A tale of Tanzania. In *Reader's Theatre editions*. Retrieved March 4, 2005, from www.aaronshep.com

Shepard, A. (1995c). A frog who went to heaven: A tale of Angola. In *Reader's Theatre editions*. Retrieved March 4, 2005, from www.aaronshep.com

Shepard, A. (1995d). The hidden one. In *Reader's Theatre editions*. Retrieved March 4, 2005, from www.aaronshep.com

Shepard, A. (1995e). The sea king's daughter: A Russian legend. In *Reader's Theatre editions*. Retrieved March 4, 2005, from www.aaronshep.com

Silverstein, S. (1974). *Where the sidewalk ends*. New York: Harper & Row.

Siebert, D. (1992). *Mojave*. New York: HarperCollins.

Siebert, D. (1995). *Heartland*. New York: HarperCollins.

Slavin, R. E. (1987). Cooperative learning and the cooperative school. *Educational Leadership, 45*(3), 7–13.

Stayter, F. Z., & Allington, R. (1991). Fluency and the understanding of texts. *Theory Into Practice, 30*, 143–148.

Steptoe, J. (1989). *The story of jumping mouse*. Blackburn, Lancashire, UK: Mulbery Books.

Thayer, E. L. (1989). *Casey at the bat*. New York: Platt & Munk.

Wilhelm, J. D., & Edmiston, B. (1998). *Imagining to learn: Inquiry, ethics, and integration through drama*. Portsmouth, NH: Heinemann.

Yaffee, S. H. (1989). Drama as a teaching tool. *Educational Leadership, 46*, 29–32.

PART III

Special Populations, Special Issues

CHAPTER 13

Reading Fluency and Comprehension in Adult English Language Learners

KRISTIN LEMS

Fluency is a concept of lively interest to reading theorists and practitioners. The term "fluent reading" is generally used to refer to reading in which a high degree of automaticity has been reached, decoding is no longer effortful, and attentional resources can be focused on construction of meaning (Samuels, 2002). It can be called a "multi-dimensional reading construct" (Rasinski, 1990, p. 43).

In this chapter, I refer to oral reading fluency as ORF, or "oral reading," rather than as "fluency," to consistently call the reader's attention to the fact that I am describing audible oral reading. "Fluency," on the other hand, refers to an abstract competence.

Oral reading fluency is important in the reading field due to its demonstrated robust correlation with silent reading comprehension and other measures of reading performance. In a wide variety of research studies, across different variables and populations, ORF assessments have been shown to correlate strongly with student scores on many reading tasks (Kuhn & Stahl, 2002). As a result, fluency measures are used in a growing number of school settings for placement, norming, referral for special services, and as a gauge of individual and class reading progress (Blachowicz, Sullivan, & Cieply, 2001), and fluency practice is becoming commonplace. Rebecca Barr (personal communication, February 2000) described the value of fluency assessment succinctly: "It can provide enough information to confirm hunches, prompt further assessment, and begin the process of intervention." Fluency is assuming its rightful place in the panorama of reading resources.

Fluency has a different definition and use in the neighboring field of English as a second language (ESL), where teachers work on developing second-language (L2) proficiency in their students. Professionals in that field use the word "fluency" to refer to a high level of proficiency and comfort level in all functions of the target language; this is entirely different from the concept used in reading fluency research. This chapter adopts the definition of fluency used in the reading field. Still, both of these widely differing concepts of fluency share the idea of effortlessness, ease, and smoothness, a notion as important in L2 listening, speaking, reading, and writing as it is in first-language (L1) reading, and whether the mode is silent or oral. In fact, "fluency" can be regarded as a core literacy construct.

Not only are fluency and comprehension highly correlated (Fuchs, Fuchs, Hosp, & Jenkins, 2001; Rasinski, 2003), but fluency practice also results in higher levels of reading comprehension (Samuels, 1979). As a result, fluency-building activities, such as repeated reading (Samuels, 1979), paired reading (Topping, 1995), timed partner reading (Goldsmith-Conley & Barbour, 2004), Readers Theatre, poetry performance, and many other practices described in this book, are becoming well established in the balanced language arts classroom (Rasinski, 2003). Along with that, fluency-building activities are beginning to appear in textbooks and articles written for ESL and bilingual education audiences as well (Anderson, 1999; Baker & Good, 1995; Li & Nes, 2001; Taguchi, Takayasu-Maass, & Gorsuch, 2004).

It is premature, however, to add oral reading fluency assessment or practice to the adult ESL curriculum because research has not yet established that there is a relationship between ORF and silent reading comprehension in adult English language learners. Until that can be established or ruled out, using oral reading for assessment or classroom practice with English-learning adults lacks construct validity.

This chapter summarizes the results of one study examining whether there is a relationship between oral reading and silent reading comprehension in adult English language learners (ELLs). The study asked three questions: First, is there a correlation between adult ELL oral reading fluency and silent reading comprehension? Second, which measure of oral reading fluency correlates better with reading comprehension for adult ELLs—words correct per minute or a fluency rubric, such as the Multidimensional Fluency Scale (MFS)(Zutell & Rasinski, 1991)? Finally, can miscue analysis of the oral reading of seven students at the intermediate level add anything to our understanding of their reading fluency?

DEFINITIONS OF FLUENCY

There is a considerable ambiguity in the reading field about the definition of fluency. Some simply call fluency "decoding plus comprehension" (Lipson & Lang, 1991). Some define it as "words correct per minute" (Hasbrouck & Tindal, 1992). Others add the element of prosody (Dowhower, 1991). Kame'enui and Simmons (2001) lament that fluency seems to have acquired a "one size fits all" quality. Shinn, Knutson, Good, Tilly, and Collins (1992), in a study of reading textbooks, found no distinction made between the constructs of fluency and decoding. Samuels, one of the authors of the automatic processing reading model, and the creator, in 1979, of the repeated reading technique, adds that "one of the indicators of reading fluency, which is not usually presented in the research literature, is the ability to identify a common word as a holistic unit" (2002, p. 170). Put in the words of a frustrated researcher, "the unsettling conclusion is that reading fluency involves every process and subskill involved in reading" (Wolf & Katzir-Cohen, 2001, p. 219).

Lipson and Lang (1991) suggest that "teachers are likely to be on firm ground if they ask not whether a student is fluent but rather, 'What can this student read fluently?' and 'Does the range of situations require expanding?' " (p. 225). Fluency is best described not as an absolute, but as a flexible ability to interact with a variety of texts, for a variety of purposes.

THE ROLE OF FLUENCY IN READING MODELS

Fluency plays an important role in some reading models. The influential automatic information-processing model of reading comprehension (LaBerge & Samuels, 1974) assigns a prime role to fluency and is cited most often in writings about fluency. In effect, the model describes an allocation of cognitive processing resources to the reading task, which evolves as proficiency increases from a focus on word recognition to a level of automaticity. When the reader reaches a level of rapid, automatic word recognition, cognitive resources are freed up for comprehension of text.

Stanovich's (1980) interactive compensatory model conceptualizes fluent reading as a by-product of, rather than a contributor to, comprehension. In this model, a smooth path of comprehension, with words rapidly accessible to the reader, allows automatic processing and maximum availability of attention for comprehension, whereas a "hitch" in word processing requires the use of other strategic systems, including those based on knowledge of syntax, morphology, expository structures, punctuation, and other kinds of literacy knowledge. In this model, then, reading fluency has a comprehension component, and is reflected in a definition such as the following: "[A fluent reader is] able to perform two difficult tasks simultaneously . . . the ability to identify words and comprehend a text at the same time" (Samuels, 2002, p. 168). If reading is defined as constructing meaning from text, then this model requires that reading comprehension figure into any adequate definition of reading fluency.

In the parallel interactive model (Rumelhart, 1980), reading is seen as a set of processing activities in which several linguistic and cognitive systems can be sampled at once. In this model, word recognition and its meta-activity, decoding, interact with other systems. Therefore, reading fluency is only one point of origin for making meaning from print and does not figure as a key measure.

Reading fluency takes on another role in reading models that look at reading as an extension from oracy (oral language) to literacy (written language), with oral language at the core of later literacy (Sticht & James, 1984). According to this theory, learning to speak emerges from listening comprehension, and both of these are preconditions of fluent reading, in which a reader comprehends a text through reading as easily as a listener can understand an oral text. A similar view is expressed in the simple model of reading (Gough & Tunmer, 1986), which states that reading comprehension (RC) is the product of decoding (D) and language competence (LC), or $RC = D \times LC$. Language competence can be described as all of the aspects of reading that do not require decoding, and this competence is sometimes used synonymously with listening comprehension. In both of these reading models, fluent reading would be considered an outcome that allows readers to achieve the top limit of their language comprehension.

Interactive models of reading (Stanovich, 2000) assign a greater role to prior knowledge (including knowledge of text features) in word recognition, and also posit that comprehension can occur from either "top down" or "bottom up," without necessarily resolving word identification before meaning can be sampled (Fuchs et al., 2001, p. 242). Since this model allows the use of prior knowledge in constructing meaning at the same stage that word identification is accessed, features of syntax, such as chunking, and features of pragmatics, such as prosody, would necessarily be included in a definition of reading fluency.

COMPONENTS OF ORAL READING FLUENCY

Oral reading is the performance measure by which the abstract construct of fluency is usually gauged. It generally includes measurement of two or more of the following five features: rate, accuracy, parsing, prosody, and comprehension—features that are at the same time both discrete and synergistic.

Rate

Rate is a critical skill in that when text is read below a certain rate, reading comprehension is unable to occur. Rasinski (2000) observed that students referred to his reading clinic scored only slightly below grade level in comprehension and word recognition, but their oral reading rate was significantly below that of their peers, making it impossible to keep up with schoolwork. Rate has been established for different grade levels and at different times of the school year (Behavioral Research and Teaching, 2005; Fuchs, Fuchs, Hamlett, Walz, & Germann, 1993; Hasbrouck & Tindal, 1992). For adults, researchers evaluating thousands of digitally recorded oral reading samples have established the rate of 140 words correct per minute as a "threshold" for reading fluency, for both native English-speaking and L2 adults (Balogh, 2005). Samuels (personal communication, March 2003) points out that it is risky to establish norms for rate unless text type and reading purpose are established as well.

Accuracy

The standard ORF scores contain an accuracy measure. Goodman and Burke (1972) set up a complex miscue-scoring inventory that has formed the basis of most accuracy scoring ever since. Something about the synergy of rate and accuracy together appears to create a strong assessment instrument. An oral reading study in which rate was removed as a factor, and only accuracy was charted, failed to have much diagnostic power (Parker, Hasbrouck, & Tindal, 1992).

Parsing

The third construct, parsing, or "chunking," is the ability to separate text into meaningful phrase and clause units. Parsing is an important measure of the development of syntax knowledge, or the grammar of a language. In addition to natural breaks that follow syntax patterns, punctuation provides signals for phrase and clause breaks, and mastery of these signals can be demonstrated through oral reading. Most L1 fluency literature does not distinguish parsing from prosody, conflating them into a single concept. However, in talking about English language learners, it is critical to distinguish whether a passage is read with correct parsing, which indicates knowledge of grammar, and, after that, prosody, which has more to do with oral production than grammar. For adult ELLs, a miscue in parsing would be more likely to have implications for reading comprehension than a miscue in prosody because of the possible interference of a foreign accent.

Prosody

In 1991, Dowhower noted that "prosody," which can be defined as reading with appropriate expression, was ORF's "neglected bedfellow." In several studies, she discovered a strong relationship between "expressive reading" and comprehension. As a result of such research, oral reading rubrics, such as those of the National Reading Panel (2000) and the National Assessment of Educational Progress (NAEP; Pinnell et al., 1995), include consideration of expressive reading, as does the MFS included in this study and in research found in several other chapters in this book. However, expressive reading by adult ELLs is complicated by interference from not only the phonemes, but the intonational patterns of their native language.

Comprehension

Finally, some definitions of fluency assume that comprehension is a constituent. Samuels's (1979) description of proficient ORF includes that the reader should be able to "comprehend while reading aloud" (p. 406). Rasinski (1990) also defines reading fluency as "those surface level or observable behaviors during oral reading that are associated with comprehension" (p. 38).

CRITERION VALIDITY OF ORAL READING FLUENCY

Many studies of students using their first language (L1) have found high criterion validity for oral reading as a proxy for reading comprehension (Hintze, Shapiro, & Conte, 1997). In three different studies, Deno, Mirkin, and Chiang (1982) found high correlations between oral reading tasks and standardized reading comprehension tests, levels higher than those with cloze or other direct measures. ORF also correlated highly with both literal and inferential reading scores on standardized tests. In one controlled study, ORF samples were able to distinguish students with learning disabilities from those from impoverished socioeconomic backgrounds or students in general education (Deno, Marston, Shinn, & Tindal, 1983). Fuchs, Fuchs, and Maxwell (1988) found stronger correlations between oral reading scores and standardized tests of reading comprehension than between standardized tests and question answering, oral recall, and written cloze. Jenkins and Jewell (1993) found oral reading to correlate strongly with reading comprehension activities. ORF was found to correlate well with teacher judgment of student progress (Hintze et al., 1997). Hintze and colleagues (1997) found that oral reading was a better measure of reading comprehension than orally answering questions on a silently read passage, whether the reading program was basal, literature-based, or whole-language-based. Several researchers found that ORF correlations held up regardless of the nature of the text (Cahalan-Laitusis & Harris, 2003; Fuchs & Deno, 1992; Hintze et al., 1997). Shinn and colleagues (1992) found that ORF rate correlates highly with any and all measures of reading comprehension, leading the authors to conclude that "CBM [curriculum-based measurement] oral reading fluency fits current theoretical models of reading well and can be validated as a measure of general reading achievement, including comprehension" (p. 476).

It may be that there is something like a "critical period" for using ORF as a measure of reading comprehension, at least for native speakers. Espin and Foegen (1996) found that, by secondary school, learner outcomes such as ability to engage in higher-order thinking skills and vocabulary knowledge are more important indicators of comprehension than oral reading, and in a study by Espin and Deno (1993), oral reading corre-lated only moderately with information-locating skills in more mature readers. Fuchs and colleagues (2001) mention a "developmental trajec-tory of oral reading fluency [that] involves greatest growth in the primary grades, with a negatively accelerating curve though the intermediate grades and perhaps into high school" (p. 240).

At least two studies have validated ORF as a measure of reading comprehension for Hispanic children who are ELLs. Baker and Good (1995) established the reliability and validity of using curriculum-based ORF assessments with second-grade bilingual Hispanic students. In an-other study, Ramirez (2001) found higher correlations between silent reading comprehension and ORF measures than between silent reading comprehension and several other measures, including simple decoding, for fifth-grade Spanish ELLs. However, studies of adult ELL oral reading fluency do not appear to have been done at this time.

L2 ADULT READING

Researchers have had to struggle to construct L2 reading models, due to their incredible complexities. A model must account for such factors as L1 literacy level and educational experiences, age at which L2 study commences, sociocultural conditions under which both L1 and L2 are acquired and learned, structural and phonetic differences between L1 and L2, and other features. While it is impossible to devote the time needed to address all of these in this chapter, a few brief comments are in order.

A number of studies corroborate that L1 literacy level is a key deter-minant of L2 reading comprehension, although the exact nature of the transfer between languages is not fully known (Bernhardt, 2000). Bernhardt and Kamil (1995) sketched a partial L2 reading model as fol-lows: "Second-language reading is a function of L1 reading ability and second-language grammatical ability" (Bernhardt, 2000, p. 803). None-theless, even accounting for these two factors, a great deal, perhaps 50%, of L2 reading proficiency remains unaccounted for at the present time (Bernhardt, 2005).

There is overwhelming evidence of transfer between languages. In fact, the central argument of those in favor of dual language, dual immer-sion, and bilingual education programs rests on this important and exten-sive body of research. However, the extent and the nature of the transfer varies widely among populations.

Fitzgerald's 1995 metastudy of research on L2 reading led her to the conclusion that, at least in academic tasks, L2 readers resemble L1 readers in substance but process more slowly. She found that the more proficient an L2 reader becomes, the more his or her processing strategies resemble those of an L1 reader. She concluded that the differences were of degree, not of kind. She also found that "considerable evidence emerged to support the [common underlying proficiency] CUP model" (p. 186) proposed by Cummins (1979, 1981), which says that language knowledge is universal at its core, with a common underlying knowledge, and that languages differ from one another in their surface manifestations.

DIFFERENCES IN L1 AND L2 ORAL READING

The significant differences in the ways that decoding, recoding, and meaning construction occur in L2 adult learners create a more complicated landscape for assessing reading comprehension and oral reading fluency than is the case with L1 children. At least three different scenarios can be described, and these contrast with L1 oral reading in important ways.

Decoding without Comprehension

In L1 reading, when an emergent reader of normal abilities is able to pronounce a decoded word aloud, the word then becomes available for a semantic match. The reader draws upon the bank of words that the image and/or sound triggers, and makes a match with a known meaning, or develops a new one from context. A fluent L1 reader can identify the words in the text as whole units and simultaneously construct meaning from them, making an effortless match between a word's written form, oral form, and meaning, as long as the word is already familiar to the reader or can be construed from context.

However, ELLs may be able to decode English words successfully (i.e., match sight and sound) because they are fully proficient in decoding the letters, but not be able to make a semantic match to the word's meaning because they are missing knowledge of vocabulary, syntax (word order), or discourse in English, the target language. Consequently, their ability to read the word aloud may not necessarily access the word's meaning. This is sometimes called "word calling."

Comprehension without Recoding (Ability to Pronounce)

On the other hand, some L2 learners may be able to recognize the meaning of a word when reading it silently but be unable to pronounce the word when reading aloud, because they do not know the phoneme–grapheme correspondences of English, or know them but cannot make the sounds. Nevertheless, they may understand the meaning of the word. For example, most Americans would recognize the phrase E pluribus unum on American currency to mean "From many, one," and although they cannot pronounce it with Latin phonemes, or possibly at all, they do comprehend it.

Decoding and Recoding with Negative Transfer

A third possibility is some combination of the above, that an L2 reader decodes and pronounces a word or string of words using his or her L1 knowledge in a way that interferes with the sound or meaning of the word in the target language. This can result from phonemic interference from L1, a false cognate, or other negative transfer from L1. Thus, a string of words could be apparently correctly rendered but not understood, or incorrectly rendered but understood, depending on the nature of the interference.

When ELL adults read aloud, they are being asked to decode the graphemes of the connected English text and map them to both the English phoneme system and the reader's semantic knowledge, while simultaneously recoding the phonemes into an oral performance, and to do it rapidly. The sheer complexity of the task would lead one to predict that their oral reading ability would tell us something about their reading process, but that differences in L1 literacy level, native language structures, and decoding and recoding ability would confound the assessment.

THE STUDY

Participants and Program

This descriptive study looked at several measures of English language proficiency for 232 postsecondary ELL students in a five-level, semi-intensive academic ESL program at a private urban university in the Midwest. Since entrance to the program required a high school diploma, it can be assumed that the students were fully literate in their native languages. Learners consisted of both working adults and younger adults who had immigrated to the United States during high school and still needed additional ESL coursework.

The first languages and levels of the 232 students are summarized in Table 13.1. Those using the Roman alphabet included the Poles and Spanish speakers; those using the Cyrillic alphabet included the Ukrainians and Bulgarians, and the Chinese used Mandarin, a logosyllabic system with a phonological component (Li, 2002). In addition, there were 10 students who represented other languages not aggregated for the study.

The program has five levels of study, from total beginner (level 1) to high intermediate/advanced students (level 5). Academic in focus, its purpose is to prepare students for transition into undergraduate study at the university. The 14-hour per week, 10-week term includes considerable study of grammar, reading and writing, language and computer laboratories, and conversation practice.

All 232 students were included in the first question of the study, about the possible correlation between oral and silent reading. The second question, in which correlations of words correct per minute and MFS scores with silent reading comprehension were compared, involved 80 mixed-level students. The third question, about the role of miscue analysis in a description of intermediate students' oral reading, used a case study approach with seven level 3 students of mixed-language backgrounds.

TABLE 13.1. Participant Characteristics by First Language and Level in Program

First language	Number	Percent
Polish	143	61.6
Ukrainian	33	14.2
Chinese	23	9.9
Spanish (Mexican)	14	6.0
Bulgarian	9	3.9
Other	10	4.3
Level 1	14	6.0
Level 3	154	66.4
Level 5	64	27.6
TOTAL	232	100.0

Procedure

Near the end of the quarter, a taped oral interview is conducted to evaluate students' oral proficiency. A 1-minute oral reading taken from the level 3 reader, but not used in the class, was added to the interviews, which were taped and timed by the assessing teacher and later coded by the researcher using a system of words correct per minute. A coding key was created to facilitate consistency in coding (Leu, 1982) and included substitutions, omissions, and insertions, which were then classified as significant (meaning-changing) miscues, other miscues, and foreign accent miscues (intelligible but with a substitution of an L1 phoneme, such as pronouncing *thrift* as *trift*). After each sample was coded, it was entered into a statistics software program. The final examination score and language laboratory final exam score were also entered. Later, 80 of the taped oral readings were rescored by two raters using the MFS. Analysis of the data included measurements of central tendency and other descriptive statistics, correlations, and regression analysis. Finally, a subgroup of seven level 3 learners was chosen from the 80 who had been evaluated using both fluency systems, and their coding sheets were examined in detail.

Instruments

Words correct per minute is the measure by which ORF has been shown to correlate with silent reading comprehension. Using a 1-minute sample has also been validated, as follows: "When a global index of relative reading proficiency is the purpose of measurement, such an index can be easily obtained within 1 minute without using a standardized test" (Deno et al., 1982, p. 44).

The study uses the final exam (FE) as the measure for reading comprehension. Final exams contain many features of standardized reading achievement tests: students cannot consult their notes or their classmates; tests are timed; students must follow directions for several task types, and the test requires vocabulary knowledge. Moreover, since the final exam is at the end of the course, all students have gone through a similar instructional experience, which added further stability to the variable. The three exams consisted of 15–17 pages each, further improving reliability, and have been refined for use in the ESL program over a number of years.

The readability level for the ORF passage was calculated using the Fry readability scale (Fry, 1977), and the instructional reading level of each class level was established by calculating the readability levels of the reading passages on each final exam. Since no scale yet exists for adult ELLs, L1 grade levels were used (Fuchs et al., 1993; Hasbrouck & Tindal, 1992); the ORF passage was found to be at the frustration level for level 1 students, instructional level for level 3 students, and independent level for level 5 students (Betts, 1946).

The language laboratory final exam (LLFE) is based on content and structures taught in the language laboratory portion of the course and consists of listening to a series of short, taped items and responding in writing with true–false, multiple-choice, or one-sentence answers.

Results

It was found that as learner proficiency in the program increased, so did the fluency score. The mean words correct per minute score increased by 23 words between levels 1 and 3, and another 19 words between levels 3 and 5. It appears that ORF rate increases in ELL adults as their general proficiency level increases.

When evaluated by first language, there were significant differences in words correct per minute, with Poles performing at the highest level, Chinese at the lowest, and the other language groups distributed between, according to their written language's similarity to the English alphabet. In FE and LLFE performance, however, there were no significant differences among the language groups.

When correlations were performed (see Table 13.2), a weak to moderate but highly significant correlation of .256 ($p \le .001$, $n = 232$) was found between words correct per minute and FE score, and a somewhat

TABLE 13.2. Correlations for Measures of Oral Reading Fluency and Other Measures

Measure	FE (reading measure)	LLFE (listening measure)
Words correct per minute	.26*	.39*
Total words read	.21*	.35*
Total number of miscues	−.29*	−.30*
Total number of sig. miscues	−.30*	−.32*
Miscue ratio	−.31*	−.41*

Note. $n = 232$.
*$p \le .001$.

higher correlation of .39 ($p \leq .001$, $n = 232$) between words correct per minute and the listening measure.

When analyzed by level in program (see Table 13.3), the correlation between fluency measures and the reading measure was stronger at level 3 than level 1, and stronger for level 5 than level 3. Using different presentations of the fluency components, speed alone was less predictive of read-

TABLE 13.3. Correlations for Measures of Oral Reading Fluency and Other Measures by Level and First Language

Measure	FE	LLFE
Words correct per minute		
Level 1 ($n = 14$)	.04	.63*
Level 3 ($n = 154$)	.27**	.38**
Level 5 ($n = 64$)	.41**	.39*
Polish ($n = 143$)	.24**	.24**
Ukrainian ($n = 33$)	.10	.53**
Chinese ($n = 23$)	.15	.51
Hispanic ($n = 14$)	.55*	.66*
Bulgarian ($n = 9$)	.52	.76*
Other languages ($n = 10$)	.30	.34
Total words read		
Level 1	.06	.64
Level 3	.22**	.34**
Level 5	.35**	.35**
Polish	.19**	.21**
Ukrainian	.12	.47**
Chinese	.01	.18
Hispanic	.47	.59*
Bulgarian	.49	.72
Other languages	−.37	−.41
Miscue ratio		
Level 1	−.06	−.40
Level 3	−.29**	−.32**
Level 5	−.46**	−.37**
Polish	−.31**	−.18*
Ukrainian	.05	−.52**
Chinese	−.30	−.25
Hispanic	−.68**	−.86**
Bulgarian	−.75*	−.85**
Other languages	−.43	−.46

Note. $n = 232$.
*Correlations are significant at the $p < .05$ level; **Correlations are significant at the $p < .01$ level.

ing comprehension than accuracy alone, and both speed and accuracy were less predictive than miscue ratio. The highest correlation of the reading measure with a fluency measure was at level 5, with miscue ratio ($r = -.46$, $p \leq .001$).

By level 5, unlike levels 1 and 3, the fluency measures become more strongly correlated with the reading measure than with the listening measure. This suggests that a certain level of listening comprehension may need to be reached before fluency measures are meaningful (Cummins, 1984).

When analyzed by first language, the strongest correlations were found for Hispanic students, where correlations reached $r = -.68$ ($p \leq .01$) for miscue ratio with the reading measure. On the other hand, no significant correlations were found between any of the fluency measures and the reading measure or the listening measure for the Chinese students, which suggests that these students may use some other means of constructing meaning from print that does not access the oral renderings of the words being read.

Finally, the listening comprehension measure was more strongly correlated with the silent reading measure than any of the fluency measures. It appears that the listening measure may be a link between the fluency and silent reading measures.

On the second question, the MFS score increased with level in program, like words correct per minute. It correlated with the reading measure at a level of .29, only slightly better than words correct per minute, and at the same level of significance. None of the subskills of the MFS (pace, phrasing, and smoothness) had higher correlations with the reading measure than the total MFS score; however, when the subskills were put in a stepwise regression analysis to predict the reading score, the pace subskill was as strong a predictor (9%) of the reading measure as the total MFS score, whereas the other two skills did not contribute to the prediction. Therefore, prosodic features did not serve as predictors for silent reading comprehension performance, whereas pace did. Like the other set of fluency measures, MFS is more highly correlated with the listening measure than with the reading measure. The correlation of MFS and the listening measure ($r = .46$; $p \leq .001$) is the strongest correlation of any of the ORF measures and either silent reading or listening comprehension.

However, the MFS had low interrater reliability, just above chance, on some of the submeasures. This is probably because of the subjective nature of the judgments raters must make about pace, phrasing, and smoothness. On the other hand, words correct per minute and MFS scores are highly correlated with each other ($r = .88$; $p \leq .001$), so the more quantifiable nature of the words correct per minute rating makes it preferable to the fluency rubric.

When the miscue analysis of ORF samples of seven level 3 students from different language backgrounds was conducted, it revealed that all of the fluency measures fail to account for some of the characteristics of the adult ELL, due to two factors: the differences between English and the L1 writing and phoneme systems from which the students come, and the issue of "foreign accents," which may "fossilize" early while reading comprehension skills continue to increase.

For L2 readers in particular, the ORF rating systems do not inform the rater whether a miscue derives from a problem with understanding the word's meaning, or in pronouncing it. For example, numerous participants in the study pronounced the word *used* with two syllables. It was impossible to know how many of them understood that the word in this article meant *secondhand*, both when mispronounced and when pronounced correctly. Furthermore, it is impossible to know whether a mispronounced rendering is developmental—that is, able to be ameliorated—or has already reached a plateau, as part of a permanent foreign accent.

ORAL READING FLUENCY IN A MODEL
OF ADULT ENGLISH LANGUAGE LEARNERS

Perhaps oral reading fluency as a measure of adult ELL silent reading becomes significant after a certain number of requisite skills are in place. These skills include a threshold level of listening comprehension (enough receptive oral vocabulary to access the English phonemic–semantic system), decoding (enough knowledge of the English grapheme–phoneme system to figure out how written words sound); and recoding/pronunciation (enough oral proficiency to pronounce some of the target words in the English phoneme system). In such a model, the critical period during which oral reading is a sensitive assessment would come into play after students reach an (as-yet-unspecified) listening threshold, and fade away when students have achieved a mature level of silent reading, as is the case for L1 readers (Fuchs et al., 2001; Kuhn & Stahl, 2002). The critical period would be reached at different times for students from different L1 backgrounds, depending on the degree of similarity between their language's orthography and that of English. However, data on the Chinese students suggests that an entirely different model may be necessary to account for the much slower rate of acquisition of the decoding skill.

Interestingly, in the study, the correlation between the listening comprehension measure and the silent reading measure remained relatively constant across levels, and the listening measure predicted 29% of the reading score for level 1 students, 25% for level 3 students, and 28% for level 5 students. The listening measure is written to match the difficulty level of the curriculum, so it becomes increasingly more advanced but retains about equal importance as the students move up through the levels. This is in contrast to the strength of the fluency measure's correlation with the reading measure, which increases as proficiency increases. One can conclude that listening comprehension continues to be a stable measure that accounts for about 25% of reading comprehension across proficiency levels for adult ELLs.

For adult ELLs, then, oral reading cannot operate as a proxy for decoding skill until the grapheme–phoneme system, listening comprehension skills, including basic listening vocabulary, and L2 recoding skills are in place. Furthermore, once the prerequisites for decoding L2 text have been achieved, other adult reading strategies take over and decoding no longer correlates highly with silent reading comprehension. In addition, even when the requisite skills are in place, other factors, such as transfer of L1 reading skills, are more influential. Still, the low to moderate correlation between oral reading and silent reading comprehension has been found to be highly significant.

CONCLUSIONS AND DIRECTIONS
FOR FUTURE RESEARCH

To make use of ORF assessments on a large scale in adult ELL teaching, two pieces must be put in place: an ORF instrument that can reliably factor in the "foreign accent" feature, and statistically valid norms for adult ELL oral reading levels.

A confirmatory study that includes an oral fluency measure, a listening comprehension measure, and a silent reading comprehension passage at instructional reading level, using students from a postsecondary ESL program, would be a useful follow-up to this research.

Despite lower correlations with reading comprehension than for L1 students, timed oral readings can tell the ESL instructor several important things. An oral reading score is sensitive to progress across levels; as student proficiency goes up, oral reading fluency goes up as well. Also, ORF scores in this study predicted 14% of performance on silent reading comprehension tasks, using miscue ratio, and miscue ratio can predict up to 37% of performance on listening comprehension tasks. Although these are small to moderate percentages, they are highly significant ($p < .001$), and can provide a valuable tool for classroom assessment.

Hearing an individual student read aloud can give a teacher valuable insight into the student's learning processes. Evidence of consistent L1 vowel interference, for example, can help ESL teachers identify the need for more explicit instruction on English vowel sounds. Oral reading also builds confidence, and this activity can be especially helpful to Chinese students, for whom decoding in English is still an unfamiliar enterprise. ESL teachers with a mixed class containing Chinese students may want to provide extra opportunities for those students to practice the decoding skill, in order to get it to a level of automaticity comparable to that of their classmates.

The study takes the first tentative steps toward bringing the ORF construct to the field of adult and postsecondary ESL teaching. It is hoped that others will be inspired to take the next steps in the journey.

ACKNOWLEDGMENT

A substantially similar version of this chapter appears in the 2005 *Yearbook of the National Reading Conference* (Lems, K. [2005]. A study of adult ESL oral reading fluency and silent reading comprehension. *Yearkbook of the National Reading Conference, 54*) and is reprinted here with permission from the National Reading Conference.

REFERENCES

Anderson, N. (1999). *Exploring second language reading: Issues and strategies.* Boston: Heinle & Heinle.

Anderson, N. (2003, March). *Metacognition and the L2 reader.* Paper presented at the annual meeting of the Teachers of English to Speakers of Other Languages, Baltimore.

Baker, S. K., & Good, R. (1995). Curriculum-based measurement of English reading with bilingual Hispanic students: A validation study with second-grade students. *School Psychology Review, 24*(4), 561–578.

Balogh, J. (2005, March). Measuring adult oral reading. In L. D. Miller (Chair), *Fluency in L2 reading and speaking.* Symposium conducted at the annual meeting of Teachers of English to Speakers of Other Languages, San Antonio, TX.

Behavioral Research and Teaching. (2005, January). *Oral reading fluency: 90 years of assessment* (BRT Technical Report No. 33). Eugene, OR: Author. Retrieved April 3, 2005 from http://brt.uoregon.edu/techreports/tr_33_ncorf_descstats.pdf

Bernhardt, E. B. (2000). Second-language reading as a case study of reading scholarship in the 20th century. In M. Kamil, P. B. Mosenthal, P. D. Pearson, & R. Barr (Eds.), *Handbook of reading research* (Vol. 3, pp. 791–811). Mahwah, NJ: Erlbaum.

Bernhardt, E. (2005). Progress and procrastination in second language reading. *Annual Review of Applied Linguistics, 25,* 133–143.

Bernhardt, E. B., & Kamil, M. (1995). Interpreting relationships between L1 and L2 reading: Consolidating the linguistic threshold and the linguistic interdependence hypotheses. *Applied Linguistics, 16,* 15–34.

Betts, E. A. (1946). *Foundations of reading instruction.* New York: American Book Company.

Blachowicz, C. Z., Sullivan, D. M., & Cieply, C. (2001). Fluency snapshots: A quick screening tool for your classroom. *Reading Psychology, 22,* 95–109.

Cahalan-Laitusis, C., & Harris, A. (2003, April). *Oral reading fluency and optimal difficulty level of a literature-based reading curriculum.* Paper presented at the annual meeting of the American Educational Research Association, Chicago.

Cummins, J. (1979). Linguistic interdependence and the educational development of bilingual children. *Review of Educational Research, 49*(2), 222–251.

Cummins, J. (1981). The role of primary language development in promoting educational success for language minority students. In *Schooling and language minority students: A theoretical framework* (pp. 3–49). Sacramento, CA: State Department of Education.

Cummins, J. (1984). *Bilingualism and special education: Issues in assessment and pedagogy.* Clevedon, UK: Multilingual Matters.

Deno, S. L., Marston, D., Shinn, M., & Tindal, G. (1983). Oral reading fluency: A simple datum for scaling reading disability. *Topics in Learning and Learning Disabilities, 2,* 53–59.

Deno, S. L., Mirkin, P. K., & Chiang, B. (1982). Identifying valid measures of reading. *Exceptional Children, 49,* 36–45.

Dowhower, S. (1991). Speaking of prosody: Fluency's unattended bedfellow. *Theory Into Practice, 30*(3), 165–175.

Espin, C. A., & Deno, S. L. (1993). Performance in reading from content area text as an indicator of achievement. *Remedial and Special Education, 14,* 47–59.

Espin, C. A., & Foegen, A. (1996). Validity of general outcome measures for predicting secondary students' performance on content-area tasks. *Exceptional Children, 62*(6), 497–514.

Fitzgerald, J. (1995). English-as-a-second-language learners' cognitive reading processes: A review of research in the United States [Electronic version]. *Review of Education Research, 6*(2), 145–190.

Fry, E. B. (1977). Fry's readability graph: Clarification, validity, and extension to level 17. *Journal of Reading, 21,* 278–288.

Fuchs, L. S., & Deno, S. L. (1992). Effects of curriculum within curriculum-based measurement. *Exceptional Children, 58,* 232–242.

Fuchs, L. S., Fuchs, D., Hamlett, C. L., Walz, L., & Germann, G. (1993). Formative evaluation of academic progress: How much growth can we expect? *School Psychology Review, 22*(1), 27–48.

Fuchs, L. S., Fuchs, D., Hosp, M., & Jenkins, J. R. (2001). Oral reading fluency as an indicator of reading competence: A theoretical, empirical, and historical analysis. *Scientific Studies of Reading, 5*(3), 239–256.

Fuchs, L. S., Fuchs, D., & Maxwell, L. (1988). The validity of informal reading comprehension measures. *Remedial and Special Education, 9*(2), 20–29.

Goldsmith-Conley, E., & Barbour, J. (2004). Timed partner reading: A practical technique for fluency instruction? *Illinois Reading Council Journal, 36*(3), 33–41.

Goodman, K., & Burke, C. L. (1972). *Reading miscue inventory.* New York: MacMillan.

Gough, P. B., & Tunmer, W. E. (1986). Decoding, reading, and reading disability. *Remedial and Special Education, 7*(1), 6–10.

Hasbrouck, J., & Tindal, G. (1992, Spring). Curriculum-based oral reading fluency norms for students in grades 2 through 5. *Teaching Exceptional Children,* pp. 41–44.

Hintze, J., Shapiro, E., & Conte, K. L. (1997). Oral reading fluency and authentic reading material: Criterion validity of the technical features of CBM survey-level assessment. *School Psychology Review, 26*(4), 535–553.

Jenkins, J. R., & Jewell, M. (1993). Examining the validity of two measures for formative teaching: Reading aloud and maze. *Exceptional Children, 59,* 421–432.

Kame'enui, E., & Simmons, D. (2001). Introduction to this special issue: The DNA of reading fluency. *Scientific Studies of Reading, 5*(3), 203–210.

Kuhn, M. R., & Stahl, S. (2002). *Fluency: A review of developmental and remedial practices* (2-008). Ann Arbor, MI: Center for the Improvement of Early Reading Achievement. Retrieved April 2, 2005, from www.ciera.org/library/reports/inquiry-2/2-008/2-008.html

LaBerge, D., & Samuels, S. J. (1974). Toward a theory of automatic information processing in reading. *Cognitive Psychology, 6,* 293–323.

Leu, D. (1982). Oral reading error analysis: A critical review of research and application. *Reading Research Quarterly, 17,* 420–437.

Li, D., & Nes, S. (2001). Using paired reading to help ESL students become fluent and accurate readers. *Reading Improvement, 38*(2), 50–62.

Li, L. (2002). The role of phonology in reading Chinese single characters and two-character words with high, medium and low phonological regularities by Chinese grade 2 and grade 5 students. *Reading Research Quarterly, 37,* 372–374.

Lipson, M., & Lang, L. (1991). Not as easy as it seems: some unresolved questions about fluency. *Theory Into Practice, 30*(3), 218–227.

National Reading Panel. (2000). *Report of the subgroups.* Washington, DC: National Institute of Child Health and Human Development. Retrieved November 1, 2002, from www.nationalreadingpanel.org/publications/sub-groups.htm

Parker, R., Hasbrouck, J. E., & Tindal, G. (1992). Greater validity for oral reading fluency: Can miscues help? *Journal of Special Education, 25,* 492–503.

Pinnell, G. S., Pikulski, J. J., Wixson, K. K., Campbell, J. R., Gough, P. B., & Beatty, A. S. (1995). *Listening to children read aloud* (Report No. 23-FR-04). Washington, DC: U.S. Department of Education, National Center for Education Statistics.

Ramirez, C. M. (2001). *An investigation of English language and reading skills on reading comprehension for Spanish-speaking English language learners.* Unpublished doctoral dissertation, University of Oregon, Portland.

Rasinski, T. V. (1990). Investigating measures of reading fluency. *Educational Research Quarterly, 14*(3), 37–44.

Rasinski, T. (2000). Speed does matter in reading. *Reading Teacher, 54*(2), 146–151.

Rasinski, T. V. (2003). *The fluent reader: Oral reading strategies for building word recognition, fluency, and comprehension.* New York: Scholastic Professional Books.

Rumelhart, D. E. (1980). Toward an interactive model of reading. In R. B. Ruddell, M. R. Ruddell, & H. Singer (Eds.), *Theoretical models and processes of reading* (4th ed.). Hillsdale, NJ: Erlbaum.

Samuels, S. J. (1972). The effect of letter-name knowledge on learning to read. *American Educational Research Journal, 9,* 65–74.

Samuels, S. J. (1979). The method of repeated readings. *Reading Teacher, 32,* 403–408.

Samuels, S. J. (2002). Reading fluency: Its development and assessment. In A. E. Farstrup & S. J. Samuels (Eds.), *What research has to say about reading instruction* (pp. 166–183). Newark, DE: International Reading Association.

Shinn, M. R., Knutson, N., Good, R. H., Tilly, W. D., & Collins, V. (1992). Curriculum-based measurement of oral reading fluency: A confirmatory analysis of its relation to reading. *School Psychology Review, 21,* 459–479.

Stanovich, K. (1980). Toward an interactive-compensatory model of individual differences in the development of reading fluency. *Reading Research Quarterly, 1*(1), 33–71.

Stanovich, K. (2000). *Progress in understanding reading: Scientific foundations and new frontiers.* New York: Guilford Press.

Sticht, T. G., & James, J. H. (1984). Listening and reading. In P. D. Pearson, R. Barr, M. L. Kamil, & P. Mosenthal (Eds.), *Handbook of reading research* (pp. 293–317). Mahwah, NJ: Erlbaum.

Taguchi, E., Takayasu-Maass, M., & Gorsuch, G. J. (2004). Developing reading fluency in EFL: How assisted repeated reading and extensive reading affect fluency development. *Reading in a Foreign Language, 16*(2) 70–96.

Topping, K. J. (1995). *Paired reading, spelling and writing: The handbook for teachers and parents.* London: Cassell.

Wolf, M., & Katzir-Cohen, T. (2001). Reading fluency and its intervention. *Scientific Studies of Reading, 5*(3), 211–240.

Zutell, J., & Rasinski, T. V. (1991). Training teachers to attend to their students' oral reading fluency. *Theory Into Practice, 30*(3), 211–217.

CHAPTER 14

Teaching Fluency (and Decoding) through Fast Start

An Early Childhood Parental Involvement Program

BRUCE STEVENSON
TIMOTHY RASINSKI
NANCY PADAK

The National Reading Panel (2000) has identified word decoding (phonics) and reading fluency as two key components of successful early reading instructional programs. Clearly, the ability to decode words accurately (phonics and decoding) and effortlessly (fluency) is essential to success in learning to read. Readers who experience difficulty in decoding words, or who must invest too much effort into decoding words, cannot be considered proficient readers who adequately comprehend what they read. The critical and essential nature of decoding and fluency make them strong candidates for instruction early in the school reading curriculum.

Given the time constraints to school-based instruction, any opportunity to expand instruction beyond the confines of the school is welcome. Home involvement is clearly one area in which reading instruction can be expanded. Indeed, the theory and research supporting the inclusion of parents in children's school learning, especially in the early years of school, is deep and compelling (Chavkin, 1993; Christenson, 1995; Crimm, 1992; Durkin, 1966; Eccles & Harold, 1993; Epstein, 1989, 1994, 2001; Henderson, 1988; Henderson & Berla, 1994; Neidermeyer, 1970; Postlethwaite & Ross, 1992; Pressley, 2002; Rasinski, 1989, 2003; Topping, 1996; U.S. Department of Education, 1994).

DESIGN CHARACTERISTICS FOR PARENT TUTORING PROGRAMS

To be effective parent tutoring programs in reading for early childhood must adhere to certain design characteristics (Rasinski & Padak, 2004). The characteristics can be used as guidelines to design programs to meet specific needs or to design evaluations of existing programs.

Use Proven and Effective Strategies

Parents often have limited time to devote to working with their children. Therefore, at-home activities must be based on proven and appropriate methods for achieving success in reading. Too often, at-home activities have questionable value for improving academic performance. Drawing and coloring pictures or cutting out photographs from magazines may not be the best use of parents' and children's time together at home. In this chapter, we look at the design components of a parent program designed to develop fluency.

Provide Ongoing Training, Communication, and Support

Most parents are not teachers. They need good and understandable training that includes demonstrations and opportunities for discussion and questions. Someone who is enthusiastic about and committed to parent involvement should provide the training.

Teachers need to understand the realities of busy family life and be sensitive to educational barriers that may impede parent–child reading activity. Some parents may feel uncomfortable reading aloud to their children because of their own real or perceived lack of reading ability. Parents of English language learners may not themselves be fluent readers of English. Parents whose own educational experiences were negative may hesitate to attend school functions. Yet all these parents want to help their children succeed. The teacher's challenge, then, is to find meaningful ways for all families to be involved in home reading activities. Making books on tape available is one way to promote all families' involvement. With some thought, resourceful teachers can find many more.

Continuing communication and support can provide parents with timely feedback about their questions and concerns, and can encourage persistence with the at-home reading activities. Support can be in the form of a regular informative newsletter, monthly sessions in the school, or offers of personal contact by phone or e-mail. Ongoing communication and support build bonds between home and school, and demonstrate to parents that other people care about their children's reading growth.

Use Authentic Reading Texts

One of the best things that parents can do for children of any age is to read to them. Reading aloud provides children with a model of fluent reading and offers parents natural opportunities to point out text features for young children. Similarly, when parents read with their children or listen to their children read, children grow as readers. Texts for these activities should be authentic (e.g., poems, song lyrics, jokes, jump rope rhymes); children should be able to read them successfully with enough support from parents. These simple activities—reading to, reading with, and listening to children—are powerful ways to promote student growth in reading.

Some parent involvement plans fail because parents lack appropriate texts or the time or resources to acquire them. Although periodic trips to the public library are advisable, requiring them as a condition of participation in at-home reading activities might discourage parental involvement. The easiest solution is to provide parents and children with reading materials. When the materials are provided, parents are more likely to remember to do the activities with their children. The materials themselves act as reminders to parents to get the job done.

Make Activities Easy, Enjoyable, Consistent, and Long Term

Parents tell us that parent involvement activities don't work if they are too complex, take inordinate amounts of time, or change from day to day or week to week. They say it's hard to develop a routine of working with their children under these conditions. Therefore, at-home reading activities need to reflect this reality. At-home activities for young children should be relatively brief (10–15 minutes several times each week), simple routines, with some variation to keep interest high. Such activities make it easier for parents and children to develop predictable, time-efficient routines. These, in turn, increase the likelihood that the at-home activities will be conducted regularly and successfully.

Consistency is important as well. Once an effective instructional routine is introduced, major changes or disruptions in the parent–child routine should be avoided. Rather, families should be able to develop a level of comfort with the routines. Variety can be introduced by changing the texts and the ways in which parents and children respond to what they read.

For parents and children to persist in academic tasks over the long term, the instructional activities must be enjoyable for everyone. A sense of informality and playfulness infused into the activities can help achieve this goal. Parents should be reminded to be enthusiastic, to provide positive encouragement, and to support their children's attempts to read. Allowing children some control over activities also lends enjoyment to the sessions. If the reading is followed by some word games, for example, children can choose the games, as well as the words, to include.

When home and school collaborate to provide regular, enjoyable, and authentic reading experiences over the long term, students benefit because they have multiple daily opportunities to grow as readers.

Provide Ways to Document Home Activities

Documenting at-home activity permits teachers and schools to monitor parent–child involvement and evaluate the program's success in achieving its goal. More important, perhaps, documentation gives parents tacit encouragement and reminds them to continue reading with their children. Parents can use a log sheet to record their work with their children over a specified period of time. Parents tell us that posting the sheet in a prominent place reminds them to do the activity. At the end of the time period, the log sheets are returned to the school and used to evaluate participation.

FAST START: COMBINING EARLY LITERACY INSTRUCTION WITH HOME INVOLVEMENT

We used these design characteristics to develop and refine Fast Start, a simple home-involvement program that has shown remarkable results. Fast Start (Padak & Rasinski, 2004, 2005; Rasinski, 1995), an adaptation of the Fluency Development Lesson (Rasinski, Padak, Linek, & Sturtevant, 1994), is a parental involvement in reading program for primary-grade students designed to get children off to a successful start through intensive and systematic parental involvement in word decoding and fluency instruction that is coordinated through the school. The program involves a 10- to 15-minute daily activity that involves parents in repeatedly reading a brief text to and with their children (Dowhower, 1994), proactively listening to their children read the text to them, and engaging in a brief word study activity with their children. Specifically, Fast Start procedures include the following:

- Parent and child work with a daily passage. The passage is short (50–200 words), usually high in predictability (patterned texts with rhyming words), and age-appropriate in terms of content. Age-appropriate verse poems and song lyrics work particularly well for grades K–2.
- Parent and child sit together in a quiet area or room. The parent reads the text to the child several times, until the child is familiar with the passage. The parent draws the child's attention to the text by pointing to the appropriate lines and words as they are read.
- Parent and child discuss the content of the passage and also point out text features such as repeated words, rhymes, alliterative lines, patterns of text, and so on.
- Next, parent and child simultaneously read the passage together. The passage is again read several times, until the child feels willing and comfortable with reading the passage on his or her own.
- The child reads the text alone, with the parent providing backup or shadow reading support. The child is encouraged to point to the words as they are read to ensure voice-to-print matching. The text is again read several times by the child.
- Finally, the parent engages in phonemic awareness and/or word study activities with the child. These activities may include, but are not limited to, the following:

  - The parent and child may choose words from the text that are of interest; this may include rhyming words, content words, high frequency words, and so on. The words are printed on cards and added to word cards from previous days. This word bank is used for word practice, sentence building, word sorts, and other informal word games and activities.

- The parent draws the child's attention to various sounds that are salient in the passage and may help the child make the letter-to-sound match. For example, the parent may say two words from the text and ask the child to clap if the words begin with the same sound.
- The parent chooses a word that contains a common word family (i.e., rime or phonogram) that is salient in the text (e.g., *ock* in *Hickory Dickory Dock*). The word is written on a sheet of paper, with the word family underlined or highlighted in some fashion. Then the parent and child think of other words that rhyme and that contain the same word family (e.g., *sock, lock, rock, clock, tock*). These words are written in list form under the original word and then practiced.

The beauty of Fast Start, as described earlier, is its simplicity and brevity. It is a simple routine that can be used again and again. Indeed, the expectation is that parents use the routine on a daily basis with their children, essentially altering only the daily passage that is employed. Similarly, the lesson routine is quick to implement. The entire lesson can be implemented in less than 15 minutes. However, in that brief period of time, a large number of words, both in meaningful context and in isolation for detailed analysis, are read and reread.

EVIDENCE OF FAST START SUCCESS

Fast Start has been implemented in a number of settings; the results of the implementations have been remarkably and universally positive.

In a Clinical Reading Program

In a 5-week pilot implementation of an adapted version of Fast Start with struggling readers in a university summer reading clinic, Rasinski (1995) reported strong correlations (ranging from .60 to .79) between degree of parent participation in Fast Start and various measures of reading achievement. Parents were introduced to Fast Start in an orientation meeting at the beginning of the clinical program and were asked to implement it daily with their children. Materials for parents were provided by clinic staff members. Students were pre- and posttested on various measures of reading proficiency. Results indicated that students who regularly participated in Fast Start lessons with their parents made substantially greater gains in word decoding and reading fluency than children who did Fast Start less consistently or not at all. These results held for children in the primary through middle grades.

In Literacy Acquisition

Another study examined the implementation of Fast Start at the critical initial stage of literacy development—the beginning of first grade (Rasinski & Stevenson, 2005; Stevenson, 2002). Thirty beginning first-grade students, representing a wide range of reading abilities, were randomly assigned to experimental or control conditions for a period of 11 weeks.

Parents and students in the experimental group received Fast Start training, weekly materials packets, and weekly telephone support. They were asked to implement Fast Start daily with their children over the 11-week trial. The time for implementation ranged from 10 to 12 minutes per day. Control group parents and students received the parent involvement opportunities typical for their family and classroom.

Significant main effects for those students considered most at risk in reading (as measured by the pretest) were found on measures of letter/word recognition and reading fluency. Indeed, among at-risk first graders, the Fast Start students made twice the progress in letter and word recognition and two and a half times the progress in fluency (correct words read per minute in reading a grade-appropriate passage) made by students in the control group, who received more traditional home involvement opportunities from the school.

Verbal and written survey information collected from the experimental group indicated generally positive perceptions of the program by parents. Comments from all Fast Start parents during the weekly telephone conferences indicated very little negative feeling toward the program. Most comments were quite positive or reflected minor concerns that were easily rectified.

School-Based Implementation of Fast Start

Padak and Rasinski (2004, 2005) worked with K–1 teachers in an implementation of Fast Start in 18 elementary schools in an urban school district over the course of the 2002–2003 school year.

Kindergarten students were pre- and posttested using Clay's observational survey (2002). Results indicated that children who were involved in Fast Start had significantly greater word vocabulary growth, attained concepts about print more quickly, and learned to identify uppercase and lowercase letters more quickly than students who did not participate in Fast Start.

First graders were pre- and posttested with the Developmental Reading Assessment (Beaver, 1997), a reading assessment that incorporates authentic reading experiences. Analysis of scores for these children showed that students who were at least somewhat involved in Fast Start significantly outperformed their non–Fast Start counterparts. These results indicate that the Fast Start program was effective in increasing children's reading abilities, regardless of their measured ability at the beginning of the year. Remarkably, even being "somewhat" involved in Fast Start was enough to lead to achievement gains.

Analyses of surveys and interviews showed that children who participated in Fast Start were overwhelmingly positive about the experience. Children noted that they liked the content of the texts and that they enjoyed working with family members. Regarding content, one child said, "I liked the rhyming words and they were funny." Another commented, "The poems were not hard or easy—they were just right." Children also enjoyed the word play activities. Sample comments show this: "They help you read a lot"; "'cause I can learn stuff—how to do the sounds and how to make all the letters"; "because I got to play with my dad."

Children firmly believed that Fast Start helped them become better readers. Their reasons for this belief centered in three areas:

- Challenging content: "Because they had lots of words I didn't know"; "The words were hard but now I'm reading."
- Encouraged reading development: "The harder it gets, the better you get"; "Because I couldn't read that much before and now I'm reading a lot of stuff"; "Because they have hard words, and the more I read, the more I know."
- Encouraged interest in reading: "Because all of a sudden I sat down and started reading"; "I read them every day after school. Sometimes I write poems myself."

Parents' perceptions about Fast Start, gathered through surveys, were also very positive. Many parents commented about their children's and their own positive response to Fast Start: "The one-on-one time was nice"; "It gave him something to look forward to every night"; "I have always loved poetry. I see the same excitement in [my child] now"; "It brought us closer together."

Parents were also very positive about the impact that Fast Start had on their children's reading ability and on whether the time they devoted to Fast Start was well spent. With regard to the former, parents commented, "[Child] is eager to read now and without assistance"; "It seemed to help him with his fluency and expression"; "It has helped him recognize words and build confidence in reading." And about spending time in Fast Start, sample parent comments included the following: "To see your child read and want to read is priceless"; "This is a nice way for the family to spend time together"; "It allows for quality time."

In general, teachers believed that Fast Start time was well spent and that their students enjoyed the activity. Although teachers were less sure about academic benefits or about parents' responses, the empirical evidence suggested that they need not be concerned. Parents in this urban district found Fast Start worthwhile, and its value was validated in the children's growth in reading.

CONCLUSIONS

Our work with Fast Start convinces us that intensive and systematic parental involvement programs at the early childhood level and focused on critical areas of the reading are possible. In every implementation of Fast Start, students made progress in their reading achievement beyond what would normally have been expected. Moreover, the research we review here suggests that parents, children, and, to a lesser extent, teachers feel that Fast Start is an engaging activity for children and parents, and a valuable tool for improving students' literacy. In an era in which parental involvement is widely advocated but poorly implemented in a systematic and ongoing manner, Fast Start presents schools and teachers with a wonderful opportunity to make strong inroads into the literacy achievement of children considered most at risk for failure in reading.

Fast Start is a program that does indeed work with children. It is not, however, the only program that might be developed and implemented with parents and children. Its design is based on an analysis of fundamental and critical aspects of literacy for beginning readers (i.e., decoding and fluency) and a consideration of features considered important for parental involvement. Fast Start is based on sound theory, research, and principles of instruction in literacy. Conceivably, other instructional programs for other groups of children and other areas of curriculum can be developed through a similar developmental process.

The essential question now is how to scale up Fast Start and other such promising programs to a level at which they will have a measurable and large-scale impact on the students' literacy development. This is not so much a question that can be answered through empirical research; rather, educational curriculum and policy development professionals must become advocates for home involvement programs.

Other questions regarding fluency and decoding instruction and home involvement deserve exploration. Can similar parental involvement programs be developed and implemented successfully beyond the primary grades? Would a program similar to Fast Start be successful as a summer education program, where the coordination with and support of the school may be less than optimal?

We also see important empirical questions related to the immediate application of Fast Start in the manifestations described in this chapter. First, does Fast Start implementation in the primary grades have long-term consequences for student literacy development? Theoretically, the answer is "yes." Students who more quickly master the basic aspects of literacy development (word decoding and fluency) should be more ready to deal with the higher, more complex aspects of literacy (vocabulary and comprehension). Although theoretically compelling, such consequences have not been empirically tested.

A second question relates to the notion of teacher buy-in of a program such as Fast Start. Results from previous work highlighted in this chapter suggest that teachers have not been as enthusiastic about Fast Start as parents and students. This finding is troubling in that we are convinced that teachers are critical to the success of home involvement programs such as Fast Start. Teachers who are less committed to the successful implementation of programs such as Fast Start are less likely to realize the full potential of the program. We suspect that many teachers have not been fully prepared in their preservice and in-service education programs to work with parents, and that many have been frustrated by past experiences in trying to involve parents. Nevertheless, home involvement programs require the proactive support of teachers. We need to learn more about the impediments to teacher involvement and ways to support teachers in their work with parents in programs such as Fast Start.

In summary, it appears that Fast Start holds great promise for both parental involvement in reading and significant improvements in reading achievement for early childhood readers. For educators wishing to use Fast Start, we suggest a focus on those students who have minimal sight word vocabularies and minimal reading fluency development, or who have experienced difficulty in acquiring these skills.

Since Fast Start seems quite effective for those students most at risk for reading failure, its use in kindergarten, first, or second grades may alleviate more serious and more costly reading failure at higher grades. It may also help school districts comply with parent involvement and reading achievement mandates.

REFERENCES

Beaver, J. (1997). *Developmental Reading Assessment*. Upper Saddle River, NJ: Pearson.

Chavkin, N. F. (Ed.). (1993). *Families and schools in a pluralistic society*. Albany: State University of New York Press.

Christenson, S. L. (1995). Best practices in supporting home collaboration. In A. Thomas & J. Grimes (Eds.), *Best practices in school psychology III* (pp. 253–267). Washington, DC: National Association of School Psychologists.

Clay, M. M. (2002). *An observational survey of early literacy in achievement* (2nd ed.). Portsmouth, NH: Heinemann.

Crimm, J. A. (1992). *Parent involvement and academic achievement: A meta-analysis*. Doctoral dissertation, University of Georgia, Athens.

Dowhower, S. L. (1994). Repeated reading revisited: Research into practice. *Reading and Writing Quarterly, 10*, 343–358.

Durkin, D. (1966). *Children who read early*. New York: Teachers College Press.

Eccles, J. S., & Harold, R. D. (1993). Parent–school involvement during the early adolescent years. *Teachers College Record, 94*, 568–587.

Epstein, J. L. (1989). Family structures and student motivation: A developmental perspective. In C. Ames & R. Ames (Eds.), *Research on motivation in education: Vol. 3. Goals and cognitions* (pp. 259–295). New York: Academic Press.

Epstein, J. L. (1994, October–November). *Perspectives and previews on research and policy for school, family, and community partnerships*. Paper presented at the Family–School Links Conference, Pennsylvania State University, University Park.

Epstein, J. L. (2001). Effect on student achievement of teacher's practices of parent involvement. In J. L. Epstein (Ed.), *School, family, and community partnerships: Preparing educators and improving schools* (pp. 221–235). Boulder, CO: Westview Press.

Henderson, A. (1988). Parents are a school's best friends. *Phi Delta Kappan, 70*, 148–153.

Henderson, A., & Berla, N. (Eds.). (1994). *A new generation of evidence: The family is critical to student achievement*. Washington, DC: National Committee for Citizens in Education.

National Reading Panel. (2000). *Report of the National Reading Panel: Teaching children to read: Report of the subgroups*. Washington, DC: U.S. Department of Health and Human Services, National Institutes of Health.

Neidermeyer, F. C. (1970). Parents teach kindergartners at home. *Elementary School Journal, 70*, 439–445.

Padak, N., & Rasinski, T. (2004). Fast Start: A promising practice for family literacy programs. *Family Literacy Forum, 3*(2), 3–9.

Padak, N., & Rasinski, T. (2004). Fast Start: Successful literacy instruction that connects schools and homes. In J. A. R. Dugan, P. Linder, M. B. Sampson, & B. A. Brancato (Eds.), *Celebrating the power of literacy: Twenty-sixth yearbook of the College Reading Association yearbook* (pp. 11–23). Commerce, TX: College Reading Association.

Postlethwaite, T. N., & Ross, K. N. (1992). *Effective schools in reading: Implications for policy planners.* The Hague: International Association for the Evaluation of Educational Achievement.

Pressley, M. (2002). Effective beginning reading instruction. *Journal of Literacy Research, 34*, 165–188.

Rasinski, T. V. (1989). Reading and empowerment of parents. *Reading Teacher, 34*, 226–231.

Rasinski, T. V. (1995). Fast Start: A parental involvement reading program for primary grade students. In W. M. Linek & E. G. Sturtevant (Eds.), *Generations of literacy: Seventeenth yearbook of the College Reading Association.* Harrisonburg, VA: College Reading Association.

Rasinski, T. V. (2003). Parental involvement: Key to leaving no child behind in reading. *New England Reading Association Journal, 39*, 1–5.

Rasinski, T. V., & Padak, N. (2004). *Effective reading strategies: Teaching children who find reading difficult* (3rd ed.). Upper Saddle River, NJ: Prentice-Hall.

Rasinski, T. V., Padak, N. D., Linek, W. L., & Sturtevant, E. (1994). Effects of fluency development on urban second-grade readers. *Journal of Educational Research, 87*, 158–165.

Rasinski, T. V., & Stevenson, B. (2005). The effects of Fast Start reading: A fluency-based home involvement reading program, on the reading achievement of beginning readers. *Reading Psychology, 26*, 109–125.

Stevenson, B. (2002). *The efficacy of the Fast Start parent tutoring program in the development of reading skills of first grade students.* Unpublished doctoral dissertation, Ohio State University, Columbus.

Topping, K. J. (1996). Tutoring systems for family literacy. In S. Wolfendale & K. Topping (Eds.), *Family involvement in literacy: Effective partnerships in education.* London: Cassel.

U.S. Department of Education. (1994). *Strong families, strong schools: Building community partnerships for learning.* Washington, DC: Author.

CHAPTER 15

Building a Focus on Oral Reading Fluency into Individual Instruction for Struggling Readers

JERRY ZUTELL
RANDAL DONELSON
JESSICA BEVANS
PATSY TODT

In his seminal article, Allington (1983) discussed fluency as a forgotten goal of reading instruction. Interest in this dimension of proficient reading was slow to develop (for an exception, see Zutell & Rasinski, 1991a), but research such as the National Assessment of Educational Progress (NAEP) study, as reported by Pinnell and colleagues (1995), and reviews such as the report of the National Reading Panel (2000) have generated considerable focus on fluency assessment and building fluency instruction into the literacy curriculum.

The NAEP study, in particular, found that fluency serves as a much better predictor of comprehension than oral reading accuracy, the traditional measure of reading instructional level. Our experiences working with struggling readers at the Ohio State University Reading Clinic have been consistent with these findings. We find that a large majority of students who come to us for assistance are relatively slow, laborious readers, even on materials on which they are able to score at the independent level for accuracy. Furthermore, they are often able to maintain reasonable oral reading accuracy on more difficult materials, although their reading rates are well below expectations for students at their ages and/or ability levels. Struggling readers at beginning levels, with minimal sight vocabularies, often read even simple, well-known, and rehearsed texts in a word-by-word manner, with little sense of meaningful language.

In this chapter we describe how we address these issues in our clinical instruction. We begin with a brief description of our instructional setting. Then we describe the general components of our program, present our beliefs about the nature of fluent reading, and discuss in more detail the instructional components that specifically address improving fluency. We conclude with a discussion of characteristics of tutors who deliver effective fluency instruction, based upon our observations and experiences.

THE OHIO STATE UNIVERSITY READING CLINIC

As with many university clinics, our program has two main objectives: (1) to provide careful, research-based, one-on-one instruction to improve the reading and writing abilities of struggling readers, and (2) to provide a supervised clinical experience for preservice and practicing teachers in order to prepare them to work with students who have difficulty in learning to read and write. In Ohio, the course credit associated with the Clinic is required for initial licensure as an Intervention Specialist and for Reading Endorsement on an existing teaching certificate or license. Tutors typically have taken several reading courses, including a required course on assessment and remedial instruction, before beginning their clinical work. Very few have had direct previous experience working one-on-one with a struggling reader.

Tutoring is done in individual carrels, under the direct supervision of a faculty instructor and an experienced graduate assistant. Sessions are approximately 50 minutes, and are done three times a week for 9 weeks during regular academic quarters, and five times a week for five and one-half weeks during summer session. Tutors change each quarter. Tutors attend class, carry out initial assessments, develop and deliver lesson plans, write personal reflections, and construct an in-depth case study report as part of course requirements.

Students with reading difficulties are referred for tutoring in a variety of ways, including by classroom teachers, school psychologists, and other school personnel, through "word of mouth" from parent to parent, and from calls to the university and visits to the Clinic website. It is not unusual to have more than one child from the same family attending, and we even have had children of former students receiving services. We charge a fee by quarter but use a sliding scale, so that no one is excluded due to lack of income. We keep a list of applicants organized by date of application and move through the list as openings become available. Students remain in the Clinic as long as the staff determine they are in need of further support and as long as the family is willing and able to maintain regular attendance. We do not serve students who have additional circumstances that we do not have the expertise to address—for example, students with severe loss of hearing or vision, or with minimal knowledge of English. However, at any given time, a significant number of our students may be diagnosed as having learning disabilities, attention deficits, and/or hyperactivity. We tend to have a mix of students in terms of gender, socioeconomic status, and ethnicity (Caucasian and African American).

INSTRUCTIONAL APPROACH

Assessment

At the Ohio State University Reading Clinic, initial assessments are used to determine instructional materials and activities, and ongoing assessments are used to adjust materials and instruction as student needs and abilities change. At the beginning of each quarter, students are tested with an informal word identification inventory (immediate and total scores) and a developmental spelling inventory (Schlagal, 1989). The results are used to make initial placements in instructional level reading texts and in appropriate word study activities. Throughout the quarter, checks of speed and accuracy are done to determine whether students should be kept at the same level or moved to easier or harder texts. Brief spelling tests at the end of each word study cycle help the tutor decide on the content for the next set of lessons. At the end of the quarter, testing on an informal reading inventory (Woods & Moe, 2002) is used to measure achievement. Results of all assessments are included in the case study report, which is used by the next tutor in conjunction with his or her own findings to make initial placements in appropriate materials.

Instruction

While instruction is adjusted to meet the literacy learning needs of each individual, plans follow a basic format consistent with the comprehensive developmental approach used at the Clinic. There are several essential components to each plan of study.

Each student is engaged in reading materials at his or her instructional level. Depending upon the ability level of the student, this reading is done orally (beginning readers), as a mix of oral and silent reading (transitional readers), or mostly silently (more advanced readers). Guided reading and discussion about these materials follows a before–during–after approach. Techniques consistent with this approach, such as the Directed Reading–Thinking Activity (Stauffer, 1980), "what we know, what we want to find out, what we have learned" (K-W-L; Ogle, 1986), and story mapping are used to frame discussion. (For beginning readers such activities aimed at maintaining and developing comprehension are often done as listening activities, since their level of understanding typically exceeds the conceptual demands of beginning reading materials.)

Each student is regularly engaged in writing. Often this writing is directly connected to reading, by way of note taking, graphic organizers, summaries, and/or responses. Writing activities follow a process model that includes brainstorming, note taking, drafting, revising, editing, and publishing.

Each student spends time working in developmentally appropriate word study activities. These typically involve manipulatives, including magnetic letters; letter tiles; onset-rime slides, wheels, or cards; picture cards; and word cards for word sorting (Bear, Invernizzi, Templeton, & Johnston, 2003). For students with a sufficient sight word vocabulary, instruction follows a modified version of the Directed Spelling Thinking Activity (Zutell, 1996). Patterns for study are chosen based on assessment results and analyses of word attack/spelling attempts during reading and writing activities. The cycle of instruction begins with high tutor input through demonstration and verbalization of decision making. Over time the student assumes more independence, and the requirements of the sorts become more demanding. Combinations of collaborative sorts, independent sorts, visual sorts, blind sorts, speed sorts, word hunting, and writing-to-the-sort activities are used. A spelling test on the final day of the cycle assesses student knowledge of the patterns studied and informs the choice for the next word study activity.

We expect these essential components to be incorporated into lesson plans on a regular schedule, though the time devoted to each may vary from session to session, depending on circumstances and the needs of individual students. Work on word attack strategies, spelling strategies, and meaning vocabulary are also regularly addressed during reading and writing activities. Word games, free reading, and reading to the student are optional activities that are regularly incorporated during time remaining in the tutoring session. This framework forms the context into which an additional component, direct instruction on reading fluency, is also often incorporated.

PERSPECTIVES ON FLUENCY

Following Zutell and Rasinski (1991b), we view fluency as having three major components: phrasing, smoothness, and pace. We believe phrasing is at the heart of fluency. Fluent readers chunk words into meaningful phrases and/or clauses. They focus on ideas. They use pitch, stress, and intonation appropriately to convey the meanings and feelings clearly intended by the author. For fluent readers, reading also appears fairly effortless, or automatic, and occurs minimally at a conversational pace. Thus, behaviors that indicate a lack of fluency include inappropriate or extensive pauses; monotonic, word-by-word, and/or choppy reading; inappropriate prosody; run-ons; multiple attempts at words or phrases; and a slow, laborious pace.

Here we also offer our own views on some aspects of fluency that we think need to be addressed and clarified.

First is the issue of reading with expression. Certainly fluent readers do often read with expression, as may be appropriate for certain texts, most clearly those related to feelings, emotions, characters, and/or dialogue. And we do often use such texts as a means to illustrate the connections between fluent reading and accessing meaning. But we also recognize that many written texts are meant to be read in a "matter-of-fact" way—for example, expository texts, content textbooks, explanations, and directions. Some students working on fluency exclusively in stories may conclude that all texts are to be read "expressively" and may therefore generate readings that do not match the tone and intent of the author, and may even interfere with full understanding. For this reason, we try to incorporate nonfiction texts into fluency instruction, even with our beginning readers, so they develop an understanding of the importance of appropriate phrasing and prosody for comprehending all manner of reading materials.

Second, we treat accuracy as a separate aspect of overall reading performance. Word errors do not all have the same impact on fluency. They can be made quickly, and not be attended to, possibly not recognized as errors, or take away time and energy during word attack, even if they are corrected. While a high degree of automatic word recognition is necessary for proficient reading and supports fluency, it is not sufficient. We have found that readers can be accurate without being fluent, and can be orally fluent without being highly accurate. This is not to say that proficient readers are inaccurate! Of course, they are fluent, accurate, and have strong comprehension. But we consider fluency, accuracy, and understanding to be integrated but separate aspects of reading performance that can be sources of strengths or weaknesses for individual students. We attempt to control the issues of word identification and word attack by focusing our fluency instruction on texts that are on independent level or are well known and/or rehearsed.

Third, our use of the term "pace" rather than "speed" is purposeful. Speed is an average, quantitative measure that may possibly reflect a mix of overly fast, unphrased reading with time-consuming word attack. We define "pace" as the typical rate of reading during periods of minimal disruption.

Thus, when working closely with an individual, struggling reader in an instructional context, we are wary of focusing exclusively on correct words read per minute, a fluency measure now so popular in large group assessments, because it may mask the interactions of various aspects of the reader's behavior. We think that attending to how a student gets to such a score is as important as the score itself. For this reason we keep track of speed and accuracy separately, rather than combine them in a single measure. Moreover, we contend that, for instructional purposes, appropriate speed and accuracy should be viewed as an outcome of (1) a focus on ideas, as manifested in reading in meaningful units, and (2) automatic word recognition, not as the goal itself.

So while we see the usefulness in having a student chart speed and accuracy for motivational purposes and as a concrete indication of fluency progress, we believe that effective fluency instruction is more than blind practice at improving the number of correct words read per minute. It includes modeling and practice of phrased reading in otherwise easily managed texts. At the same time, effective fluency instruction must be supported by a strong word study program (as outlined earlier), in order to develop the extensive sight vocabulary and automatic word recognition that help students manage progressively more difficult texts more easily.

ACTIVITIES SPECIFICALLY FOCUSED ON IMPROVING ORAL READING FLUENCY

Fluency Instruction for Beginning Readers

In our clinical work we encounter a number of primary-grade students who have very limited sight vocabularies, such that they are unable to read all but the simplest texts on their own. They may not yet have internalized the voice–print match and need direction in tracking print, matching the spoken word with the written one. Others may be "glued to the print" (Chall, 1996), proceeding word-by-word through simple, predictable picture books. On the other hand, some struggling readers in this range may use predictability and memorization as a means to avoid text rather than to engage it. The challenge at this stage is for students to become word-oriented and to develop an expanding sight vocabulary while maintaining a sense of language, meaning, and ideas in their reading.

We address this issue with a cycle of instruction combining elements of Reading Recovery (Clay, 1993) and the Language-Experience Approach (Stauffer, 1975). In this cycle we use leveled books, beginning with simple, highly memorable texts, and progress to more complex, less predictable ones (Peterson, 1991), so that students must gradually rely less on memory and more on the text and their own word knowledge.

Day 1 begins with an introduction to the book using an informal predict–read–confirm/revise structure. The tutor usually does the first reading but may encourage the student to participate through choral or shared reading. After this reading, the tutor and student discuss the characters, events, outcomes, vocabulary, and illustrations as relevant to understanding and enjoyment. Then the student reads the text at least once, with support from the tutor as necessary. The purpose of this day is to provide the student with a thorough knowledge of the text that will support future readings and free the student's attention to examine the details of words in those readings (Morris, 1993).

Day 2 begins with a brief review of text content followed by student independent reading and rereading. Here the student may need to use word attack skills and strategies discussed beforehand and receive tutor encouragement and support to solve unknown words. The tutor now also begins to move words out of context by creating sentence strips to be matched back to the text, and by cutting the strips into individual words to be identified and reassembled into text sentences and new ones. Previously unknown words that are now more easily identified are marked as candidates for the student's word bank. The tutor may also ask the student questions about particular word features to encourage attention to detail (e.g., "Find the two words on this page that have double letters.").

On days 3 and 4 the student rereads the text with a specific focus on reading fluently. The tutor encourages and supports this by reminding the student of the qualities of a fluent reading, possibly demonstrating on a section or sections of text. The tutor may also engage the student in echo reading, in which the student reads a phrase, clause, or sentence immediately after the tutor, echoing his or her phrasing and prosody. Attention to words continues with more work assembling sentences, identifying and matching words in and out of context, and reviewing words in the word bank. Unknown, difficult words are typically discarded. Games such as Concentration and Go Fish played with words from the word bank may be used to reinforce word learning.

For day 5, the final day of the cycle, the tutor types a copy of the text on plain paper, and the student reads the text independently from that copy. The tutor times the reading and keeps track of errors and self-corrections. Reading the text away from its book format serves several purposes. Some students depend on picture cues and split their attention between text and pictures, well beyond the point at which this strategy is productive. Removing this source of information encourages them to become text-oriented. Many young struggling readers initially lack confidence in their ability to read text without picture support and resist doing so. This procedure helps them build confidence in their ability to read longer sections of text independently. It therefore prepares them for the way text is presented in traditional testing situations, including the informal reading inventory at the end of the quarter. And using this standardized format at the end of the cycle enables the tutor to obtain more reliable information about the student's speed and accuracy and his or her readiness to move to slightly more complex and demanding texts.

On this day, the tutor also presents the new words learned from the story in isolation for quick identification. Those easily identified words are added to the student's word bank. As the student becomes more proficient in word learning, a larger proportion of new words is learned and kept.

When tutors and students are working with easier texts in this range, daily activities go quickly due to the simple, brief nature of the texts. In these circumstances, they may be working with three different texts within a session, with cycles for each started on different days. As levels increase and activities with them take more time, they may work with only one or two texts. At the upper range (approximately Reading Recovery levels 14–16), only selected sections of the text may be used for fluency practice and the speed and accuracy check.

When students read with at least 95% accuracy and reasonable fluency by the end of the cycle, and they are adding many new words to their word banks, they are working in texts that are appropriately challenging. When students are reading with independent-level word accuracy (97%) with clearly comfortable fluency and are adding almost every new word to their word banks, the tutor should move them to more demanding texts. Regular checks of speed and accuracy at the end of the cycle provide ongoing assessment data for tutors to use in best matching students and materials.

Fluency Instruction Beyond Beginning Stages

Students at the equivalent of Reading Recovery levels 16–20 or above (approximately early second-grade level) have sufficient sight vocabularies to read instructional-level texts without the extensive support of the beginning reading cycle. They are also able to read easier texts independently, though these are often at a considerably lower level than age- and/ or grade-level expectations. Still, they often read even independent-level texts slowly and laboriously. They need direct instruction in reading fluently. For these students, we include two separate components in their instructional plan.

They read materials at their instructional level to provide an appropriate challenge, a chance to accelerate their instructional level, and the opportunity to work on word attack strategies in context.

For a direct focus on fluency, the tutor and student select a manageable section of a text at high instructional or independent level. This may be a new text or a favorite one that was used earlier as an instructional selection. Texts should have natural language patterns that are reasonably familiar to the student.

On day 1 the tutor begins by reminding the student about the specific purpose of the activity. Together they review the aims of fluency practice—to develop quick and easy reading, to produce reading that "sounds like talking," and/or to read in phrases and clauses to support understanding. They may also focus on specific aspects of fluency that the reader struggles with (e.g., choppy reading, slow pace). The student then previews the material silently to locate and resolve any meaning or sight word difficulties (with the help of the tutor as necessary). Next, the student begins to read the text orally. During this reading, the tutor may decide to model fluency directly in several ways: by taking turns reading parts of the selection, by modeling a section and then having the student read that section, and/or by focused echo reading, in which the tutor breaks the text into phrases, clauses, or sentences, and the student reads each, immediately following the tutor, maintaining direct visual focus on the text (as opposed to simply repeating what the tutor has said). On this day the student may also listen to a taped professional, or to the tutor reading, as he or she follows a written copy of the text. Finally, a "more formal" independent student reading may be done for taping and for charting speed and accuracy. This forms a baseline of comparison for later readings.

On day 2 the tutor and student briefly review day 1 activities and performance. They listen to the taped reading from the previous lesson, discussing the strengths of the student reading and improvements that might be made. The tutor may decide to provide further modeling of specific sections, again using listening to a model, shared, choral, and/or echo reading, as appropriate. When the student feels ready, a reading is taped and charted, as on day 1. The tutor and student then compare performances across the lessons. Depending on the results and individual motivation, the student may decide to do a second taped reading and charting.

Day 3 may include some activities similar to those on day 2, but in an abbreviated form, and with the primary focus on reading and assessment. Then comparisons of performances across multiple days and readings are compared and discussed. Comparisons may also be made between performances across texts in order to focus on progress and motivate the student to continued effort.

These two cycles of instruction for building fluency are different according to the needs of readers at different stages of development. In the first, a focus on fluency is integrated into heavily supported instructional-level reading, because students at this level are not yet in control of the sight vocabulary necessary for independent reading. In the second, fluency is addressed separately from instructional-level reading, in order to minimize the need for word attack and to free the student's attention to focus specifically on qualities directly related to fluency.

But there are also essential components common to both formats. Both are built around multiple readings combined with teacher modeling and discussion to clarify the concept and make it concrete and specific for the student. Both begin with high teacher support and move to more student control and independent performance by the end of the cycle. While the beginning cycle tends to be longer because of its multiple purposes, in both situations tutors are encouraged to use their judgment in adding or reducing the number of days in the cycle, depending on student performance and attitude.

It should be noted that one way in which both cycles differ from some other approaches to fluency instruction is that the end of the cycle typically does not depend upon the reader reaching a predetermined speed or number of correct words per minute. A tutor does have the option to extend the length of a cycle if he or she judges that the additional time will add significantly to the student's performance. The tutor may also suggest targets within a cycle to give the student manageable and concrete goals. But having a fixed goal can be unrealistic and not account for individual differences in vocabulary, structure, and match to the student, even though the texts are judged comparable by readability formula and/or tutor judgment. Spending too much time on a text often leads to boredom, decreased motivation, and a loss of focus. Furthermore, requiring an inflexible level of "mastery" for each individual text is likely to limit the number and variety of texts with which a student can work.

We believe that variety contributes significantly to student interest, experience, learning, and transfer. So we find it more productive in the long run to work a significant but limited amount of time with a single text, allowing the tutor to incorporate a greater variety of texts into the student's experience. Similarly, for the beginning cycle, we do not require students to learn all new words from each text before moving to a new one. We are less concerned about specific words than with the overall growth of known words. By definition, high-frequency words tend to repeat across texts, which provides additional opportunities for them to be learned. We are confident that the number of words and the rate of growth will increase as students develop an understanding of how words work. This development is supported by the range of moderately frequent words encountered across a variety of texts (Henderson, Estes, & Stonecash, 1972).

CHARACTERISTICS OF EFFECTIVE TUTORS WHEN WORKING ON FLUENCY

While the cycles of instruction described earlier provide clear structures for fluency instruction, they involve more than simply carrying out a specific set of procedures. Their successful implementation depends considerably on the skillfulness and judgment of the tutor, who makes ongoing decisions about text selection, when to provide feedback, and what kind of feedback to provide. In our work with tutors and students, we have observed that tutors who are more successful in delivering fluency instruction often have several characteristics in common. Here we offer a brief discussion of some of those characteristics.

- We have found that inexperienced tutors often tolerate less fluent reading than we do. Effective tutors have a clear sense of what a fluent reading should sound like. They are attentive and not reluctant to intervene when the reading begins to break down. They focus on positive behaviors, and they do so in specific, explicit ways. They avoid vague or blanket positive support and are careful not only to discuss but also to demonstrate differences between fluent and less fluent readings. In particular, effective tutors recognize appropriate and inappropriate pitch, stress, and intonation and provide explicit and specific models and comparisons between appropriate and inappropriate prosody. They notice and intervene when students are reading faster but not more prosodically.

- Effective tutors are aware of the importance of matching the difficulty of the text to the purpose of the instructional activity. They are vigilant in monitoring student performance to insure that fluency work is done in texts that require minimal word attack. On the other hand, they work to increase the level of texts their students can read at an instructional level in order to accelerate reading development.

- Effective tutors also match their response to word errors differently when working on fluency as opposed to when focused on "word work" in instructional level texts. For fluency, they provide difficult words quickly and in a low-key manner, so as not to disrupt the flow of the reading.

- Effective tutors include narrative and expository texts in fluency practice and illustrate/coach how to read in idea units in these texts. Beginning tutors often tend to focus exclusively on texts with dialogue for practice on "expression." But, overall, a limited number of the texts that students need to read contain large stretches of such dialogue. Effective tutors understand the importance of developing and maintaining fluency across a variety of texts and writing styles by focusing on ideas as the units of processing.

- Effective tutors rely more on demonstration than on telling, but they also explain clearly what students should be attending to in their demonstrations and in listening to tapes of their reading. They use taping, charting, and reviewing performance as a means both to focus students' attention on specific aspects of their behavior and to illustrate student improvement.

• On the other hand, effective tutors try to avoid making readers too self-conscious. Struggling readers are typically anxious about their ability and performance. If they are nervous and overly focused on how well they are doing, they may not be able to engage the text fully in the very ways that support fluent reading. Ideally, effective tutors create situations in which students get so "wrapped up" or "lost" in a text that they are focused on discovering and understanding rather than on individual words and how they are reading.

• When using buddy and echo reading techniques, effective tutors move from a focus on individual phrases, clauses, and sentences to larger, manageable chunks (e.g., two to three sentences). They are sensitive to students losing focus if chunks become too long or unmanageable, but they understand that their goal is to stretch students' efforts to use larger chunks and to maintain fluent reading over large sections of text.

• Some students read fluently enough during instruction that focuses their attention directly on fluency but revert to the slow and/or choppy reading to which they have become accustomed in other reading situations. Effective tutors encourage students to maintain focus and pace across reading activities, so that fluent reading becomes the natural, automatic way in which they engage texts.

CONCLUSION

Both current research and clinical experience indicate that fluency is an essential component of proficient reading. In our program for struggling readers, fluency instruction is embedded in a comprehensive program that also includes instructional-level reading, developmentally appropriate word study, writing, and comprehension instruction. Within such a framework, fluency is addressed specifically and directly through cycles of instruction that include clear and explicit explanations of the concept, demonstrations and modeling, independent-level reading, repeated readings, and feedback. The specific tutor characteristics and behaviors discussed in this chapter have a direct impact on the effectiveness of instruction. Reading educators would be well advised to address these qualities directly when preparing tutors to work with struggling readers.

REFERENCES

Allington, R. L. (1983). Fluency: The neglected reading goal. *The Reading Teacher, 37*, 556–561.

Bear, D., Invernizzi, M., Templeton, S., & Johnston, F. (2003). *Words their way* (2nd ed.). Columbus, OH: Merrill.

Chall, J. S. (1996). *Stages of reading development* (2nd ed.). Fort Worth, TX: Harcourt Brace.

Clay, M. M. (1993). *Reading Recovery: A guidebook for teachers in training.* Portsmouth, NH: Heinemann.

Henderson, E., Estes, T., & Stonecash, S. (1972). An exploratory study of word acquisition among first graders in a language-experience approach. *Journal of Reading Behavior, 4*, 21–30.

Morris, D. (1993). The relationship between children's concept of word in text and phoneme awareness in learning to read: A longitudinal study. *Research in the Teaching of English, 27*(2), 133–154.

National Reading Panel. (2000). *Report of the subgroups: National Reading Panel.* Washington, DC: National Institute of Child Health and Development.

Ogle, D. (1986). K-W-L: A teaching model that develops active reading of expository text. *Reading Teacher, 39*, 564–570.

Peterson, B. (1991). Selecting books for beginning readers. In D. DeFord, C. Lyons, & G. Pinnell (Eds.), *Bridges to literacy: Learning from Reading Recovery* (pp. 119–147). Portsmouth, NH: Heinemann.

Pinnell, G. S., Pikulski, J. J., Wixson, K. K., Campbell, P. J. R., Gough, P. B., & Beatty, A. S. (1995). *Listening to children read aloud: Data from NAEP's Integrated Reading Performance record (IRIP) at grade 4* (Report No. 23-FR-04, prepared by the Educational Testing Service). Washington, DC: Office of Educational Research and Improvement, U.S. Department of Education.

Schlagal, R. (1989). Constancy and change in spelling development. *Reading Psychology, 10*(3), 207–232.

Stauffer, R. G. (1975). *Directing the thinking process.* New York: Harper & Row.

Stauffer, R. G. (1980). *The language-experience approach to the teaching of reading* (2nd ed.). New York: Harper & Row.

Woods, M., & Moe, A. (2002). *Analytical Reading Inventory* (7th ed.). Columbus, OH: Merrill.

Zutell, J. (1996). The Directed Spelling Thinking Activity (DSTA): Providing an effective balance in word study instruction. *Reading Teacher, 50*(2), 2–12.

Zutell, J., & Rasinski, T. (Eds.). (1991a). Fluency in oral reading. *Theory Into Practice, 30*(3), 242–227.

Zutell, J., & Rasinski, T. (1991b). Training teachers to attend to their students' oral reading fluency. *Theory Into Practice, 30*(3), 211–217.

CHAPTER 16

Fluency from the First
What Works with First Graders

ELFRIEDA H. HIEBERT
CHARLES W. FISHER

Huey's review of research (1908/1968) revealed that psychologists recognized the relationship between rapid recognition of words and meaningful comprehension of texts as early as the 1880s. When cognitive scientists revived interest in reading fluency in the 1970s (LaBerge & Samuels, 1974), special educators integrated the construct into interventions with struggling readers (Fuchs, Fuchs, Hamlett, Walz, & Germann, 1993). However, fluency was not emphasized in mainstream reading programs or assessments. It was not until the National Reading Panel's (2000) report and the inclusion of fluency as one of the five reading domains within the Reading First/No Child Left Behind Act (U.S. Congress, 2001) that fluency was brought to the forefront.

While the Reading First mandates begin with first graders, the nature of appropriate fluency instruction and/or interventions with first graders is not clear. Whole-language theorists recommended repeated reading of texts with young children (e.g., Holdaway, 1979). However, the research evidence from this procedure has been limited and has been confounded by the type of text that whole-language theorists recommended for this activity—predictable text. Available evidence suggests that many beginning readers may repeat the words in predictable texts but they may be overrelying on their aural memory, rather than attending to the written words (Johnston, 2000).

An examination of studies used in the meta-analysis conducted by the National Reading Panel subgroup on fluency (Hiebert & Fisher, 2005) showed that subjects in the studies were at least second graders, with third grade being the most frequent grade level. Furthermore, most participating students, with the exception of one or two studies, were struggling readers. Therefore, the prototypes for fluency interventions were developed for a target population of struggling readers beyond the first grade. The needs of children at the early stages of reading may differ, especially when these beginning readers also are learning to speak the language of instruction.

In this chapter, we review the results of a study (Hiebert & Fisher, 2004) in which groups of predominantly English language learners were involved in repeated reading. The two treatment groups differed in the kinds of texts that they read, but, regardless of text type, they read the texts repeatedly. The students in the control group were exposed to texts that have a high level of potential for accuracy (e.g., Stein, Johnson, & Gutlohn, 1999). However, these students were not asked to reread these texts systematically. We use these findings to suggest features of beginning reading instruction in which first graders become fluent from the start.

REVIEW OF RESEARCH

The study and the recommendations for first-grade programs presented in this chapter draw from several areas of research: (1) research on the development of oral reading rates, (2) characteristics of first-grade interventions and fluency, and (3) the role of repetition of words in texts.

Trajectories of Oral Reading Rate

From the end of grade 1 through the end of grade 4, a student's reading proficiency relative to peers stays stable (Juel, 1988). Without an intervention, it is highly likely that those first graders ending the year in the 25th and 50th percentiles will be the same students in the 25th and 50th percentiles as fourth graders. Thus, even though national norms (Behavioral Research and Teaching, 2005; Good, Wallin, Simmons, Kame'enui,

& Kaminski, 2002) are gathered on cross-sectional samples, these data do indicate the trajectories followed by students in particular quartiles.

Figure 16.1 provides end-of-year reading rates from grades 1–8 based on recently reported national norms (Behavioral Research and Teaching, 2005).

An examination of patterns of end-of-grade performances indicates that the 25th and 50th percentile groups made progress comparable to that of students in the 75th percentile group from year to year. When the 75th percentile group levels off at sixth grade, the growth of the 25th and 50th percentile groups also stops. According to a study that was part of the 1994 National Assessment of Educational Progress (NAEP; Pinnell et al., 1995), few fourth graders who read fewer than 125 words correct per minute (wcpm) attained a proficient or higher standard in silent reading comprehension on a grade-level passage. Not until eighth grade do students in the 25th percentile group attain a rate of 125 wcpm.

The performances of students over first grade deserve attention, because it is at this point that the discrepant patterns begin. Fluency rates for five percentile groups at the middle and end of first grade, drawn from the norms reported by Good and colleagues (2002), are provided in Figure 16.2. The patterns in Figure 16.2 indicate that, at the midpoint of grade 1, when fluency norms are first tracked, students in the 25th and 75th percentile already differ substantially. At the same time, the difference between students in the 25th and 50th percentiles is not substantial.

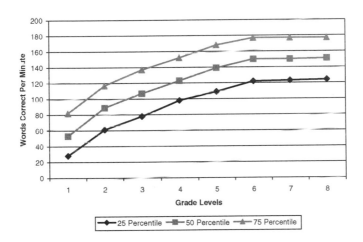

FIGURE 16.1. Typical reading rates for students at grades 1–8 (based on norms reported by Behavioral Research and Teaching, 2005).

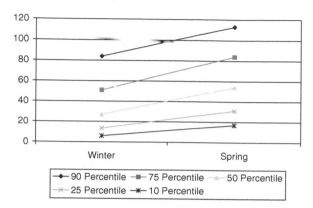

FIGURE 16.2. Mid- and end-of-first-grade rate of reading levels (based on norms provided by Good et al., 2002).

However, from the middle to the end of grade 1, the 50th percentile group achieves growth in words correct per minute that is comparable to the 75th percentile group: 30 wcpm for a single term. During no other time period will students make growth at this speed in a single term. However, the students at the 25th percentile make almost half this increase during the last semester of first grade. While students in the 25th percentile group over the next school years will achieve growth comparable to that of students in higher percentile groups, comparatively less growth during the second half of grade one means that these students will be reading at rates that are below grade-level expectations. The question here is whether concerted interventions during the last half of first grade can decrease this gap between students at the 25th and 50th percentiles.

First-Grade Interventions and Changes in Fluency Levels

As was demonstrated earlier, the students in the meta-analyses of the National Reading Panel were older, struggling readers. The recommendation for repeated reading has been consistent in first grade. However, data on fluency have not been reported in the intervention reports (e.g., Pinnell, Lyons, DeFord, Bryk, & Seltzer, 1994). Furthermore, the interventions include a range of activities beyond the repeated reading task.

A study by Jenkins, Peyton, Sanders, and Vadasy (2004) is an exception in the early reading intervention research, in that fluency data were gathered and all activities were similar for students except for the types of texts used for repeated reading. In the Jenkins and colleagues study, first-grade students read a text twice at introduction and once more in a subsequent lesson. Since Jenkins and colleagues needed to use available texts, the characteristics of the texts varied even on the target dimension of decodability. During the third portion of the study, when a substantial amount of the growth in first graders' proficiency occurs (e.g., Good et al., 2002), both sets of texts had high percentages of decodable words: 80% for the more decodable treatment and 69% for the less decodable treatment. Furthermore, the percentage of words among the 300 most frequent words was similar at this point as well: 21 and 24%, respectively, for the more and less decodable conditions.

After the 25-week individual tutorial, both groups of students read non-phonetically, controlled texts at 35 and 37 wcpm compared to 26 wcpm for control students. On phonetically controlled texts, the students in the more decodable group read at 42 wcpm, the less decodable read at 41 wcpm, and control students read at 28 wcpm. Differences between students in the repeated reading condition and in the control group were significant on both kinds of text, but not between different text conditions. The average reading rate for the two types of texts across the two treatment conditions was 38 wcpm, or the 33rd percentile in spring of grade 1 (Good et al., 2002), while the control group's mean of 30 wcpm was at the 24th percentile. The expenditure involved in individual tutoring for 4 days of each of 25 weeks is substantial. However, the Jenkins et al. (2004) study suggests that the opportunity to read repeatedly can affect the reading rate of first graders.

Repetition of Words and Fluency

A set of critical issues that have been debated more than investigated over the past several decades have to do with the amount of repetition and the unit of linguistic information (i.e., word, phoneme, rime) that beginning readers require (Hiebert & Martin, 2002). A related issue is the rate at which beginning readers can assimilate new linguistic information and how the size of the unit influences this assimilation. The factors of repetition and pacing in beginning reading materials have been sorely neglected over the past two decades as philosophies of text have been promoted (Hiebert & Martin, 2002). For young children who are learning to speak English at the same time they are being asked to learn to read, these issues are paramount.

Much of the existing knowledge on repetition stems from the work of Gates (1930), who did several quasi-experimental studies of children's recognition of high-frequency words in first-grade classrooms with particular kinds of materials. He called his primary experimental texts the "60" materials, referring to the presence of one new word out of every 60 words. In at least one context, Gates compared the 60 texts with texts in which one word out of every 14 words was new. Gates concluded that "this group of bright pupils could not go ahead with this material without supplementary work" (p. 37). The supplementary work that Gates described was 20 minutes of word study and 30 minutes of reading phrases, sentences, and paragraphs on worksheets, blackboards, and so on. According to Gates, the students in this classroom, whom he described as high-ability, required additional exposure to the words. As the latter description indicates, Gates differentiated the rate of repetition according to students' IQ. Based on his investigations, Gates reported the number of repetitions required for students of different IQ levels. Students in the average IQ range required 35 repetitions; those in the 60–69 IQ range required 55; and those with IQs from 120–129 required 20 repetitions of a word to recognize it.

Gates's (1930) conclusions became the basis for the creation of first-grade textbooks read by several generations of American children. While providing a commendable start in the research, Gates's work was based on a particular type of text—narratives limited to the most frequent words. As analyses of these texts would show several decades later, the text style and content that was possible with the first 300 words were sufficiently stilted and artificial to create problems in comprehension (Amsterdam, Ammon, & Simons, 1990). Subsequent research also demonstrated the manner in which word characteristics influenced word repetition. Research on word imagery, for example, showed that beginning readers learn words with high-imagery values (e.g., *apple*) more rapidly than words with low-imagery values (e.g., *is*) (Hargis, Terhaar-Yonkers, Williams, & Reed, 1988). Furthermore, when the decodability of words was manipulated along with concreteness and imagery value, high-imagery, decodable words were learned more quickly than other groups of words, including high-imagery, less decodable words.

While evidence points to the fact that word characteristics influence the number of repetitions beginning readers require to recognize a word, it is likely that many beginning readers—especially those who are learning to speak English at the same time they are learning to read it—require at least several repetitions of a word to remember it, even if the word is highly meaningful and phonetically regular. There is also evidence that researchers, policymakers, and textbook publishers have not been concerned with the repetition of words in texts for beginning readers over the past two decades. For example, Foorman, Francis, Davidson, Harm, and Griffin (2004) reported percentages as high as 70 of single-appearing words in the units of current first-grade textbooks. A response to this finding of many single-appearing words in first-grade textbooks is that the word has been replaced by the phoneme as the unit of repetition in first-grade textbooks, according to the policies of America's two largest textbook adoption states, California and Texas (Stein et al., 1999). The research foundation of the number of repetitions that are required to know a phoneme in *any* word is nonexistent (Hiebert & Martin, 2002). Furthermore, many single-appearing words are multisyllabic words that can be difficult for beginning readers to decode.

Neither the learning of individual nor of groups of phonemes has been addressed from the perspective of English language learners. By contrast, a robust literature exists on the nature and size of vocabulary for adult learners of English as a foreign language (EFL). According to Nation (1990), learners of EFL require a productive vocabulary of around 2,000 high-frequency words plus the strategies to deal with low-frequency words. Nation estimates that an additional 1,000 high-frequency words are needed by EFL learners to be successful in English university programs.

The 2,000 words identified by Nation (1990) are the 2,000 headwords from the General Service List (West, 1953). Bauman (n.d.), in revisiting the General Service List, has identified a group of related words (e.g., *acts, actor, actress, action*) as well as verb forms (*acts, acted, acting*) and plurals (e.g., *actors, actresses, actions*). The result of Bauman's additions is a list of 5,500 words. Nation advocated the use of texts written to reinforce the core vocabulary (in his case, 2,000 headwords from the General Service List) with EFL students. The issue of repetition is not raised. Furthermore, adult EFL students can presumably read in their native languages.

The repetition of a core group of words characterizes the interventions in which the fluency levels of students have changed (Hiebert & Fisher, 2005). However, in reading policy, there have been two different approaches. In one, the phoneme is the unit of repetition. In the other, words—with particular characteristics of those words—are the unit of repetition. To date, there has been no comparison of naturally occurring texts with these two units of analysis. The study (Hiebert & Fisher, 2004) summarized in this chapter addresses this issue.

DESCRIPTION OF STUDY

The question addressed in the Hiebert and Fisher (2004) study was whether the fluency trajectory for students in the bottom quartile can be changed. We are not suggesting that all students can attain the rates of students in the first quartile. However, in that students at the 25th percentile performed quite comparably to their counterparts at the 50th percentile in mid-first grade, our interest was in whether these students could attain higher levels of fluency.

The study was implemented with first-grade, English language learning students during the final trimester of the school year. Students attended two schools in which the number of native Spanish speakers was in the range of 92–97%. Students from a particular class were assigned to one of three groups: (1) single-criterion (SC) text intervention, (2) multiple-criteria (MC) text intervention, or (3) control. There needed to be at least six children from a class who participated in the intervention groups, since classroom instruction was controlled by having the same project teacher work with one SC text and one MC text group, each with three students. Only when there were more children than there were slots for the intervention in a particular class were children assigned to the control group. This procedure yielded 27 students in each of the two intervention groups and 10 students in the control group.

Instruction

Students met in small groups with a project teacher for 24 half-hour sessions over an 8-week period. Project teachers were provided with lesson plans developed by the investigators for each text. Time allocations were provided for each of four activities: (1) word card activities that used two words with particular letter–sound correspondences from a text (6 minutes); (2) three readings of a new book: teacher-led read-aloud with a retelling by students of the story, paired reading, and choral reading (10 minutes); (3) writing words on individual chalkboards (5 minutes); and (4) reading an additional book or rereading books from previous lessons (9 minutes).

Texts

The texts used in the SC condition were the decodable books of the Open Court program (Adams et al., 2000). The underlying curriculum and accompanying teacher guidance for this program systematically introduces beginning readers to phonemes. The texts in the MC condition were the little books of the NEARStar program (Pacific Resources for Education and Learning, 2003). These books were written to systematically introduce beginning readers to three types of written words: (a) words with common and consistent letter-sound patterns, (b) high-frequency words, and (c) high-imagery words (see Hiebert, Brown, Taitague, Fisher, & Adler, 2003, for further description).

Both the SC and MC programs provide 40 eight-page books in their beginning reading level. Characteristics of the texts in both the SC and MC programs are summarized in Table 16.1, and illustrations from each of the programs are given in Table 16.2. The data in Table 16.1 indicate that both programs emphasize short vowels at the early level used in this intervention. The texts at the beginning of each 40-book program had approximately the same number of words, although the number of words per text increased more rapidly in the SC program than in the MC program. Total number of words was kept equivalent by using 30 SC texts (1,689 words) and 35 MC texts (1,667 words). The 40th text of each program was withheld for use in assessment.

The programs were different in number and kinds of unique words. The SC program had 296 unique words, 70% with short-vowel patterns and an additional 10% among the 100 most frequent words. Of the 145 unique words in the MC program, 58% had short-vowel patterns and an additional 23% were among the 100 most frequent words.

Assessments

Assessments were individually given to students before and after the intervention. The assessments consisted of two groups of words presented individually at 3-second intervals on a computer: (1) short-vowel words

TABLE 16.1. Features of Four Examples of First-Grade Texts

	Total/ unique words (#)	300 most frequent words (%)	Short- and long-vowel patterns (%)	r-controlled and diphthong vowel patterns (%)	Multisyllabic (%)
Study: Open Court	1,689/296	26	58	4	11
Study: NEARStar	1,667/145	51	41	5	3
DIBELS 1.2	609/246	50	21	7	21
Classroom decodables	1,218/461	27.5	26	9	37

TABLE 16.2. Excerpts from Four Exemplars of First-Grade Texts

Program	Excerpt
Study: Open Court	*Nan's Family*
	On the mat.
	Sam sits on his mat.
	Pat sits on Sam.
	Tim sits on Pat.
	Nan sits on Tim.
	Tip sits on Nan.
	Tip.
Study: NEARStar	*My Mom*
	See my mom.
	See me.
	Feet to feet.
	See my mom.
	See me.
	Hands to hands.
	I love my mom!
DIBELS	*Spring Is Coming*
	It has been so cold this winter. The wind blew and blew. It rained and rained. The days have been gray and dark.
Classroom decodables (at time of study)	*Sunny's Buddy*
	Sunny's new friends played games. They ate jelly treats, drank fizzy drinks, and got dizzy dancing. What a nutty, silly bunch! Then everyone went home.

and (2) high-frequency words and a set of text reading measures that considered rate of reading, accuracy, and comprehension: (1) first-grade passages of the Texas Primary Reading Inventory (TPRI; Texas Education Agency, 2002) and (2) the 40th texts of the SC and the MC programs.

Results

The three groups did not differ on any of the pretest measures. On the posttest, the main group effect was not significant for the 3-second recognition of phonetically regular words but it was for all three measures of words correct per minute (the preprimer text of the TPRI and the 40th texts from both the SC and MC programs). Post hoc analyses showed that the difference on the preprimer text of the TPRI was between the two intervention groups and the control group, as evident in the gain scores: 23 for the SC group, 27 for the MC group, and 10 for the control group.

Similarly, for the 40th SC book, the control group's gain of three words was significantly less than the SC's gain of nine words and the MC's gain of 11 words. On the 40th text of the MC program, post hoc analyses showed that the MC group performed significantly better (gain of 23 wcpm) than the SC group (gain of 13 wcpm), and that both intervention groups had significantly higher performances than that of the control group, whose gain was 2 wcpm.

IMPLICATIONS AND DIRECTIONS

Before describing the implications of the findings for first-grade fluency, it is important to identify what was not addressed in this intervention. First, the intervention did not engender a spirit of "reading faster" among these first-grade readers. While students were timed during the assessments, teachers neither timed students during lessons nor did children chart their times, as is often the case in fluency interventions with older, struggling readers. The intervention was aimed at increasing the amount that first graders read.

Second, the intervention was not extensive. The 12-hour intervention is the same amount of time that California is mandating for recipients of Reading First grants during a *single* week of school. Even within a 12-hour period, students in the two interventions made gains beyond those of students who received classroom instruction. The students in the SC group made a gain of 2.9 wcpm on the TPRI for every week of instruction, close to the three words per week that Fuchs and colleagues (1993) have proposed as an ambitious goal for closing the achievement gap. With a gain of 3.4 wcpm, students in the MC group exceeded this ambitious goal. Students in the control group made progress but were moving at a rate that left them far from the goal of 50 wcpm that has been identified as necessary by end of grade 1 if students are to attain adequate reading levels in subsequent grades (Fuchs et al., 1993; Good et al., 2002).

What the two interventions did address was having students repeatedly read accessible text. We use three words from the previous sentence to describe what we believe to be critical if the students in the bottom quartile are to have a different reading trajectory: *accessible, text,* and *repeatedly.*

"Accessible"

According to the potential for accuracy criterion, in which the instruction of phonemes is used as the criterion for text difficulty (Stein et al.,

1999), the decodable texts that were part of classroom lessons during the last quarter of grade 1 should have been accessible. The potential for accuracy perspective holds that if all of the graphophonics relationships have been presented in lessons in the teacher's manual, students should be able to read the words in a text. However, the assumption that all children learn the patterns after a handful of lessons has little empirical foundation. The data on reading rates at mid-grade-1 that are presented in Figure 16.2 indicate that on a passage such as *Spring is Coming* (a typical DIBELS [Dynamic Indicators of Basic Early Literacy Skills] 1.2 benchmark passage that is excerpted in Table 16.2), half of the national first-grade cohort takes from 1 to 4 minutes to read the five sentences or phrases on the DIBELS Benchmark Grade 1.2 assessment. On indices of high-frequency words and monosyllabic simple-vowel-pattern words, the DIBELS text is considerably easier than the grade-level decodable that students in the study were reading in their classrooms. By the fourth quarter of grade 1, the content of the decodables emphasizes four affixes: -ful, -y, re-, and un-.

"Text"

In one of the few investigations of the ratio between word study exercises and text reading, Gates (1930) concluded that students did better in a classroom where they saw words in texts of a variety of types (poems, informational, narrative) than in worksheets and other exercises. Gates's conclusions need to be understood in the context of the words that he emphasized—high-frequency words rather than phonetically regular words. However, the issue that Gates raised—the ratio between word study and text reading at different points in reading development—has received little subsequent attention. In designing the instructional routine for the study, particular choices needed to be made about both the kinds of word study and the ratio of word study to text reading.

Several different kinds of word study were provided in the instructional routine: talking about the words, discriminating critical features of the word patterns auditorily, and spelling words. The contribution of certain kinds of word study activities to student achievement cannot be isolated in the Hiebert and Fisher (2004) study. Nor can conclusions be made as to the appropriate ratio of word study to text reading. Both activities are likely critical. But available evidence does show that students require opportunities to apply the information taught and practiced in word study exercises in the texts that they read. All the word study instruction in this study was directly connected to the words students read in their texts.

While having little guidance as to the amount of text reading beginning readers require, a goal in designing the instructional routine was to increase substantially the amount that students read as part of the lesson. Data from previous decades indicate that the amount that students read in classrooms is critically related to their reading achievement (Fisher & Berliner, 1985). From the best available data (Allington, 1984), the amount that low-performing first graders typically read during classroom instruction is approximately 27 words per half-hour.[1] In both treatments in the study summarized in this chapter, students read approximately 6,500 words over a 12-hour period, or approximately 270 words per half-hour. The intervention increased 10-fold the amount that students were reading in their first-grade classrooms.

For English language learners, we predict that the reading of text is particularly important. We base this prediction on the results of a recent study of native-Spanish-speaking first graders learning to read in English. Vaughn and colleagues (in press) reported a sharp difference between children's performances on measures of word recognition and fluent reading. On average, students who participated in a reading intervention had posttest scores that placed them at approximately the 55th percentile on the word recognition test and 11th percentile on the fluency measure. Although not as great as the difference between word recognition and fluency within the intervention students, the discrepancy between posttest performances on word recognition and fluency was also substantial for control group students: approximately the 32nd percentile on word recognition and 7th percentile on fluency.

Many programs are directed at increasing the amount that students read at home—and this goal is a worthy one. The amount that students read at home varies substantially, according to percentile levels (Anderson, Wilson, & Fielding, 1988) and the differences accumulate, making an ever-increasing achievement gap (Cunningham & Stanovich, 1997). However, if students are not reading voraciously in their classrooms, it is hard to expect that they would read voraciously at home, especially when language and cultural patterns differ in the two contexts. If English language learners are to read voraciously at home, they also need to read voraciously at school. Voracious reading presumably begins with students having frequent opportunity to read in their classrooms.

---

[1]Allington (1984) calculated that low-achieving students read 400 words over a week of 90-minute reading periods (450 minutes of instruction = 7.5 instructional hours): 400 words/7.5 hours = 53 words per hour.

"Repeatedly"

Repeated reading of texts can be seen to be critical for English language learners in that it supports them in becoming fluent with particular texts. It also increases the amount of exposure that students have to words. At the current time, the state-adopted textbook program used in the schools where the intervention was conducted provides approximately 10,000 words in the decodable and anthology components of first grade. Across 180 instructional days, students are provided approximately 56 words per day, or 280 words per week (even less than the low-achieving students in Allington's study in 1984). While the amount of reading that is required to achieve particular levels of fluency has yet to be substantiated, providing students who learn to read in school approximately 56 words a day is likely insufficient to become literate. However, when these texts are read three or four times, first graders will be reading approximately 1,000 words a week rather than 280. Students who do not have frequent occasions for text reading outside of school appear to benefit from even a short period of scaffolded reading, as occurred in the study summarized in this chapter. At the present time, we do not know how much guided and repeated reading is needed to develop fluency. However, it is clear that if fluent reading is to be developed among English language learners, the amount of exposure to text that students have in classrooms needs to increase.

ACKNOWLEDGMENTS

An earlier draft of this chapter was funded by the U.S. Department of Education under award number R203F990026 and has been presented to the Pacific Resources for Education and Learning as Deliverable V.2.1. The content does not necessarily reflect the views of the U.S. Department of Education or any other agency of the U.S. government.

REFERENCES

Adams, M. J., Bereiter, C., McKeough, A., Case, R., Roit, M., Hirschberg, J., et al. (2000). *Open Court reading.* Columbus, OH: SRA/McGraw-Hill.

Allington, R. L. (1984). Content coverage and contextual reading in reading groups. *Journal of Reading Behavior, 16,* 85–96.

Amsterdam, A. L., Ammon, P., & Simons, H. (1990). Children's elicited imitations of controlled and rewritten reading texts. *Journal of Educational Psychology, 82,* 486–490.

Anderson, R. C., Wilson, P. T., & Fielding, L. G. (1988). Growth in reading and how children spend their time outside of school. *Reading Research Quarterly, 23,* 285–303.

Bauman, J. (n.d.). *About the General Service List.* Retrieved November 3, 2004, from jbauman.com/aboutgsl.html

Behavioral Research and Teaching. (2005, January). *Oral reading fluency: 90 years of assessment* (BRT Technical Report No. 33). Eugene, OR: Author.

Cunningham, A. E., & Stanovich, K. E. (1997). Early reading acquisition and its relation to reading experience and ability 10 years later. *Developmental Psychology, 33*(6), 934–945.

Fisher, C. W., & Berliner, D. C. (Eds.). (1985). *Perspectives on instructional time.* New York: Longman.

Foorman, B. R., Francis, D. J., Davidson, K. C., Harm, M. W., & Griffin, J. (2004). Variability in text features in six grade 1 basal reading programs. *Scientific Studies of Reading, 8,* 167–197.

Fuchs, L. S., Fuchs, D., Hamlett, C. L., Walz, L., & Germann, G. (1993). Formative evaluation of academic progress: How much growth can we expect? *School Psychology Review, 22,* 27–48.

Gates, A. I. (1930). *Interest and ability in reading.* New York: Macmillan.

Good, R. H., Wallin, J. U., Simmons, D. C., Kame'enui, E. J., & Kaminski, R. A. (2002). *System-wide percentile ranks for DIBELS Benchmark Assessment* (Technical Report No. 9). Eugene: University of Oregon.

Hargis, C. H., Terhaar-Yonkers, M., Williams, P. C., & Reed, M. T. (1988). Repetition requirements for word recognition. *Journal of Reading, 31,* 320–327.

Hiebert, E. H., Brown, Z. A., Taitague, C., Fisher, C. W., & Adler, M. A. (2003). Texts and English Language Learners: Scaffolding entrée to reading. In F. B. Boyd & C. H. Brock, with M. S. Rozendal (Eds.), *Multicultural and multilingual literacy and language: Context and practices* (pp. 32–53). New York: Guilford Press.

Hiebert, E. H., & Fisher, C. W. (2004, April). *Effects of text type on the reading acquisition of English language learners.* Paper presented at the annual meeting of the American Educational Research Association, San Diego, CA.

Hiebert, E. H., & Fisher, C. W. (2005). A review of the National Reading Panel's studies on fluency: On the matter of text. *Elementary School Journal, 105,* 443–460.

Hiebert, E. H., & Martin, L. A. (2002). The texts of beginning reading instruction. In S. B. Neuman & D. K. Dickinson (Eds.), *Handbook of early literacy research* (pp. 361–376). New York: Guilford Press.

Holdaway, D. (1979). *The foundations of literacy.* Sydney, NSW, Australia: Ashton Scholastic.

Huey, E. B. (1968). *The psychology and pedagogy of reading*. Cambridge, MA: MIT Press. (Original work published 1908)

Jenkins, J. R., Peyton, J. A., Sanders, E. A., & Vadasy, P. F. (2004). Effects of reading decodable texts in supplemental first-grade tutoring. *Scientific Studies of Reading*, 8, 53–86.

Johnston, F. R. (2000). Word learning in predictable text. *Journal of Educational Psychology*, 92(2), 248–255.

LaBerge, D., & Samuels, S. (1974). Toward a theory of automatic information processing in reading. *Cognitive Psychology*, 6, 293–323.

Nation, I. S. P. (1990). *Teaching and learning vocabulary*. Boston: Heinle & Heinle.

National Reading Panel. (2000). *Teaching children to read: An evidence-based assessment of the scientific research literature on reading and its implications for reading instruction*. Washington, DC: National Institute of Child Health and Human Development.

Pacific Resources for Education and Learning. (2003). *NEARStar (Levels 1–3)*. Honolulu, HI: Author.

Pinnell, G. S., Lyons, C. A., DeFord, D. E., Bryk, A. S., & Seltzer, M. (1994). Comparing instructional models for the literacy education of high-risk first graders. *Reading Research Quarterly*, 29(1), 8–39.

Pinnell, G. S., Pikulski, J. J., Wixson, K. K., Campbell, J. R., Gough, P. B., & Beatty, A. S. (1995). *Listening to children read aloud: Data from NAEP's Integrated Reading Performance Record (IRPR) at grade 4*. Washington, DC: Office of Educational Research and Improvement, U. S. Department of Education.

Stein, M. L., Johnson, B. J., & Gutlohn, L. (1999). Analyzing beginning reading programs: The relationship between decoding instruction and text. *Remedial and Special Education*, 20, 275–287.

Texas Education Agency. (2002). *Texas Primary Reading Inventory*. Austin, TX: Author.

U.S. Congress. (2001). *No Child Left Behind Act: Reauthorization of the Elementary and Secondary Education Act* (PL 107–110). Retrieved April 10, 2003, from www.ed.gov/offices/oese/esea/.

Vaughn, S., Linan-Thompson, S., Cirino, P. T., Carlson, C. D., Pollard-Durodola, S. D., Cardenas-Hagan, E., & Francis, D. J. (in press). First-grade English language learners at-risk for reading problems: Effectiveness of an English intervention. *Elementary School Journal*.

West, M. (1953). *General Service List of English words*. London: Longman, Green.

APPENDIX Multidimensional Fluency Scale

Name _____

	1	2	3	4
Expression and Volume	Reads in a quiet voice as if to get words out. The reading does not sound natural like talking to a friend.	Reads in a quiet voice. The reading sounds natural in part of the text, but the reader does not always sound like they are talking to a friend.	Reads with volume and expression. However, sometimes the reader slips into expressionless reading and does not sound like they are talking to a friend.	Reads with varied volume and expression. The reader sounds like they are talking to a friend with their voice matching the interpretation of the passage.
Phrasing	Reads word-by-word in a monotone voice.	Reads in two- or three-word phrases, not adhering to punctuation, stress and intonation.	Reads with a mixture of run-ons, mid sentence pauses for breath, and some choppiness. There is reasonable stress and intonation.	Reads with good phrasing, adhering to punctuation, stress, and intonation.
Smoothness	Frequently hesitates while reading, sounds out words, and repeats words or phrases. The reader makes multiple attempts to read the same passage.	Reads with extended pauses or hesitations. The reader has many "rough spots."	Reads with occasional breaks in rhythm. The reader has difficulty with specific words and/or sentence structures.	Reads smoothly with some breaks, but self-corrects with difficult words and/ or sentence structures.
Pace	Reads slowly and laboriously.	Reads moderately slowly.	Reads fast and slow throughout reading.	Reads at a conversational pace throughout the reading.

Scores of 10 or more indicate that the student is making good progress in fluency.   Score _____
Scores below 10 indicate that the student needs additional instruction in fluency.

295

Index

Page numbers followed by *f* indicate figure; *t* indicate table.